"Sellers captures the people in her life in spare, perfect strokes. This is a memoir devoid of bitterness. . . . Unless I've got prose blindness, Sellers is an ace. . . . Her calm, glass-half-full-to-overflowing worldview could, in another writer's hands, veer toward treacle, but she pulls it off beautifully. I predict exciting things for her: critical acclaim, hearty sales, and, perhaps best of all, long lines of strangers at every reading."

—Mary Roach,
The New York Times Book Review

"Never forget a face? What if you couldn't remember any? Sellers . . . learns to appreciate the upside: Being blind to faces makes it easier to see herself and those she loves as they really are."

—*People* (four stars)

"Although [Sellers] can't recognize others, in this book she has managed to find herself." —*O, The Oprah Magazine*

"A brilliant memoir that is part love story, part detective work. Having learned to negotiate the territory between what we see, what we think we see, and what we miss, this wonderful writer manages to capture the pain and the joy found in the mysteries of the mind and heart. A fascinating, disturbing journey, by turns hilarious and heartbreaking."

—Abigail Thomas,
author of *A Three Dog Life* and *Safekeeping*

"Poignant . . . though prosopagnosia is the narrative vehicle, the memoir is really about the legacy of mental illness. . . . [Sellers] makes impressive use of well-chosen details." —*The Boston Globe*

"Sellers seems to have inherited both the batty, charming side of her parents' personalities as well as their forbearance in the face of insanity. . . . [Her] understanding of the loneliness and fears that drove them makes one thing certain: Instead of an ability to recognize faces, she somehow ended up with a bigger heart."

—*The Atlanta Journal-Constitution*

"A powerfully moving account of a childhood lost and regained."

—Diane Ackerman,
author of *The Zookeeper's Wife* and *Dawn Light*

"Every reader loved this plucky self-portrait." —*Elle*

"[A] stunning memoir . . . paced like a work of suspenseful fiction . . . Sellers's writing is sprightly, even funny; this is a memoir to be devoured in great chunks. The pleasure of reading it derives both from its graceful style and from its ultimate lesson: that seeing our past for what it really was, and forgiving those involved, frees us up to love them all the more, despite their (and our) limitations."

—*BookPage*

"Heather Sellers is a glorious writer. *You Don't Look Like Anyone I Know* is an astonishing book."

—Jane Hamilton,
author of *A Map of the World* and *The Book of Ruth*

"Gripping . . . a beautifully written reflection on the ability to see and, ultimately, understand the incomprehensible . . . [Sellers's] story is less about neurology and more about clarity." —*Library Journal*

A True Story of Family, Face Blindness, and Forgiveness

RIVERHEAD BOOKS *New York*

RIVERHEAD BOOKS
Published by the Penguin Group
Penguin Group (USA) Inc.
375 Hudson Street, New York, New York 10014, USA
Penguin Group (Canada), 90 Eglinton Avenue East, Suite 700, Toronto, Ontario M4P 2Y3, Canada
(a division of Pearson Penguin Canada Inc.)
Penguin Books Ltd., 80 Strand, London WC2R 0RL, England
Penguin Group Ireland, 25 St. Stephen's Green, Dublin 2, Ireland
(a division of Penguin Books Ltd.)
Penguin Group (Australia), 250 Camberwell Road, Camberwell, Victoria 3124, Australia
(a division of Pearson Australia Group Pty. Ltd.)
Penguin Books India Pvt. Ltd., 11 Community Centre, Panchsheel Park,
New Delhi—110 017, India
Penguin Group (NZ), 67 Apollo Drive, Rosedale, Auckland 0632, New Zealand
(a division of Pearson New Zealand Ltd.)
Penguin Books (South Africa) (Pty.) Ltd., 24 Sturdee Avenue, Rosebank,
Johannesburg 2196, South Africa

Penguin Books Ltd., Registered Offices: 80 Strand, London WC2R 0RL, England

The author gratefully acknowledges permission to quote from W. S. Merwin, "The Nomad Flute," from *The Shadow of Sirius*. Copyright © 2008 by W. S. Merwin. Reprinted with the permission of Copper Canyon Press, www.coppercanyonpress.org.

Out of respect for their privacy, names and identifying details of some of the people who appear in these pages have been changed.

Book design by Nicole LaRoche

First Riverhead hardcover edition: October 2010
First Riverhead trade paperback edition: October 2011
Riverhead trade paperback ISBN: 978-1-59448-540-4

The Library of Congress has catalogued the Riverhead hardcover edition as follows:

Sellers, Heather, date.
You don't look like anyone I know : a true story of family, face blindness, and forgiveness / Heather Sellers.
p. cm.
ISBN 978-1-59448-773-6
1. Sellers, Heather, date. 2. Women authors, American—biography. 3. Face perception. 4. Prosopagnosia. I. Title.
PS3569.E5749Z46 2010 2010010228
818'.609—dc22

PRINTED IN THE UNITED STATES OF AMERICA

10 9 8 7 6 5 4 3 2 1

Penguin is committed to publishing works of quality and integrity.
In that spirit, we are proud to offer this book to our readers;
however, the story, the experiences, and the words
are the author's alone.

For my mother, and for David,

who gave her to me.

She is going, and she is gone, and

I am thinking of her the whole time.

I am always thinking of her.

I have with me
all that I do not know
I have lost none of it

—W. S. MERWIN

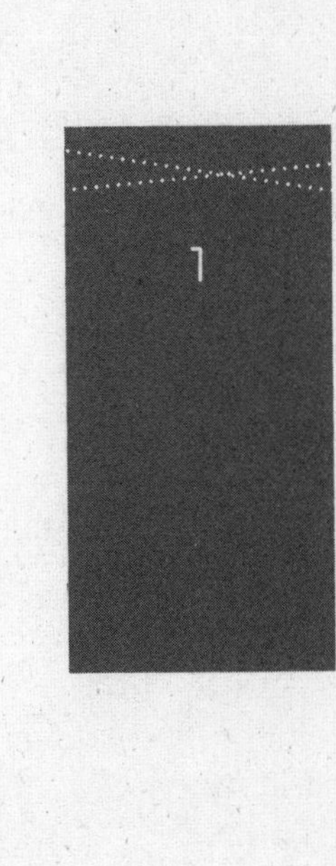

One

We left for the airport before dawn. Dave was driving. His sons, David Junior and Jacob, were in the backseat. I was thirty-eight years old. The landscape we were leaving was like the landscape in a children's book. Shiny new cars beetled to office buildings. Below, the Grand River curved like cursive drawn with a thick silver pen across our part of Michigan. We zipped past bare sun-warm fields on the outskirts of Grand Rapids, down the new highway to the airport, and I snuggled into Dave. I had a strong *family* feeling. I was eager for him to meet my wild daddy, my dear peculiar mom. Dave was willing, the boys were excited. None of us were awake yet.

Earlier that week, I'd come back to Michigan from upstate New York, where I was working as a visiting writer during my sabbatical year, so we could all go to Florida together. Dave had picked me up at the airport. I saw him before he saw me, walking down the corridor, past the narrow sports bar. Dave always wore running shoes and his walk was a distinctive leaning-forward walk, springy and gentle. I'd noticed this was how fine runners walked: head level, leaning forward. "You're going forward, not up and down," Dave's coach had told him, driving the bounce out of his step and converting it to speed. In college, Dave had been All-Conference. He'd run with Brian Diemer, the Olympic medalist, and Greg Meyer, the last American to win the Boston Marathon. Dave's event was the 10K. Over and above being fast—five-minute-mile fast—the 10K required terrific strength and focus. That pace had to be maintained for a long time, for half an hour. The biggest problem wasn't getting tired, it was drifting, getting lost in the monotony. Dave had a secret trick. He knew how to make himself see the beautiful cornfields near Caledonia, where he liked to run, instead of what was right in front of him. He could teleport, or bilocate. Dave was confident and sure of himself and calm and humble, all at once. His walk: fast-slow, leaning forward like he wanted to get where he was going while a large part of him was just along for the ride. The entire effect of Dave was hopefulness in running shoes.

I ran up to him and threw my arms around him and stretched up to kiss him; he drew back, pressing me away.

It wasn't Dave. I had the wrong guy.

Dave—my real Dave—came up a moment later; we laughed about my mistake. I was embarrassed he had seen me hugging another man. "So many people here look like you!" I said. "We need to move. To a place with fewer Dutch people." This had happened numerous times before, my mistaking someone else for Dave.

He told me I was funny, and he steered me toward baggage claim.

....

It had been a decade since I had taken anyone home to Orlando. I rarely visited. The last time I'd seen my parents was three years earlier; the visit had not been a success. My dad could be difficult. My mother could turn on a dime. I'd cut the trip short.

I'd told Dave everything—my dad's drinking, my mom's fragility—and Dave was sensitive, nonjudgmental, insightful. His first wife was a severely disabled schizophrenic: the bar for normal behavior was set reassuringly low. Whenever I called home to check on my parents, Dave held my hand while I shouted into the phone. He even talked to my father a few times. We'd been dating only a few months, and I was temporarily living in another state, but Dave and his sons felt like my family.

Everything was all planned out. My father lived by the airport: we'd drive by his house and the boys could go for a swim in his pool; we'd have a quick lunch. Fred would want to toast to something, so we'd have drinks, play cards, then go up to my mom's for dinner. She was making a roast, shrimp, four vegetables—corn, green beans, beets, carrots—and pies. "I know midwestern men," she'd said. "And I know you don't make pies yourself, Heather. Men *like* pie. I know you don't like for me to tell you helpful little things, but it wouldn't hurt for you to learn a pie or two."

We'd spend the night at my mom's house. She was setting up pallets for the boys on her living room floor. I'd assured her Dave wouldn't mind a cot in her study; I'd be happy in the guest room. The next day, we planned to take her to Disney World with us. I could see us on the Mad Hatter teacups, spinning, screaming our heads off, ecstatic. The Mad Hatter had been my favorite ride when I was a kid, and later, when I worked at Disney. No ups and downs, no scary things jumping out at you as you churned through dark water tunnels with strangers. You just *spun.*

Then maybe the boys would go swim in the Atlantic while I stole away to give my speech on the writing process. My speaking engagement was how we were paying for the trip, but I was keeping the talk a secret from my mother: I didn't want her to come.

The last time she'd seen me speak in public was when I was a graduate student and she visited a class I was teaching on Hemingway's short fiction. She'd promised to sit quietly in the back, but she raised her hand anyway. "Didn't Booth Tarkington sell more copies that year? By a *long* shot?" That evening, she supplied me with a numbered list of twenty-three items "to work on." *Make more eye contact. Learn the students' names.* She'd tallied the number of times I'd said *um.*

I felt bad about it, but I didn't want my mother in my world. I was never sure what she would do.

Dave felt it was important I work hard on getting along with her, let her have her way. "She's seventy-three years old," he kept reminding me. "Value the little time left."

So we'd have quality time with her, I'd do the speech in Winter Park on the sly, then I'd take the boys and Dave to my twentieth high school reunion. Dave felt this was too much for one trip, but to me it felt like success, redemption. I wanted my parents and my entire high school to see that everything was okay, that I'd turned out great. Anyway, to be around my parents, we needed a schedule, plenty to do. We had to keep moving. This was the extent of my worry. I was proud of this handsome man who was in love with me, and I was in love with his kids, whose grades had gone from Ds to mostly Bs since I'd come into their lives. As the four of us walked into the airport together, I felt, for the first time in my life, normal.

As we queued in security, Jacob pressed through DO NOT ENTER emergency-only glass doors at the new checkpoint, sending Kent County International Airport Terminal B into lockdown. An alarm buzzed and would not stop buzzing. Men in black uniforms ran toward us from every direction.

"Didn't you see the signs?" a guard demanded. Dave bristled.

David Junior assumed his favorite tae kwon do stances, the fancy forms, high block, low block, banking off the row of seating, and posing, striking air.

Jacob clung to the other side of the glass, stranded. He shrugged his shoulders nervously. He looked scared and sorry. He placed his hands on top of his head and shook his legs out, one after the other.

We were moved to a much later flight.

It was pitch-dark when we landed on the shimmering runway in Orlando.

“Am I turning here, sweetheart?” Dave said. He squeezed my thigh in a way that I hated. “We’re coming up to a red light,” he said. “Where am I going?”

“Go left,” I said, hoping for the best. Curry Ford Avenue? I knew something from my childhood happened on this street. Curry Ford. I didn’t know where it was exactly in relationship to where I needed to be. I rolled down my window. The October air was sweet. The last time I’d visited, it was summer, and Fred and his brother Donny had been on what they always called a fishing trip, their name for a bender; there was never any traveling or any catch.

“You seem a little tense,” Dave said, stroking my arm.

“I’m not,” I snapped. “Turn here.”

Junior told me not to worry. “We’re used to killing zombies all over the world, Heather.” He leaned forward and patted me on the shoulder.

Finally, we pulled into Fred’s driveway.

“Okay, now, boys,” Dave said. He counseled them on how they couldn’t run around or talk too loud or rifle through things, and not to ask to swim; wait until Fred offered. He spoke softly and they sat calmly in the back seat and listened. Junior nodded.

I needed to be in there giving Fred a similar consultation. *Don’t hit me or the boys. Don’t pinch people. Don’t yell. Don’t tell nasty jokes or pee off the back porch.*

Then they were out of the car and running around in the

yard, which had gone to sand and seed. The house looked terrible, gutter hanging off the front, shutters broken and peeling, loose bricks lying at all angles on the front walk, abandoned. Someone had intended to make repairs, but they hadn't gotten very far.

We stood on the stoop, Dave with his arm around me, his politeness like a silver cape around him, around all of us. The boys stood behind us, painfully well behaved. It was like we were time travelers—I felt we'd come from somewhere so far away. I rang the doorbell, half expecting electrocution: the doorbell had lost its cover, and wires stuck out of the socket. At the same time, I half expected applause from within. I felt like a magician: *Et voilà! A little family!* At thirty-eight, I felt late for my own life.

We waited out the long sequence of chimes, *dum, dum, dum, da dum, dum dum dum dum dum da dum.* From inside, *Wheel of Fortune* went to commercial. A ball game blared from a scratchy radio.

Junior socked Jacob, who protested. Dave stepped back and stood between them, putting an arm around each son. He looked over the wall. "No one is swimming in that pool," he said. Even in the dark, the water smelled green, and when I looked closely, it was—thick green soup. The boys moaned and my heart sank. I'd promised them a swim. I'd promised them sandwiches, cards, a fun grandfather. Where was everybody? I pressed my hands to my face.

"You don't just go in your own house?" Junior said. His voice was loud.

"Boys," Dave said very quietly. "'Member?"

I knocked, hard. I rattled the latch, and the door just opened. I could hear snoring.

Jacob said, "This one time, The Flash, you know The Flash, he ran so fast he outran himself and touched his own back. It makes no sense. So cool. One time he died, and then he outran death when death came to claim his soul. That's pretty fast. Outrun death. Gotta be pretty quick."

I smiled at Jakey. Whenever he sensed I was nervous, he introduced a superhero. I rubbed the top of his head. I stepped inside the house. Cigarette smoke, television, mustiness. "Fred," I called out, sweetly. "It's us! We're here! Fa-red!"

Then I stopped and rubbed my hands, like I was trying to erase the knocking. I did not want to go farther.

Two

In 1977, it was me and my mother, the two of us against the world. I was thirteen years old and I loved and hated her and loved and hated myself in equal, constant conflicting portions. Our old truck, which she'd named Suzy, wouldn't start most mornings—not easily. It was winter, we were on our own, and my mother said this was just the worst possible time for anything to be breaking down, so of course that's why everything was. "We are essentially doomed," she said.

All night, like every night, she hadn't been able to sleep. She woke me up when she heard rapping. She woke me again when she heard breathing. There was someone in the house. We huddled under her stale, lotion-smelling covers. I thought I could hear breathing, but I wasn't sure. At dawn, she got dressed. We would try to track down the vehicles she'd seen the day before, the suspicious vehicles that had no license plates. Someone was up to something. The night before, she'd tracked them almost all the way to the coast. The shocking part of it? They were government vehicles. She'd taken notes with the little notepad and Cross pen she kept with her, even in bed. We were going to head out and find the caravan, pursue this.

It was pitch-dark, freezing. I stood in the driveway in my mother's bedroom slippers and old ruby rayon robe, peeling the blankets off Suzy's hood. A rusted-out pea-green Datsun pickup, Suzy always stayed in the driveway. No one else on Buckwood Drive parked in their driveways, but our garage was stuffed to the ceiling with my father's abandoned projects, and you couldn't even walk in there. In winter, we covered the hood with my father's old army blankets. I liked tucking Suzy in and I liked unpeeling her and layering the blankets in the truck bed. It was comforting to make a nest back there with the leaves, the red gasoline can, a naked faux Barbie I'd stashed by the hump, an off-brand girl.

I patted the hood and pressed my cheek to the cold metal. I pretended Suzy had to be babied, but really I hoped Suzy would die soon. Then someone would have to step in and rescue us. My father had been moving out and back in with us—mostly out—for as long as I could remember. My mother blamed herself, but she said it didn't help that I was always so difficult, always after attention. Men couldn't put up with a lot of domestic drama, she said, her hands on her head, pulling at her hair. They wanted two things: food, and I'd figure out the rest.

I got Suzy's engine started, then went back inside the house and told my mother how ridiculous this was, the early hour, the futile hunt. But truly, I didn't mind getting up at dawn and driving around. It gave me a chance to look for my father. It gave me a chance to see the world.

Mom placed her cardboard box on the seat between us. In her box was her purse, wrapped in a plastic Zayre bag, a nasty old apple, bits of aluminum foil, a thermos of coffee, and a plastic container of water. There were old Triscuits in used waxed paper, carefully folded into a tight envelope, mom origami.

If I directed my mom not to use the box, not to carry it into the grocery store or my school or J. C. Penney, for example, she said, "I don't care what people think. I hate sheep. Most people are sheep. Not your old mom! I like how I am." The box sat between us like a pet. I didn't like it even to touch me.

I put my feet on the seat to avoid the cold air coming in. Suzy's floor was rusted-out lace. Mom's pale pink bedroom slippers transformed my real feet into mouse-looking feet. I tucked them under my butt and shivered.

"What if she doesn't start," Mom said. She closed her eyes. She held the steering wheel in her hands as though gently shaking Suzy by the neck.

"It starts, it starts," I said. "I started her up earlier."

"She's not starting, Heather. She's not starting."

"You aren't engaging the clutch. You have to press down."

"Oh my gosh in heaven," she said, peering down at the pedals accusingly.

If I made my mother think I was in on her plan, I could sometimes redirect her. I'd help her look for the threatening trucks, then casually suggest a troll through Holley Apartments' dirt parking lot. I wanted my father back. We weren't making it without him. For months I'd been calling his work number after school, letting it ring for hours. He never picked up his phone. I wanted to know: Could you make a phone ring for an eternity? Or at some point, does the operator step in and put a stop to it? *You're done trying! No one is home!* I could try him only after school when my mother was out job-hunting. She did not want the phone used for any reason except an emergency.

Secretly, I was thinking about maybe moving in with my father. What had happened to him? Where was he? Did he really have a new family, as the neighbor girl, Chantelle, had suggested over a year ago, flipping her gross new bra straps with her witchy index fingers? Reaching inside her own shirt and *snapping.* I hated that Chantelle. She lied about little things; she seemed obsessed with sex talk. She said, "Heather, you're such a dip." She couldn't believe I didn't know what a rubber was. Of course I said I did know. *You really don't,* she said. *I can tell. If you know, then why won't you say?*

I don't want to say.

After he first left, I'd received a postcard from my father, postmarked, thrillingly, Bonn, West Germany. In it he said to tell my mother not to worry so much and he was hoping to get a goat when he returned to Florida—they were incredibly destructive animals. Would I like a goat? He said he'd forgotten to pack socks and underwear. I thought if only he had me, if only he'd taken me with him, I would have provided underwear, I would have brought socks. He'd signed the card with his giant trademark cursive *F.* In the upper left-hand corner of my homework that fall, I'd started putting a big *H.* It could also be used for personal tic-tac-toe. I only played myself. I pretended *not to know what I had just done.* That was easier than it sounded, but it was still a kind of trick.

Now, Mom and I were lurching down Summerlin at a speed so slow I was sure it was illegal. Suddenly Suzy started choking and rumbling. We lurched forward.

"Oh my gosh."

"What," I said, looking around for the convoy, or for a tire to have flown off the ancient truck.

"The front door. I am suddenly not at all sure I locked the front door."

So we went back, as we always did. My mother loped out of the truck and up to the house. When she came back, she got in, lurched us halfway down the driveway, then said, "Can you run quick, check the door, honey, would you? I'm just not certain. Would you double-check?"

I lunged out of the truck and hurtled up the driveway in the dark, but there were pink edges around the sky now. It was freezing.

I twisted the knob.

The door was locked.

But it wasn't completely shut and I was worried about my outfit. It was what my mom would call a "getup." We weren't going to be able to walk around in these clothes. What were we thinking? She was in plaid pants from the 1940s, a plaid shirt over another plaid shirt. Her hair was in curlers. She was always in curlers; even her driver's license photo was in curlers. They wouldn't let her change it. I'd called the secretary of state and pretended to be her. My accent came out British, vaguely like a queen. No new photos.

"Heavens to Murgatroyd!" I'd said, enjoying my voice. Whoever this person was, I liked her.

I pulled the door closed, quiet but hard. This was good strategy. She'd think, *My thorough, safe, conscientious, beautiful daughter.* I'd get points.

I was hardly back in the truck when, *boom*, she was out to check again. She took her purse. My mother didn't trust me with her purse. Each night she hid it somewhere or slept with it. She would not leave me alone with her purse. This was because I ransacked her things regularly and read all the mail that came to the house. Every afternoon, I got off the school bus and went straight to the mailbox, collected the mail, and read every word of every piece—everything. I even tried to read the long-paper lawyer mail, thick packets of gobbledygook, worse than my textbooks. It always spelled doom: foreclosure, divorce, escrow, custody. My father was suing her and she was throwing away the paperwork. The lawyer letters were getting longer, the envelopes thicker; she was ordered to show up for court dates, and I had a very strong feeling she was not showing up. She kept saying to me, over and over, "It's the children who are victimized in these situations. The children! They are the ones who suffer." She wanted me to get my own lawyer and pay for it myself. If I didn't have representation, the court system would run over me.

Sometimes there was an envelope with a check from Fred Sellers. No return address. No note. The address on the check was 701 Buckwood Drive: our address. We were eating way-more-than-day-old from the Merita outlet store, and twenty-for-a-dollar lime and lemon-lime yogurts that were past their prime. I begged, "Cash one check! Please! It's our own money!" But my mother argued that if she took the money, she'd be construed as condoning the divorce, and she couldn't condone divorce. She'd been raised Catholic, she had married for life.

"But you won't even take me to church," I pointed out.

"Honey, you're haranguing me again. Please. I can't take your pressuring me all the time. I'm on the very brink."

It was getting light out. My mom hunched over the steering wheel, squinting as though we were pressing, blindly, into stiff wind, dense fog. She was driving about four miles per hour. I watched the speedometer closely.

"You can go faster, Mom," I said. "This is hard on your clutch. This is what is wearing out the clutches so fast, the guy said. Remember? You are riding the clutch."

"Thank you, honey," she said. "I'll try to do better. Now, eyes peeled. This is where I lost them last night. I think right in here. Can you see anything?"

We mounted the on-ramp for I-4. On the highway, a steady stream of vehicles passed us, honking. She rolled down her window and waved them on, grimacing. After a while, she honked back. "Mr. Big Hurry!" "Mr. So Important!" "Mr. Better Than Everyone Else! Here's a toot for ya! Back at ya!" She shook her tiny, papery fist. I scrunched down in the passenger seat.

"Let's go home," I said. "I'm already going to miss the bus."

"I have a hunch," she said, glittering. "Let's just try the

parking lot at the oil company. I think that's where they might gather to stage."

"No," I said. But I didn't care. First period was band. Kyle Roberts, Duane Bacon, and Keith Landreu. Keith was a lanky, pimpled, rail-skinny boy with thick, frizzy, curly hair, the kind that moved independently of him, giving his head a fragmented, lopsided, ridiculous effect. I couldn't help liking him for that. But Kyle and Duane were horrible boys who called the teacher gay and said nasty blow-job-type things to us winds. *You like flowers, right, Heather? So why don't you put your tulips on my organ?* More than once, Duane Bacon had put a note in my flute case. I knew it was him. He wanted to make me talk. He wanted to lick my feet.

Being late meant I would miss band. But being late for the bus meant my mother would drive me, and she'd insist on walking me to the doors, carrying that crazy box.

"You need your headlights on," I said.

"My headlights are off for a reason, Heather honey. Oh my gosh—look. See those vehicles up ahead?" Her voice shifted into a football-stands yell. "Good girl, Suzy! Well, they aren't getting away with it! I'm going to get to the bottom of this."

The caravan of trucks ahead of us didn't have license plates, and they did look creepy. There were a couple of military bases around Orlando . . . but still. It was weird. We followed them down the off-ramp at Colonial. We turned, after them, to the right. This was the way to the base and to the beach.

"No!" I cried. "Mom. No. I have school!"

"Aha!" she said, and she tapped the steering wheel. "We're on 'em!"

Ahead of us, the trucks were ghostly-looking in the foggy dawn. They were flatbeds, with giant hoops covered in taut camo canvas, like a military *Little House on the Prairie*. Soon, their taillights were way ahead of us. We were doing nearly forty mph, warp speed for Suzy, but five mph below the posted minimum.

I rolled down my window. I took the apple from the box.

"Honey," she said.

"I know," I said. "It's nippy. So? Sue me."

I palmed the apple and then winged it ahead as the icy air took bites from my face. I knew I wouldn't hit the trucks, but I wanted to try. I wanted to say, "We're back here!" I wanted to say Hello and Help. I wanted to say Get Me out of Here. I wanted to ruin my mother's plan, be part of it, both at once. The world absorbed the apple without a sound. It was as if it had never existed. Wind flashed into the cab and whipped my hair into my mouth, my eyes. I rolled up the window and watched the road sliding under the broken-out bits of floorboard, hoping to see the apple or at least some applesauce.

We drove in silence for a long time. I thought of my homework, in my satchel, undone. And how hard it was to know which was worse. This or band.

* * *

We didn't look for my father that day, but we did on other days. We'd saddle up Suzy, check the door countless times, and set out at the crack of dawn.

Chantelle Jenkins, the neighbor girl who enjoyed telling me

about where her father put his pee-pee in her mother, was the one who told me my father lived at the Holley Apartments; she'd been swimming there, with her father and my father's new family. I told her my father was in Germany and I told her she was obstreperous and mendacious. She knew penis this and gonads that, but I knew some words too. Chantelle said I was a freak. I told Chantelle she was so normal, she was devoid of interest. She was like a fake person. Plastic. "You're like a toy," I said.

We discovered the Holley Apartments were not named for the plant. There was no landscaping whatsoever. As we chugged around the dirt circle that was the driveway, I looked around for someone like my father. The apartments were cement block, painted pink. As far as I could see, there was no pool.

"It was worth a shot," my mother said. She looked happy and calm, tooling around the circle.

I convinced her to go around again. I wanted him to see us, to understand that we knew all about his other family and his horrible new life. I believed that if he knew we knew, he'd feel so terrible, so ashamed, he'd come back and be happy with us. His real family.

"Let's ask at the office," I said. "For their manifest." I loved the word *manifest.* It sounded nasty, but it wasn't nasty, it was powerful and intimidating.

She said we couldn't go in like this. "They'll think we escaped from the asylum!" she laughed. "Look at us."

"This is how we look, Mom," I said, bored and flat and as dully as possible.

I pressed my face against the cold glass of the window and looked hard at the metal doors, the dark cars, as we were driving away. I wondered whether, even if I caught sight of him or his car, I would say so to my mother. It would feel like I was ratting him out. I didn't want to sic her on him. I just wanted him to remember me, to *see me.* Maybe I could dash out and talk with him alone, without her. I looked hard for a sign of him. His golf clubs. A pile of junk.

"This is a bust," she said, and we headed for home. I had a nervous school stomach. What if one of those men in front of the apartments *was* my father? What did he look like now? What if we'd driven right past him? I looked back. Maybe a good man in a suit with a briefcase and shiny shoes was chasing us down the road, waving, *Wait up! Wait up!*

Along Orange Blossom Trail, there were men with beards, barefoot, shuffling along, drinking out of paper bags. Out in front of GIRLS! GIRLS! GIRLS! girls sat on stools and waved. I waved. A shirtless man waved back.

My mom said she didn't think it was a very good idea to encourage that sort of behavior. And in that moment, I thought, I will dedicate my life to encouraging that sort of behavior.

"Mom," I said, "here's the turn. Go, go, go. Don't stop on green, don't stop on green." Behind us, a truck was flashing its headlights, the driver snarling.

"I can't get over at the last minute!"

"You can get over!"

"I can't!"

We missed, again, the turn toward home.

Three

The night before we left Michigan for Orlando, Dave and the boys waited in the parking lot while I ran to Walgreens. I'd ordered triple sets of a dozen photos: the boys at the beach, the dogs and boys in the park, the boys in the fall leaf piles, the boys playing Nintendo, the boys and Silly String, holding the dogs in my backyard—all of us, including the dogs, grinning like lunatics. I wanted to give sets to my mother and my father so they could put us in frames, display us as family.

There was a line for photos, and I thumbed through *People* as I waited. I tried to stay up on the stars' pregnancies and meltdowns so as not to be a complete cliché as an English professor. It was hard to just keep a hand in, though. I recognized the names—Jennifer Aniston, Angelina Jolie, Britney, Jessica—but not the faces. It was like high school. All the popular girls made sure they looked exactly alike. It would be a life's work to really know who was who. I was trying to sort out the women when a young man came up and stood right next to me, way too close. I pulled back, my heart beating wildly. I was just about to shout for help. I held tight to my purse. He had a backpack pressed to his chest—was he shoplifting?—and a ball cap on. He tried to hug me.

"What are you doing?" I said very loudly, and people in line turned to me. The man laughed and tried again to hug me.

"No!" I said. I walked toward the doors, where there was usually a cop.

"I want this," he said. "Heather." He shook my shoulder. We were standing in front of a display of bagged snacks.

It was Junior. He dropped the backpack to the floor and used both hands to shake me.

"What are you doing?" I said. "What are you doing?" It seemed like a mean trick he was playing.

When I got back in the car, Junior was already telling his dad and Jacob what had happened. I'd squealed like a girl, he said, the whole store freaked out.

"I thought he was a shoplifter," I said. I laughed.

Junior said, "You thought I was a homeless person. A criminal! The look on your face!"

In the car, Dave had put his arm around me. I leaned on his shoulder. He asked me if I was okay. "Are you sure about all this, sweetheart? Have you taken on too much with us three guys and this big trip, this trip home?"

I admitted, quietly, I was just a little nervous about flying. I turned to the backseat and told Junior I was really sorry. I was just tired. I felt crazy, wrong, stressed-out. It was Orlando: I was tense because we were going home.

He said there wasn't anything to be sorry about. "No worries," he said. "I thought it was funny."

This kind of confusion had happened before. Sometimes I didn't seem to recognize the boys. I was afraid I did not love them. Or I was mentally ill. Or both.

After knocking and knocking on my father's door, we walked in and there we stood, watching a man asleep on the small curved gold crushed-velvet sofa. His snoring was so loud, with such chest heaving and such dramatic pauses between breaths, it was like watching a zoo animal. The timing was somehow off, the snore not in sync with the breathing. The boys couldn't stop giggling. They were falling on each other.

The house was cluttered, but furniture was missing. The end tables and side chairs were gone. The photos were gone from the mantel, except the one of me in my pink prom dress, standing next to my father. Piles of mail, magazines, newspapers, covered the dining room table, save for a little carved-out space at the end where my father's office chair sat. At his place, on a weathered yellow place mat, three ashtrays smoked, filled with dead and dying cigarettes. The boys looked cold and scared and small. I put my arms around Dave and held on.

"I think Louise has moved out again," I said. The televisions and radio blared. The sleeping man had to be Donny. He had the Donny shape: doughy, mountainous, scars on the fronts of his shins and knees, a Frankenstein.

"No woman lives here," Dave said loudly, "that's for sure." I was surprised at his tone, how hard it was. I'd expected things to be so different here, just because we were coming down.

Why would I have thought that? Meanwhile, Junior had spied the organ and was running his hands up and down the keyboard, which had never worked. Jacob was picking at both eyebrows, thumb and forefinger riffling through the crop of hairs, plucking.

"So, where's Fred?" Dave said. He stroked my back and I pulled away.

I walked down the hallway in the dark. Behind the closed door of my old bedroom, I heard a man coughing—not my father's coughing—and strange sounds, sex whimpering and elevator music oversimplified, a porn soundtrack. Whenever Fred's current wife, Louise, took off, my father took in drifters, non-vets he met down at the Legion, men who promised to barter maintenance work for rent. They stole his money; he wrote them large checks and told me they were his friends, leave him alone, mind my own business. His sister had quit speaking to him because of it. All his tools were long gone, along with my grandmother's silver, crystal, and china, his newer computer, a bed. They were good men, he said. He knew them.

"We can go," I said to Dave. "Where are the boys?" A jug of gin sat on the mail on the dining room table. "We should go, we should go," I said. This was my father's house, so none of this chaos was really a surprise. But my father had wanted so badly for me to get married and have kids, and here I was, delivering something so close after all these years. With this visit, we were finally going to transform into a normal family unit. In my mind, I had swept out the mess, edited out the vulgarity. How could I have been so naive?

"I feel like we have to make sure he's okay," Dave said.

"GODDAMMIT!" a man yelled, and Donny stirred.

And there he was, my father, rolling in from the back room in his wheelchair, trying to stub up over the track of the sliding glass doors.

Dave went to help him. He knelt and pulled on the wheel that was stuck. My father struck him on the shoulder.

"What," my father yelled, scowling. He looked as mad as I had ever seen him. "What the hell are you people doing in my house?"

"It's Dave, Heather's Dave. It's your daughter," Dave said. "See? It's your Heather."

Dave took a step back and knelt down again to look up at Fred. I did not come closer. I was worried about where the boys were.

Fred was drooling. Since his stroke, he was always in shambles, tilted. He looked like he was a pile of pieces of a man. His hair was white strips to his shoulders, stiff and unwashed. He jerked his head back and looked into my eyes. Tears came streaming down his cheeks, and he smiled and then grinned wide. He pointed with his good hand.

"She fat," he said. He laughed hard. "What the hell took you so long?"

I said I was sorry we were late, and sorry we had to leave so soon, but Mom was expecting us. "I'll be back," I said. And I took his damp, cold hand and pressed it between my hands. I wasn't sure the boys should see him.

"I'll be back soon," I whispered in his ear. "I'll be right back."

"No," he said. "No, no, no, no."

Donny sat up, but he did not appear to wake up.

"No," Fred said. "Look at him. No."

My mother had designated a gas station near her house as the place from which to call her before I arrived, to give her what she always called "fair warning." Dave and I found the gas station or what had been the gas station; it had been razed. Now it was a pile of concrete and rebar, rusted rods jutting out at crazy angles. Concertina wire surrounded the lot.

"Now what?" Dave said.

"Everything's changed! This wasn't like this before," I said. "Could I use your cell phone to call her?"

"You keep saying that," David Junior said from the backseat. "'Everything's changed. Everything's changed.'"

"Boys," Dave said. He never yelled at his kids. He whispered. When he had to give direction, he pulled them into a gentle hug and whispered into their ears. The wilder they got, the quieter he got, and the closer he pulled them to him.

Dave handed me his cell phone so I could call my mother. She needed this specific amount of time, the time from here to her house, to be ready. I'd always called from here; she counted on it. Meanwhile, Dave turned us down a street I didn't know even existed. It was pitch-dark, but the night sky over Orlando looked awake and sparkly, like blue velvet.

Dave said he wanted a beer. I tried not to look at him when he said this. When I first met him, he was in AA. Now he drank a beer or two every evening. I usually joined him and it felt okay to me, casual, in check. Plus, Dave was an ardent Libertarian. He put great stock in leaving people to themselves, not making policies and laws. Most laws were, in his words, redundant and unnecessary. Trust each person to do the right thing—that was his philosophy. Mind your own business. Let people make their own choices and live with the consequences. He had a code. He talked about it quietly, with a kind of regard that made me trust him. I knew he would never cheat on me. His code included loyalty, caring for his family, and doing the right thing. Dave carried a copy of *The Federalist Papers* in his glove compartment. He knew the Bill of Rights by heart. He knew when and how and why America went off the gold standard, and he worried about integrity and how people could be raised and educated to think for themselves. He was in the NRA, which concerned me: I didn't want to sleep in a bedroom where there were guns. If we fought about these things, he always won because he knew countless facts. He'd been on the debate team in high school, going to State. I'd never known anyone who cared so deeply about *the right thing*. So, when it came to drinking, I didn't worry about him losing control. This man collected coins and stamps and vintage toys. And Hazel Atlas kitchenware from the 1930s. This was a man who, though he didn't cook, adored green glass dishes and who believed we should back up our promises with *gold*. Beer was not a problem.

"Excellent idea," I said, regarding the beer. "But not to take inside, right? And not to drink in the car." He'd have to drink it in her driveway, on the sly; my mother wouldn't let alcohol in the house. I was happy for her to think he was a non-drinker. She would *love* the Libertarian stuff, the march-to-your-own-drummer routine, the almost militant privacy stuff. She would eat it up, and I was pleased about this connection they would have, but I could see slipping out myself for a sip of beer to take the edge off. More than a sip.

With my encouragement, we pulled into a Texaco. The gas station speakers blared Tom Petty's "American Girl." Three scruffy stringy men, red-tan Orlando men, crystal-meth jittery, stood by the gas pump smoking. It was one of those places that looked like it was on the verge of explosion.

Dave patted my leg three times with his palm. *Okay, now.* He reached under the seat for his wallet, feeling around with both hands.

"I'm fine," I said.

"A little tense," he said. He laid his palm on my knee and squeezed. "It's okay," he said. I hadn't told him about what the boys had seen in my father's house. I had found them out in the garage, where Fred had a VCR and a computer, and on both screens there'd been porn playing. I'd steered the boys gently to the car, apologizing. How had I not understood this kind of thing was going to happen? That the boys would see exactly this?

"Do we need anything else?" Dave said after a moment, chocking his chin.

I thought, *Yes.* We need anything else. We need everything else.

The phone rang and rang in my mother's house. I shivered in the weirdly warm air next to the car. I envisioned us seated around her dining room table, playing Password. A family experience, a fun night for the boys. I loved looking at the words in the slim red and brown sleeves, the little blue window magically revealing the one word you could not say. Eating Chex Mix like we used to do, me and my mom and my brother. I think we ate Chex Mix. I remembered making Chex Mix, vats of Chex Mix. Didn't I?

I didn't see Dave in the store. A tiny elderly woman at the counter, nervous, was staring at me, hard. She looked angry, angry at me specifically.

I leaned in the back window. The boys fanned themselves with Magic cards tucked between their fingers.

"Are you starting with a human character?" Jacob said to Junior.

"Half human." Junior was a stick, a daddy longlegs.

"Half?" Jacob said. Dave said he and Jake looked alike, but I couldn't see it for the life of me. Jake had long blond hair, thick bones, huge steel-gray blue eyes, the kind of eyes that said, *Please.* Not a question. A reminder.

I didn't know if I could leave the boys alone in the car here.

A couple of days ago, Dave had run into Sarah, their mother, in a convenience store near home. She'd asked him for three bucks. He had tears in his eyes when he told me. I leaned against him and whispered, *I'm so sorry,* and felt his heart beating scared-hard. Not fast. Hard. I hadn't met Sarah yet. Part of me hoped I wouldn't ever have to. Large parts of me hoped this. Almost all of me. I was afraid of her, afraid she'd try to kill me for taking her sons, making them my own. "A lot of guys say their ex-wife is psychotic," Dave had said to me once. He'd pointed to his chest. "*My* ex-wife is psychotic." At first I'd been alarmed by Dave's story: Sarah had been in the state mental hospital; he had to leave her in order to keep the boys safe. But he understood mental illness; I loved how he talked about it. I'd been obsessed with R. D. Laing and radical psychiatry in college, and Dave had similar views. Diagnoses, Dave thought, were rough guesses, blunt tools, always more inaccurate than they were helpful. Dave said mental illness was not really anything separate from who the person was; it wasn't illness as much as it was intensification. He believed mentally ill people had a lot more control than they let on. They partly made themselves crazy, intentionally, because there was a kind of power and freedom in abandoning this reality, these rules. They enjoyed it sometimes. He said some mentally ill people you feel really bad for. Some, he felt, would have been very difficult people anyway. Mental illness didn't really change people. It just made them more of who they were going to be anyway. Mental illness was less like obliteration, more like italics.

I started telling the boys how excited my mother was to have something akin to grandchildren—she would treat them like princes. I was pretending the Fred stop hadn't happened. Junior said he could go for a pop.

"You're already finished with the last one?" I said.

"Heather," Jacob said. "You keep buying smalls. We drink liters. We drink liters!"

I didn't want the boys to move. I didn't want to lose them. I told them to stay put and I scooted across the greasy parking lot, past the smokers and the pumps, leaping across the oily blurs on the cement. I opened the door, and the hard-staring, tiny woman flew out, shaking her head, gaze fixed on the sidewalk just before her. She had on a hat, sunglasses, thick new white sneakers, and a jacket; she seemed ostentatiously incognito as she clutched a gallon of milk and her purse to her chest. She dashed past me, and I could feel the heat coming off her body. She didn't look back. She ran to the edge of the parking lot and disappeared into the night.

I went in the store. The clerk behind the register had kinky red hair, brushed into submission. Her pale pink T-shirt read I COULD GO FOR A NICE STIFF ONE. The I in STIFF was a martini glass, tilted. I strode directly to the back. The area was labeled with big red plastic letters, spinning on fishing line: C O L D B E E R. Three men stood with the fridge doors open, moving as if in slow motion, pulling out their cases. I called out, turning around and around, "Dave? Dave? Dave?" I peered down the hall that led to the bathrooms. I had the cell phone in one hand and the walkie-talkie in the other. I'd bought walkie-talkies for the trip because I was afraid we would lose each other, that I would not be able to find the boys.

I decided to stay in one place to be easy to find. I waited for Bob Seger's "Hollywood Nights" to end, but it was one of those songs that ends three times, and each time I got faked out. Even though I knew all the words by heart, I really didn't.

No Dave. Finally, I went back out.

Dave was behind the wheel, pulling away from the pump, inching up to the store, his face a messy mix of worry, impatience, confusion, doubt. Behind the wheel he held up his arms, as in *What's wrong?* combined with *I gave up*. I got in.

"You saw me," he said. "You were looking right at me. And then you just walked right past me like I was a stranger."

I shrugged. "I didn't see you."

"You were dissed, Dad," Jacob said. "It happens."

I buckled myself in and kissed Dave on the cheek and tucked myself into my family feeling, and very quietly, without a word, we drove to my mother's house.

Four

Set inside my mother's front door was a tiny wood door-within-the-door, a little window with spindles. I knocked and it flipped back, as if by itself.

"Can I help you?" My mother's wary voice came out of the tiny door-within-the-door.

"Mama, it's us!" I said. I had my arm around Dave. "So sorry we're *so* late. We just tried to call. All these delays." Why wasn't she opening up?

"Hi, Pat!" Dave shouted.

"Grandma!" Junior sprang from his kneeling position at the doorbell and plastered himself against the front door. He poked his fingers between the wood spindles of the little opening and wriggled them inside. "Gammy!" he said, in the voice used to summon a very small child or a new puppy. "I see you! Yes I do!" he yodeled. "Peeka peekaboo!"

I loved that Junior called my mom "Grandma," although I knew she'd be startled and unhappy. I wanted her to see his crazy sweetness for what it was, nerves and love. This was a kid who hugged strangers, who talked to everybody, who took a bow when he entered a shoe store, the dry cleaners.

With both hands, Dave pulled Junior back from the door. "Slow down, big fella," he said in his soft voice. "Easy now, son."

"Kind of awkward," Jacob said quietly. "I don't think she wants us to come in there."

"Shh," Dave said. He cupped my shoulders in his big hands and whispered into my ear, "It's okay. She leads a real quiet life. Three big Michigander men banging her door down—give her space, sweetheart." He was holding me back. He was talking very slowly. Dave was a quality engineer for Steelcase, the largest office furniture manufacturer in the world, but he had worked in construction before, and before that he had worked the night shift as a security guard at Pine Rest, the mental hospital in Grand Rapids, where Sarah had later ended up as a regular patient. I imagined him using these skills—loud and slow speech, creating space and time around the person, entering very slowly and possibly sideways—in his previous line of work. In his marriage. Now with my family.

The little gate in the door clicked shut, and I heard bolts sliding back, a chain, clicking, unlocking.

My mother looked so tiny, so rigid, like wire. Her face was very, very wrinkled, like crumpled paper, very tan. She looked a dozen years older than when I'd last seen her, not two or three. She cowered, tiny, afraid. I wanted to hug her. I wanted to rub lotion on her and feed her pudding and air out this house, which smelled of old clothes and bug spray and dust. It was seventy degrees outside and she had the heat on.

She shook her head. She wouldn't look at me. She kept her eyes on the floor. "I was a terrible, terrible mother. I know you don't like me. It's okay." She hunched her shoulders and gave a wan smile. She looked bereft, so frail. I wished I'd come down more often, sooner. How much time did she have left?

I said, "Well, it's so great to be here and to see you. I'm so happy for you to meet the boys." They were waiting, just out of sight, on the other side of the door. Dave thunked the suitcases onto the stoop.

She shook her head and looked at me suspiciously as though she knew me from somewhere dangerous, *America's Most Wanted*. "No," she said. "No, Heather. But it's okay. You're embarrassed of your old mom. Who wouldn't be? I'm not blaming you. I was just surprised. Did you have a wonderful time with your father? How is he? I need to get down there. I've been remiss."

"Mom," I said. "I'm not embarrassed of you." I could hear the edge in my voice.

Dave poked his head in the door. "Hello there," he said, soft and friendly. "We just saw you at the store, I think. Good to meet you." I thought: He's making this up. I assumed he was trying to be extra nice, to make her feel at home.

She ran. She ran from the door back into the depths of the house.

And then I saw her shoes. Those boxy white shoes. How could I not have recognized my own mother?

The table out in the Florida room was set for four, goblets and silver and pale blue linen napkins, her best dishes. She had a vase of fresh flowers—camellias—and at least six empty serving dishes set out, each laden with a silver spoon or serving fork.

She came back out, looked stressed and wary; she was all business. She set Jacob to peeling cucumbers. Junior filled glasses with ice. In the living room, I noticed she'd set stuffed animals on fresh pillows, and she'd turned two sets of bed linens into welcoming rolls.

"So, honey, I got back from the store in the nick of time. I quick ran out and got an extra gallon of milk! I'm a little flustered, I guess." She was poking rolls in the microwave, bending at the waist to be on eye level with it. "I thought: *Boys! Boys need milk! They need milk!* I remember how much your brother used to go through, my gosh in heaven I should have invested in a cow!" Her eyes glittered. She leaned against the counter as though holding it up against great force. Then she hopped back to the oven. "What was I doing?"

After dinner, Dave took the boys on a walk around the neighborhood so my mom and I could get caught up. He whispered to me, "Let her be how she is, be nice, honey." She closed and locked and chained the door behind them and turned to me and said, "Do you help him with his grammar? Did he go to college? You know how I value education. I was so surprised to hear grammar mistakes coming out of such a nice man! I know you can be so diplomatic. It's one of your best qualities. The teacher! Your father and I are so proud. If only you had a job that paid you what you are worth! Have you considered trying to find something more lucrative?"

I looked into her taut face, turned up at the ceiling, all serious and imperious. I'd seen her wince and purse her lips when Junior said "aksed" and Dave said "we seen."

"Why don't we clean up and we can talk," I said, taking the higher ground.

In the kitchen she said, "I can tell you are a big help with those boys. What's the name of the big one? Remind me."

"David Junior?"

"Oh, yes, yes, David. Of course. I'm not one to call people 'Junior.' " She smiled and plunged her hands into the sink full of clear, clean water. "It's akin to Bubba. Or Jimbo! What are some people thinking? I'm one to go by just the proper names. Not nicknames."

"But two Daves," I said. "It would be confusing. You know?"

Lowering her voice, she said, "There are things you need to know, and things I need to tell you." She said she and the phone company were working on discovering who was listening in on her calls: someone was patching in. Abruptly she said, "How long do you think they'll walk? How much time do we have?"

I said maybe they'd walk around the block, or maybe down to the canal. We worked on the dishes and she described, at great length, the trouble she had with dogs going to the bathroom in her yard. She'd put up a sign, but it had been stolen. Then she said, "What about the boys' mother? Is she in the picture? Does she accept or reject you?"

Dave didn't want me to tell this story. But I wanted to tell it. I wanted her closer to me, so much closer. If I told her Dave's secrets, I felt we would have a real conversation, something meaningful we could exchange between us.

I said, "We should sit down." I turned off the water.

"Uh-oh," she said. She ran to the table and slung herself into her chair, leaned forward on her elbows. I sat across from her.

"He had to put the boys first, you have to understand, Mom. He would have never left his wife, their mom, if it wasn't what was best for the kids." I left out the two subsequent marriages. I wanted the story to knit us together, yes, but with comfortable, loose loops. We didn't need to choke.

"I admire that," she said, nodding seriously, stirring her cold coffee with her finger. "I like midwestern men. I really do." She licked her finger. She held it there before her lips. "I've always thought death would be better for children than divorce."

"She's not dead," I said.

My mother looked disappointed.

I told her everything I knew. Almost everything. Once I got started, I couldn't stop. My mother leaned in, listened closely, nodded supportively. How Dave's wife got sick after they got married, and worsened after the boys were born. The terrible episodes of psychosis the pregnancies had triggered, the hospitalizations, how hard it had been for her to care for the boys when she came home. I told how Dave found out her parents had known she'd had serious mental illness—chronic undifferentiated paranoid schizophrenia—and kept it from him.

"Oh, heavens," Mom said. "They palmed her off!"

I said, "He really is a great guy."

This was going well, for the most part, I thought. This was so much better than at Fred's. I told her how Sarah was convinced that her mother had been buried alive. She set up camp at the graveside, certain she could hear her mother's muffled screams; they'd take her away and she'd find her way back. She could not believe her mother was dead.

My mother was horrified and rapt, and I went on in great detail: the faith healers, the demon exorcism—how Sarah's father, though a successful doctor, didn't believe in mental illness or treatment or medication, because of the religion he and his people practiced. They were descendants of the nineteenth-century Dutch immigrants who'd founded a tiny Christian enclave a couple hours west of Detroit. *In isolation is our strength* was their motto. The joke was that they were the only group in the history of the world to flee religious tolerance.

I left out parts too. The custody battles and legal issues, the financial devastation, the trailer park fire. Dave had taken the boys to another town, then to his mother's. I simply explained how good Dave was. He'd fought hard to raise the boys on his own, to keep them safe. Her family, it seemed, had consistently refused to believe anything was wrong with Sarah. They blamed Dave. He should go to church. He should not speak of mental illness.

"Almost cultlike!" Mom said. "Heather, by the way," she said abruptly. "Can I get your help with ideas for window treatments? I am stuck. Stuck, stuck, stuck!" She patted at her head with both hands. "I'd so wanted to have this addressed before you came down. Can I pay you for your advice? You are so good with these things. I think you should become a home decorator! I do!"

"Window treatments?"

"I'll pay you. A consultant's fee." She grabbed her purse from the chair beside her and dug out her checkbook. "How much do ya charge?" she said, affecting a western cowgirl accent. "Name your price."

I went over to the windows in the Florida room. Blankets were looped over the curtain rods. Blue calico curtains hung under the rods, and behind the curtains the windows were shuttered tight.

The boys came back. In her silvery "Company's here!" voice my mother said if the boys helped dry dishes, we could have an ice cream party. I gave her a little hug and said thank you. She froze, grimaced.

I needed a little air.

In the driveway, breathing in the scent of jasmine, camellias, grass, my head cleared. I felt like I was inside a bottle of perfume: small, romantic, and good. Fred's house was another land. Mom's house was better. Mom was okay. Barefoot, I walked down to the street.

It was a lot for her. I'd fast-forwarded my life, collecting a man with older children. She hadn't had time to get used to things. Tomorrow would be smoother: we'd all be used to each other.

At the canal, I sat on the cement wall. The purple-green water sparkled in the starlight and streetlight. It felt cooling and soothing on my feet. I'd never been afraid of snakes or gators or dark water. I lowered my legs, up to my knees. It felt as though I were erasing, dissolving, inch by inch. It felt fabulous.

When I got back to my mother's, Dave was standing at the edge of her driveway, furrowing, looking up and down the street for me. I ran up and hugged him, hard. I whispered, "I just needed air. Sorry. Everything okay?"

Dave said there'd been a change in plans, that I shouldn't get upset.

I looked at the car and saw the backs of the boys' heads in the backseat. "Where is she?" I said. "What's going on?"

My mom appeared on the stoop under the yellow lightbulb, apron on, arms crossed. She looked bigger somehow—not just bones and air, like before, but as though there was metal in her, rods. Two words popped into my head: *mean streak.*

She said, "Dave, could I have just a moment alone with my daughter?"

"Of course," he said, at the same instant I said, "No." We walked up to the stoop. We were back where we started.

Dave made a stiff, partial bow. He jangled the car keys. My mother drew back, pressed herself against the front door.

I grabbed Dave's hand. "You can talk to both of us."

"Heather," my mother said. She stood as she had been, arms crossed, fierce, steady.

"Mother," I said.

"Before," she said, "I could look the other way. You understand. But now that there are children involved, I'm not going to be able to condone your lifestyle anymore."

"He's standing right here!" I said.

Dave put his arms around me and whispered into my ear, "I'm going to go ahead and sit in the car, sweetheart, while you and your mother talk, and it's okay, okay, it's all okay." He squeezed my arm. He told my mother it was very nice to meet her and she thanked him for understanding, as though the two of them were together on a higher plane.

I'd been gone for, what, ten minutes? What had happened in there?

"I told Dave I will pay for a room at the Jamaica Palms," my mother was saying. "Can't we just have a nice time together? Please? I have looked forward to your coming for so long! But honey, I can't have your lifestyle in my house. I wasn't raised like that. I didn't raise you to flaunt—"

The Jamaica Palms motel was next to the razed gas station. The rooms were rented by the hour, had been for years. The pool was filled with trash bags and broken glass.

"I told them you wanted to be a grandma. I told them you *love kids.*"

"I wish people would stop using that word!" She clasped her gray, veiny hands to her ears. "I can't take this!"

Dave drove us to another gas station. He sent the boys in for candy. The two of us agreed that Dave should take the boys back to Michigan. I cried. I wasn't sad the boys were leaving; I was glad of that; it didn't seem safe here for them. It was that I'd been so wrong, so profoundly confused.

We found rooms near the airport, at a brand-new hotel. It smelled acrid, like a cheap new toy. The boys spent half an hour going back and forth between our adjoining rooms, locking and unlocking the inner doors, then they headed for the pool with their dad, who took two tall beers and no towels. We'd all go to Disney in the morning. They would then fly home. I'd do my speech.

When they came in, I woke up but pretended to be sound asleep.

"You're playing possum, honey, but that's okay, you get your rest," Dave whispered in my ear. "Go to sleep now. It's safe and good here." He stroked my back in long soothing stripes, using both hands. Sometimes, when I slept in a bed not my own, I woke up screaming, unsure of who I was, where I was, what had just happened. Now I rolled over and curved into him. I could feel his heart beating, his good breath.

In the morning, the boys didn't want to wake up. Disney was for much younger children. Did they have to go? Yes, I said. We needed to do one fun thing while we were here, or I'd feel too awful. Dave shaved, showered, and ironed his pants. He ironed for all occasions.

We drove out to Disney. The highway out there passed a trailer park where I'd once lived with my dad, then a duplex of cement blocks, painted brown, that we'd rented for a while, and my old junior high. I kept quiet about these places. I pretended I didn't recognize anything. I stopped saying everything had changed. This part of town hadn't at all.

"Heather. Now, here's how you make a fist," Jacob said out of the blue. "No. No. That's a terrible fist."

I tried again. I tucked my fingers into themselves, and rolled them into my palm tightly, so I was clawing myself inside my fist.

"You are going to end up with broken hands." Jacob's massive hands curled into themselves. He unpeeled my fingers. "You are not protected at all. You're very vulnerable." He handed back my hand. He leaned over the seat, hung there, looking at me hard. "Do you *want* to die?"

"No," I said. "I must live."

An hour later, Jacob and I were draped on a bench across from the long, snaking line of people outside of what he called The Swamp Ride, hot, sweaty, tired, and cranky. Dave and Junior were in line for Space Mountain, or maybe by now riding it: Who knew? Jacob hated rides. Dave hated how costly the food was. Junior hated the lines. The whole place was for six-year-olds, he said.

"Do you read me?" Jacob said into his walkie-talkie. Feedback bristled into the echo. His leg hairs grazed my leg.

"Ten-four," I said. "Over." We were wasting the batteries big-time. We were burning up time and battery power and we were melting.

"Dad really is a ninja," he said, out of the blue, confidently robotic. And I agreed. Dad was a crafty, sly ninja.

Disney was ten degrees hotter than Orlando, and everything had changed. The flower shop where I'd worked was gone completely. Toys and Dolls, where I'd stocked Madame Alexanders and giant Poohs, was now high-end electronics.

"You're breaking up," Jacob said. "You're breaking up. I'm going! Down!" He plunged from the bench to the red concrete and seized up, lying on his back, flailing on the concrete. He did this sometimes, as a joke. He was ten. It was hard to remember, because he was so tall and his hands and feet were so enormous. The Dutch were a big people. "Wha-a-a-z-*zup*!" he chortled on the sidewalk, convulsing in a dying way.

A group of pale wide tourists approached with a phalanx of strollers. Jacob didn't move. He lay at my feet and the stroller babies peered down at him, agape, drooling, like he was the most glorious aspect of Disney thus far.

The largest man, in a Tigger ball cap, said, "Can we ask your mom to take our picture, buddy?"

Jacob shrugged and closed his eyes. "Whaz-*z-u-u-p.*" He waggled his tongue and shook his hands, thumb and pinkie out, loose fists, crazy. The tourists waggled away and still Jacob didn't get up off the sidewalk. "It's going to take the rest of the day to find our car again. Don't we have to get to the airport like kind of soonish?"

I gave him five bucks to get a Coke.

And that's when I lost him. He didn't come back. I waited for fifteen minutes, maybe half an hour. It seemed endless. And then I did everything wrong. I left the scene. I did not make a grid. I wept. I worried and I walked in circles, spotting one Jacob after another—none of whom recognized me—while an endless loop of "It's a Small World" played in my head.

I needed to regroup. Then I'd make my way to security and

fill out the forms. I'd guided weepy, terror-stricken people through the Lost Child Process many times, when I'd worked here. A man was sitting on a bench in Tomorrowland, in the one spot of shade in all the Magic Kingdom. There looked to be plenty of room for me.

I tried the boys again on the walkie-talkie.

"Hey, sweetheart," the man on the bench said. "*There* you are."

I jumped back, dropped the radio.

It was Dave. I yelled at him. Where had he gone? I had lost Jacob! He pulled me to him. Everything was fine.

"We're up here," Junior said, and there they both were, Junior and Jacob, hanging like giant zoo animals in the fake tree above our heads.

Dave hugged me, hard. He smelled like sun and peaches.

"She looked right at me. She looked *right at me*," Jacob said. "I was all like, 'Follow me,' and you saw, Heather. You looked right at me. You were right with me!"

"I didn't see," I said.

I changed clothes for my talk in the parking lot. I crouched behind the dumpster and slipped on my fuchsia floral Betsey Johnson skirt, the most expensive skirt I'd ever bought: three figures and not on sale. I saved it just for giving readings. It had a lace-trimmed flounce around the hem and an easy elastic waist. The skirt sashayed from adorably sexy to comfortable and forgiving in one fell swoosh.

I would like to have been, as a person, more like this skirt.

I put on eye shadow and bright pink lipstick, then brushed my hair in the side-view mirror, pulling wild front hunks back with a barrette and blanketing the unruly rear central zone with a swath of straighter, more compliant front-zone hair.

As I stood up and hitched my skirt and pressed the top to my skin, I suddenly had a strange sinking feeling that the clothes weren't going to stay on. They felt slippery, see-through.

Up sailed a perfectly manicured woman with a cap of sleek ash hair. *Lula Mae* was on her large name tag, perfectly positioned on the breast of a crisp green linen suit. Lula Mae was a manicured lawn.

"Hey, Heather!" Lula Mae called, as though we were on opposite shores, and Estelle, name-tagged, leggy, a strong kind of pretty, sailed up right next to us. "Hey, girl, you made it!" Estelle handed me an envelope, my check. I loved conferences, festivals of labeled strangers

"You are our most requested speaker ever," Lula Mae said as we scooted across the lawn.

"Last year you were so great," Estelle said. "Just so great. Are you going to get frisky up there again?"

I didn't know if this was a warning or a request. I confided that the reason I was late was my mom. I wasn't sure how much longer she could live on her own.

"It can come on *fast*," Estelle said. We paused, and she took my arm and held it gently, like you would a small wildcat. I let my arm be in her arms.

"We just put my mom in a place," Lula Mae said. "Hardest day of my life. Hardest day of my entire life, let me tell you."

"What place?" I said. She said she'd give me the numbers: her lawyer, the place, a great social worker.

"And here's your friend Joe," Estelle said. "I'll let you say hello."

Joe gave me a good clean hug.

"Is your hair different?" I asked him. He said no. "Is something different?" I noticed my southern accent had returned.

Joe ushered me into the auditorium. A tiny white-haired woman who looked exactly like my mother—white pants, blue linen shirt—scooted down the corridor, looking scared and eager to please and polite. It was my mother. I couldn't believe she'd found out about the speech. I was happy to see her, and terrified too. Perhaps she'd gone through my briefcase. She often said, "I'm not one to go through people's things!" It made me think, the way she said it, that she went through people's things all the time.

I braced myself to introduce her to Joe, but she walked right on past us. It was not my mother. I could tell from the way she walked away: she had my mother's head, but not her back or her gait. A group of other women welcomed her into their circle in the back of the room, by the coffee station, breaking instantly into a wave of warm kind laughter. She was a sturdier woman than my mother had ever been, with wide shoulders, with friends.

I read from one of the stories in my new book.

When I'd first written and published the stories, I told everyone they were autobiographical. The mother was difficult and overbearing, the daughter clever and thwarted, bent on rescuing the troubled brother. And until this moment, on this day in Winter Park, with Lula Mae smiling and nodding in the back by the doors, I'd thought this was true. As I read now, however, it seemed as though the story had been written by a different person, about people I never knew, people who were nothing like the parents I had just seen through the eyes of Dave and the boys. How could I have thought this was autobiographical? I ended the reading early, stopping in midparagraph after about ten minutes.

The first question was from a man at a front table.

"Are these stories autobiographical?" He'd stood up to speak and he remained standing. "I read a review that said this is autobiographical. And that's the trend, I know. But these people—this strains at our belief. There are dysfunctional families. But there isn't anything like this. This strains credibility."

I saw he was angry. I smiled. I sipped water. I looked around the room. I looked at my watch. I said, "That's an excellent question. I've been thinking about that all day, and just as I was reading . . ."

There was a long pause. Everyone was waiting for me either to take offense or to say something intelligent about autobiography, fiction, narrative distance, the ethics of writing about family members. I was waiting for the man to sit down. I didn't know what to say. Finally, I said something I had heard Rick Moody say about the movie of his book *The Ice Storm*. The movie, he'd said, was like the evil twin of the book. Autobiographical, I said, was more like autopilot. When we wrote fiction, some kind of automatic story generated itself, based on what we knew about what we saw. I gabbled on and on about how the deeper truths emerge, how truth is embedded in intention, not fact. When I noticed that two women in the front row were taking notes, I shut up.

After the talk, I sped down the twisting brick side streets of Winter Park, passed the golf course, turned around, lost, passed the golf course again. I was looking for a busy road—any busy road. I plunged back into traffic, honking, honking, sorry. I pulled into a restaurant on 17, a Chinese place that had been elegant to me from afar when I was a child. I was always begging my mother to take us there. The restaurant was closed. It had a pay phone outside, by the red-leather-upholstered front doors. I'd loved those doors, like vertical couches. As a kid, I'd always thought bad people would bounce off and good people would slip inside. Once my mother drove me around back and said, "See? See? Filthy. No way will you get me in there. Not if you paid me would I eat in a place like this."

On the phone now, I told my mom the boys were safely on their way home, and she said how nice it was to meet them.

I swallowed hard. Did she not remember kicking us out, me and Dave and the boys? To prevent myself from saying anything unkind, I said, "I can't hear you!"

A siren passed, leaving my ears ringing. I reminded my mother I had my reunion and then I'd be home; it might be late.

"You won't be here for dinner?" Her voice was metallic.

"I'll be at the reunion. I signed up for the food."

"Where?" she said. "What food?"

"The old gym."

"That was torn down years ago!" she said. "Gotcha."

I hung up. I banged my head on the red cushion door of the dream restaurant of my childhood, a door that was tattered, slashed, and grimy. And much harder than it looked from the road.

Five

When I was fourteen I wanted a living bra in the color "nude." Lisa Colpac had a nude living bra, she'd had one since she was eleven and a half. She brought the box to school. She was the nicest, coolest girl in my class. Through junior high, she allowed me to copy her math, though I wasn't allowed to approach her or talk to her out loud or pass her notes anymore. She told me I scared boys away, particularly Trey. She loved Trey. I just wanted a bra. I did not have breasts. But I had pain.

I wanted anything—anything: panties, pants, a hairbrush, a couch, the bra—in the color called nude. L'eggs panty hose in nude, in their silver plastic egg, would have made me happy for the rest of my life. I wanted things in the new "wet" look too. I was fourteen years old, I whispered to my mother. I needed to shave my legs, wear white Levi's cords, wear Candie's, keep a comb and lip gloss in my pockets and use both every few minutes. I was the lowest person at my latest school, Cherokee Junior High. There was one other person who was like me, not talking, head down, eating lunch alone, weirdly dressed, no comb: a boy named Ricky Spees. People said he was my boyfriend. He was not at all my boyfriend. We never spoke to each other or to anyone else. He was a frightened, terrible boy in high-waisted pants and clodhoppers. Like me, he was a nervous wreck, an idiot, a ghost. I steered clear of that boy. I thought of him as a suicide risk and also contagious.

My father had moved out of the Holley Apartments and was living somewhere in Winter Park or north Orlando. I knew from eavesdropping on a call he made to my mother that he had been to Germany, and he was back. He was working and he had two girlfriends. "Livestock," he'd called the girlfriends. My mother had wept into the phone.

At the house on Buckwood Drive, my mother was cemented in her bedroom for days at a time. I mostly wanted to go away to anywhere else. When I mentioned to my mother that I would *love* to go to prep school, she said under no circumstances. With what money? And with my record?

I wasn't sure exactly what she meant. I didn't have a record. Until last trimester, when Lisa Colpac moved to sit next to drippy Trey, I'd made straight A's. But I didn't argue. Record, okay, I have a record. Can I buy a bra? With my own money?

Never, she said.

My mother had to stay in the dark. She called it a headache. It seemed more like cancer to me. Something large. A head death. She was half asleep, almost frozen. I could poke her with a pencil or tap a book on her forehead, and I did, and she would not move; her eyes were open. She wasn't dead but she was. It was strange, boring, and smelly; an aroma of old peaches and fur. She couldn't have any light on her, or any moving air. I looked for words in the school library's psychiatry books to locate my mother. I found *catatonia*, but I was sure she was just faking being frozen. My father had left her because she wasn't any fun, and she was trying to get him back. She could, for example, get up whenever she wanted to. She just didn't want to, most of the time. Meanwhile, I was supposed to be doing laundry, studying, ironing, being quiet, not leaving the house, not turning on the radio, not answering the phone, never letting anyone in the house. I could go to school but nowhere else.

Every afternoon after school, while my mother fake-slept, I went into the bathroom, sat on the low counter, and slowly took off all my clothes. I looked at every inch of my body. I inspected the parts between parts. I pretended I was my lover. I looked at everything—everything—I tried to see inside. It was nerve-wracking and delicious. I was *making* myself into myself. Why not go for gorgeous?

Once in a while my mother banged on the door, rattled the knob. "What are you doing in there? Come out. Right now. You know I don't like locked doors."

I smelled my armpits. I needed deodorant. I went to her bed, clothed again, and pleaded my case. She said no, no, no. "I'm not ready to get into that sort of thing," she whispered. "Smell me," I said. "I stink." She said she didn't think it was that bad yet.

She owned two bras. They were the creepiest things. I couldn't even try them on. I didn't want what was on her body to touch my body. When she wasn't so sick, she hand-washed them. She slept in one or the other, under her flannel nightgown, under her robe—even in late spring, even now that it was roasting outside. The off-duty bra always hung on the bar over the toilet, nooselike.

I wasn't going to survive if I stayed with her. I was turning primitive. I was starting to eat paper again, like Ricky Spees. I had to have paper in my mouth all the time. I was beginning to crave rocks under my tongue. I had looked up this affliction, too, and discovered it had a name, a history: *pica*, the craving for unnatural substances. It was rampant among the retarded. It was a sign I was under great duress. I was eating my Ticonderoga pencils. I was eating the metal. I knew I had to get away from her. I felt like I was carrying on, just trying to get attention with my paper- and pencil-eating and stone-sucking. But I couldn't stop, either. I just pretended I was pretending.

I knew my father would buy me what I wanted: a bra, something in the color called nude. People in bras didn't suck rocks or eat paper. I decided to insist on moving in with him.

My father was not convinced this was a good idea. He believed I was troubled. *Emotionally disturbed*—those were his words, and he'd gotten them from my mother. I had heard them use this phrase on the telephone when I was eavesdropping, which I did as frequently as possible. My mother would not agree to even a trial period. She told him I was in serious trouble. I had to be closely monitored. I'd caused untold problems. She didn't believe my father's lifestyle could safely incorporate a child. "I am not a child!" I wanted to yell into the phone. I held my breath. I was no trouble. I was *nothing.* I was turning into a bizarre person because of my mother—I was sure of this—and if I could just get away from her, in a nice way, not to be mean, I would turn into the super-fun person I was meant to be.

"Hang up, Heather. Now," my mother said every few minutes during these conversations, like a pre-recorded message.

Finally, though, my father said he'd take me. He was doing it to make my mother mad, not to make me happy, but I didn't care. I just wanted out of her house. He liked to have fun, I liked to have fun. My mom did not like fun.

The man who came to pick me up, several days late, was a stranger, an interesting stranger, who, if he had not sounded like my father, would have caused me to call the sheriff. I knew he was my father when he whacked me on the butt and said, "Let's hit it. Burning daylight, why is it you ain't ready?" This sounded *exactly* like my father.

He'd permed and dyed his hair into a frizzy golden Afro. He was grinning nervously, fiddling with a bolo tie studded with a turquoise the size of a baby's palm. He was wearing cowboy-style jeans, tight, and ostrich-skin cowboy boots. He was jumpy, tapping one foot then the other. I stood there, gaping. I looked at his belt, expecting to see a holster, handguns. *Fred* was written there, in tooled white letters, *Fred Fred Fred.* The belt was cool. I would love a belt like that with my name. Anyone's name.

I wanted to get in his car and be gone, before my mother came home and everyone changed their minds about everything. But it was so much harder to go with him than I had thought it would be. Without me, I worried, my mother would kill herself. She'd threatened this so many times that I suspected it had become an idle threat. But what if she actually did it? Would it ruin my whole life?

"I'm ready," I whispered. "Let me get my stuff."

In his gigantic brown Oldsmobile Delta 88, he lit a cigarette even though one was fuming in the ashtray. He said we could eat at any restaurant I wanted. It was four in the afternoon. This was the opposite of anything my mother could even conceive of, and it was exactly what I wanted. "Steak 'n Shake!" I said. I'd been to so few restaurants, I knew each one by heart.

"Gary's Duck Inn," he said. He banged the steering wheel.

"Where is this place?" I turned off the blaring radio.

He turned it right back on. "I don't need a lot of static. That's going to be rule number one. Don't give the Grand Poobah any static."

When I buckled up, he said, "Don't do that."

I unbuckled.

"You want to be able to get free. You want to get the hell out." We rared out of the driveway like the car was on fire.

I looked at the Grand Poobah. All I could think of was static.

He took a glass off the dashboard and slugged it back as we careened across Orlando. This could go anywhere, it seemed, and that seemed like the best thing that could happen to me. My dad was back.

He reached down under the seat—we were over the center line now—and from a white plastic flask refilled the glass between his legs.

"Isn't that Gary's Duck Inn?" I said, pointing to a sign in the shape of a giant faded brown duck.

We veered down a side street and through a trailer park. We passed a woman in a see-through top with two little kids wearing only diapers. She looked beautiful and exhausted. She looked exactly how I felt. I watched her out the back window. I was going to get my dad to buy me a bra, and new clothes to go over it, nude shoes, a cute wet-look purse, and makeup.

I took a piece of ice from the drink between his legs. It tasted bitter, like a broken branch, and my stomach tightened and rolled over, and over again. I opened my window and spat it out.

"That's not water," I said. "Gross."

"I'm not thirsty," he said. "For water."

At the Duck Inn, he wept openly, blowing his nose and wiping his face repeatedly with his white cloth napkin. He said he should never have left a child with our mother. She was an emotional wreck, a person hell-bent on unhappiness for mysterious, unknowable reasons; maybe I could shed some insight. She'd ruined me. He wondered how I would ever make it in the world, having been exposed to so much lunacy.

I thought I should know the answers to his questions. I pretended I did know and wasn't allowed to say. This habit of mind—pretend to know, pretend it's not allowed—was how I was sorting my life.

It was too late, he said. I was completely ruined. The woman had single-handedly turned me into a head case.

"I'll have fish in the bag," I said. I ordered fish in the bag because he thought that was the funniest-sounding dish. It frustrated him, but I ate the bag, too, the blackened and browned parchment paper melting in my mouth. This was the life I wanted and deserved: fancy dinners, freedom, new clothes, normal things. I put my feet up on my father's side of the booth, sat back, and finished my water, ate my ice. I was a clever and companionable person, wise beyond my years, and fun.

After the Duck Inn, we went to the Rexall, where my father believed I needed to purchase unmentionable female items, and where I spent as much of his twenty bucks as fast as I could: giant silvery dark plastic sunglasses, hot-pink nail polish, Bonne Bell Lip Smackers, a puka-shell necklace, Maybelline mascara, green flip-flops, and Hawaiian Tropic suntan lotion. These were the things I wanted, the things I'd wanted for years. I sat in the backseat in order to apply the oil properly.

He pulled into the parking lot of Oak Ridge High School. It was nearly six, but the lot was full of cars. The schools were in double sessions in those days because Florida was booming. But I refused to go into the office and enroll for fall. I crossed my arms. I closed my eyes, zipped my mouth, crossed my legs, put on my seat belt, hugged myself. I could not change schools again. My mother had enrolled us in a different school every single year of our lives, some years making us switch in the middle of the year, always sending my brother and me to different schools. I knew no one at Oak Ridge. It was a poor-kid dangerous school with terrible teachers. I had to go to Boone. I knew people—Lisa Colpac, Keith Landreu, Duane Bacon, Ricky Spees—who would be going there. At Boone, I'd have a chance. With my father and this whole new life, I had a chance.

He hollered at me while I held tight to myself and kept my eyes shut. He said, "Ah, goddammit," and I looked at the cloud of hair shining in the sun like frizzled aluminum foil and thought, *I can't really be related to this man.*

In the trailer on McLeod Road, my father pulled a giant jug of gin off the counter and filled a glass that was sitting in the sink. Then he added an ice cube.

One bedroom was all filled up with his bed. You crawled across it to get to the closet. The other bedroom was filled with a lathe, a table saw, boxes of tools, piles of wood. In the jalousie window porch attached to the front of the trailer, a white dog slept on a brown La-Z-Boy. My father said, "Sleep here with Dolly, girl child." He laughed.

"Is there a pillow?" I asked after a little while.

He pointed to the love seat. "Cushions. Many cushions," he said. He patted the back of the love seat. "Good furniture."

I missed my mother, but I knew that would pass; I just had to get used to him. I wasn't going to cry over stupid pillows. Dolly didn't get up from the recliner. I wondered if she bit.

My father had a couple of drinks while listening to the

radio. He went to the bathroom with a fresh drink and a fresh cigarette: he lit one off the other. Then he left. I followed him to his car. He would not say where he was going.

The Olds idled under the giant jacaranda tree. It was good to be outside. The sky was purple. I never wanted to live anywhere else but Florida, it was so beautiful all day and then night was dressed up, with jewelry, so you didn't have to be. I leaned on the hood. "Don't go!" I said. "Let's play a little cards. Take me with you." I peeked at him through the windshield. He was in a cloud of smoke.

He snorted and laughed, then slung ice out the window and backed out as I slapped along in my new flip-flops, holding on to the door frame. "Well, at least tell me when you'll be back." I was like the new dog.

"Classified!" he hollered. He banged my hands with the heel of his hand. Then he lunged down, mouth open. He was going to bite; he meant it. I drew my hands back. I watched him, in a cloud of orange McLeod Road dust, as he turned into the night.

He slept during the day. For dinner, he brought us Chinese food, or we went to Jin Sha, sometimes to Gary's. And then he went out. I huddled with Dolly in the recliner, night after night, and turned on the porch television so that the noises wouldn't startle me as much. All over the trailer there were giant flying cockroaches. You could see their eggs along the inner edge of the television screen. There were lizards on the ceiling, roly-polies everywhere, living and dead. There was

Raid in the kitchen, but I hated to fill my own room up with that white dusty spray; it made me nervous for Dolly and nervous for the geckos, which I hoped ate the roaches and not the other way around. I focused hard on the television, although nothing really made sense. My mother had never let us watch television. Now it was like I didn't know how. I couldn't figure out the plots. Maybe she really *had* ruined me.

Toward the end of the summer, enrollment paperwork came from Oak Ridge High School; I threw it in the trash. One day in August, after my father had been gone for two days and counting, I drank part of a beer. Then I called up Boone High School. My daughter, I told them, would be enrolling. I told them she was interested in band and acting, and asked if there were any clubs. Spanish? Debate? Chess? I gave my mother's address.

Men came by, looking for Fred. When they pounded on the thin flexible door, I hid beside the oven, praying they wouldn't come in. I couldn't put the chain on the door because then Fred couldn't get back in. Fred let Dolly run wild, but if she was home when strange men came by, she barked and growled, and I held her and she held me, her long legs and splendid cool paws on my chest. It turned out there was room on the brown La-Z-Boy for both of us. I thought Dolly and I were a lot alike. It was the best worst summer of my life.

There wasn't a particular day I realized my father was wearing women's clothes—that he wore a bra to leave the house, under his guayabera, that he wore panty hose. At first I thought he had on bandages, then that he had to wear support hose for something medical, something urgent. The realization that he painted his fingernails and toes, shaved his chest, wore women's clothes when he went out at night (I saw heels and dresses in the backseat of the car—where did he change into them?), seeped into my knowing and I kept blotting it, erasing it. I never saw him in a dress. I assumed, just below the level of conscious knowing, that he was gay. I didn't know about cross-dressing; I knew, the way kids know, that this way of being had to stay secret. I knew the only way to keep a secret was to pretend I didn't know. In the weird way of kid thinking, I believed that if I didn't know, no one would.

And with this mind-set I went through all his things. In his dresser and closet were pornography and ladies' lingerie, high-heel pumps, gobs of panties, wadded-up dresses, all too large for me—not that I would have put any of these things on my body. I came across a book labeled *The Nothing Book,* red with a white dust jacket. For a long time, I left it in the box where I'd found it, scared to open it—I assumed it was pornographic. But one night I opened it and it was blank, every page.

This, I knew, was for me.

I wrote and wrote and wrote; I quickly filled the book. Poetry, mostly, filled with flowers and unicorns and knights and stars and phrases like *two hearts beating as one.* There was sex, but it was subtle. Not like in the porn magazines stacked in the bathroom, in the hall, on the kitchen counter. I knew the poems were terrible, but I memorized them and recited my work to myself in the shower. I thought it was very likely I would be "discovered."

My poems were all for a boy. A made-up boy, but he didn't

feel made up. He was from England. He was based mostly on Keith Landreu, a tall, gawky boy in my grade who sometimes affected a British accent, wore sunglasses, gave poker instruction in the halls between classes, and bragged about being the youngest member of Mensa. He said he was a member of the Communist Party. I adored him and detested him and sort of wanted to be him.

School started. I was getting rides to Boone from neighbors most days. Fred seemed to have forgotten I was supposed to go to Oak Ridge. One night a pair of headlights came trundling up the drive and around the duplex and beamed into the kitchen. I cowered by the oven in my panties and my dad's white undershirt. Dolly, like Fred, was out rampaging in the night. Cockroaches flitted. Moths beat against the door. No car door slammed. No one came. I crab-walked across the floor, slowly peeled myself up against the door until I could look through the greasy curtain out the little screen window. The truck was parked under the giant jacaranda. Its long witchy branches made creepy weblike shadows in the light. My father's rifle stood in the corner by the fridge like a prosthetic limb. I wished I had the guts to kill a man if I had to. I cried if a door banged shut, if there was a gust of wind. I didn't even like scabs.

The engine cut off. The headlights stayed on. Someone got out of the vehicle. In the headlights I could see only a silhouette of a tiny person. Then I could see that the person was wearing curlers, and a kerchief, and holding a purse in one hand and picking up sticks with the other, as though attempting to clean up the lawn. This could only be my mother.

I went outside. I was so happy to see her. I didn't want to be, but I was.

"Heather Laurie," she hissed, "get back in there and put clothes on right now, right this instant, my gosh in heaven!" She looked around frantically.

I wanted to stand in the yard in my underwear. This was how I lived now. This was not her jurisdiction. "Hey, Mama," I said. I sounded southern from living with my father.

She shielded her eyes. She scuttled back to the truck.

I wanted her to come inside with me, but I didn't think my father would want me to invite her in. I would have to hide the porn, the gin bottles, the panty hose. So I went around Suzy and climbed in the passenger side.

"Mama," I said. "What are you doing. It's about midnight, or after." I slid my foot against the opposite shin, rubbing out bugs.

"I can't talk to you in that condition, go put on clothes." She was still whispering. "I hate these trees," she said, peering through the windshield into the night. The giant jacarandas loomed over the tiny truck, the trailer. "And I am worried sick about you." She said the school had called. She knew I was missing whole days. She said she could be arrested.

That made me laugh; I couldn't help it.

"It's not at all funny," she said. "Not remotely."

But I couldn't stop. I liked the idea of my mother being arrested.

We had to roll up the windows, the bugs were so bad.

Between us was the box with her thermos, the little packets of food in waxed paper, used waxed paper. "I hate those trees because the root systems ruin septic, they ruin the foundation of houses, they take over the world and cause so much destruction. So much destruction."

"How are you, Mama?" I said. I had never gone this long without seeing her. Against her, after this absence, I could see how different I was, how much living with my father was changing me. I wasn't ashamed to walk around in my underwear. I wasn't eating paper anymore. I had tiny breasts. I was bolder. Keith Landreu had started writing me notes. I had written him back a poem. I had a sense that the way I lived now was preparing me for some great thing. If I could love these people, Fred and my mother, who could I not love?

"How am I? How am I? What kind of question is that? Sick. Worried sick, constantly, every single minute of every single day, that's how I am. How else could I be? This is not an environment for a child, Heather. As I think you full well know. Your father—his lifestyle . . ."

No, no, I told her. It was all fine. I did not tell her Fred was home all day, that he seemed sick and in pain and spent all his time in the bathroom. I admitted I missed some school. I did not admit I was failing math and maybe other morning classes. I was going to get caught up.

The truck, with no air, was sweltering. My mother stared out the windshield. Her face was a knot, her mouth no bigger than an almond.

She turned to me. She was hard, like a stick. She ticked off a list. I hadn't been in school. I ran around with boys. She knew for a fact. I couldn't try to wriggle out of it. I couldn't lie to her face.

"I've followed you, Heather. I have the license plate numbers. I know who those boys are and I know where their mothers live and I am poised to take action. I want you out of this environment. I can't live like this. My precious only daughter. My gosh in heaven."

I didn't want to go back inside alone. Under his ostrich boots, my father wore panty hose. He had taken my brand-new Sally Hansen Sweet Roses nail polish. I'd found it by his shaving stuff, and the next time I saw his nails they were my color. I wanted to tell my mother what I had seen. I wanted to ask her what it meant. But I never spoke of it. This is called loyalty to parents' pain.

We sat in the truck and cried separate cries.

My mother started coming by regularly. Night after night we sat in my father's driveway. I remembered my mother's good things: her white bedspread, her pretty flowered dishes, the way she sprayed for bugs. How the air was close but not smoky: you could breathe. There were a few palmetto bugs, but those you could sweep outside. She always had sweet rolls. She didn't ever leave the house at night. She was conservative, strict, but now that seemed good in a parent. I wanted to go back to her house, but I couldn't go back to her rules: no makeup, no wearing black, no shaving my legs, no telephone talking. Walk, she said, on your knees, in order to protect the carpeting. Walk on our knees? To protect the carpeting? I wanted to please her. I wanted the carpeting to last. But it was *carpeting.* Surely we were supposed to walk on it upright, like everyone else. I could not crawl through my life.

I'd sit with her in old Suzy until she fell asleep, and then I would sneak back inside and fall instantly asleep in my recliner. When my father roared up in the Olds, radio blaring, I would sit up fast. Sometimes I would see Suzy scuttling down the opposite track of the driveway, rocking slowly over the jacaranda roots with great effort, like an ancient, pea-green lizard.

Then Fred would burst in. "Womp up some breakfast, girl child! Let's get up! Burning daylight!"

I would cook us eggs and grits and sausage and he would say, "It's not too bad. It's not too, too bad. I would almost call it edible."

Six

I had barely glanced around the crowd in the ballroom downtown where the reunion was being held, when a man in khakis and a blue oxford shirt, a giant backpack slung over his shoulder, came bounding up to me.

"I might owe you a huge apology," he said. "I think perhaps I treated you a bit badly. But you know your mother." He laughed, but it was more like polite gasping for air. His curly hair was short on top, long on the sides, a style called mullet. He wore a gold stud.

I smoothed my slippery pink flowered skirt and tugged it back up at the waistband. The reality was that these kinds of snug and fussy-pretty clothes always felt at odds with me, like they were trying to fling themselves off my body.

"Keith Landreu," I said as I checked his name tag. *Curls so soft,* they'd called him. He'd been bookish, nasal, inept at sports, rumpled, everything I'd adored. "Oh God. *You're* here?"

Bad Company pulsed over the speakers. "She came to our

house," he said. "I've always wanted to e-mail you. I've Googled you, Heather. Probably too much. Congratulations, by the way. Your book looks fabulous. I have to read it. Anyway," he said, drawing a sip of beer, "I know I should have handled things better back then. But I honestly didn't know what to do." He laughed nervously. He waited for me to say something.

We'd talked, all through tenth and eleventh grade, about getting married. He'd walked me to all my classes. And then one day when I came to his locker before homeroom he didn't even look at me. He turned his back and walked away. We hadn't spoken since.

He leaned forward, lowering his voice. "Your mother told my mother she would sue for statutory rape if I ever came near you. She scared the shit out of us. My mother forbade me to have any contact with you whatsoever. So that's why I did what I did. I should have explained. I've been wanting to for, like, twenty years." He managed half a laugh.

I'd never heard any of this about my mother. She went to Keith's house? How had she known where to go? My mother never went to people's houses.

I looked around for someone else I knew. But all I saw were strangers. I'd come here to show my high school classmates I'd turned out normal. I wanted them to know that the girl who'd eaten paper and rolled rocks around in her mouth now gave speeches, had published a book. I wanted someone who knew me then to know me now. But I didn't know any of these people except for Keith.

He tapped my arm. "So, hey. Do you still have our book?" I could smell his beer breath. I took a step back.

"The book?" Of course I still had the book. *The Nothing Book.*

"Remember our poetry?" He smiled broadly.

"Not really," I lied. "I don't know what happened to all that stuff."

"I still have the jacket," he said, nodding sagely, conspiratorially, as though we were both in this conversation, together. "The blue jacket? That we—you know. On. You know my brother was in love with you. You knew he named his daughter Heather Laurie, right?"

"No, no," I said, feeling dizzy. I didn't know. I wanted a glass of wine. I wanted to go home. I said, "You had a brother?" I stepped back. He moved closer and the mirror ball flashed little pocked diamonds all over his skin.

"You remember Todd and Steven. Steven loved you, too, but not like Todd. Todd's wife looks exactly like you, it's so weird. Really, like, weird. We always talk about this. He hasn't contacted you? Ever? I'm surprised, frankly. I want you to meet my wife, Jane. She's here. Let's find her now." He sounded like a teacher. He slung his backpack over to his other shoulder. "You're going to love Jane. She's just been promoted to dean."

I told him I would be right back, I needed to use the bathroom. I walked, fast, back the way I'd come in, past the registration table. "Forgot something?" the woman said.

I did not need to pee and I was not peeing. I was sitting on the toilet in the cavernous empty bathroom in the Marriott at the Bob Carr Performing Arts Centre, getting my thoughts together. I washed my face and stared at it in the mirror. I studied my eyes, the scars that drew across my cheek, bubbled on my upper lip. I always forgot about the scars, from a car accident

I'd had in my late twenties. I never imagined my face with them. This face, these small dark eyes—this was not what I thought I looked like. But no one looks in a mirror and sees what they expected to see. I leaned closer and tried to imagine what Keith saw when he saw me. I put on more pink lipstick, lipstick I'd bought just for this trip, in a shade to match my flowered skirt. I checked my teeth, wiped off the excess. My eyes looked small and hard and wrong, shut down, frantic.

Keith was leaning against the floral-papered wall right outside the ladies' room. He was alone. He was holding his backpack in front of him, limp in front of his knees.

"So, yeah, don't go yet," Keith said. "You just got here." He seemed to be blocking my way. "I wanted to ask you: Did everyone in your family end up in a mental institution. Or were those just rumors?"

"Keith," I said. I leaned against the wall opposite him. Clearly, he had a theory about my family, and I didn't want to hear it. Keith and his wife, I knew, were historians. This is what they did. They constructed histories. I wiped my face and tried to focus.

In my childhood, there was just enough material—a few weeks of piano lessons, a few months of private flute lessons, a short, humiliating season on the swim team, which I dragged down to new lows until I was asked by the coach to quit—out of which I could, when I got to college, and later, when I met Dave, construct a story that both sounded normal and was true. Now, with Keith looking at me, hopeful and concerted, I closed my eyes. I'd left out so much. I'd left out so much for so long. I hadn't forgotten my history. I'd just worked around it.

There were ways you could know a thing and not know it.

It was like another me knew and that me and this me had never conversed. Compartmentalizing, wasn't it? Except that when you compartmentalized, you put some things away to concentrate on other things. This was different. It was more like a ship had gone down, long ago. And the surface of the water heaved and changed and darkened and calmed. I didn't envision what was below. It was another world. There was enough going on in the world above water, getting my Ph.D., getting tenure, writing my collection, trying to figure out how to be a mom to Junior and Jacob, to make things good with Dave. My above-water life was the one I lived. The underwater, dark life—I never forgot about it, exactly, but it had no corresponding parts in the light up above, in my current reality.

And until now I hadn't run into anyone who held my past and this present in the same light. What I had done, I saw now, was stitch around the dark parts, making a shape, a presentable story of my family. Everything I told was true: I simply found the signposts in my life that other people could reference—swim team, babysitting, kickball, strict mothers, skipping school—and steered my story by them.

"I absolutely have to go now," I said.

Keith put his hands on my shoulders, gently. "Heather, no," he said. "I have so many questions. How did you get out?"

"What do you mean?" I said. Did he think I'd been in an institution too?

He waved his hands around, as though stirring a soup sky. "I find it miraculous we were able to get out. I want to know: How did you do it? You had it so bad. My God."

I asked him again. "What are you talking about?" He didn't have it bad. I didn't have it that bad. Is this what he'd always thought?

His face brightened. He held his pointer finger in the air. I could see him in his classroom at his university. "Remember how you drove me around in your dad's car, when you were, like, *fourteen*?" He was smiling and nodding, his mouth open. "God. Remember those horrible clothes you wore?"

Those clothes. The strange, outdated pants and blouses my mother got from the Cancer Society thrift shop. I didn't know Keith had been ashamed of those clothes too. I didn't know he'd seen anything at all.

"Aren't you married?" Keith said. "I heard you were." He stroked his chin, like an impression of a professor. "Yet you do not wear a ring."

"I wish you the best. I gotta scoot. I have to see my mom." I walked toward the front lobby but he tucked right along beside me, loping, matching my steps.

"Your mom. Oh, God. There is so much I want to talk to you about. There is so much I want to know, go over and everything, compare notes. I want to get copies of any letters you still have. The poems. Do you have the blanket? Can we go somewhere and talk, or tomorrow, are you coming to the picnic? Can you come with us?" He dropped down to the floor and unzipped his backpack.

"That house," he said, digging. "Your mother's house. My God. It was like a war zone. What was up with your mother? What was she, paranoid schizophrenic?" He peered up at me, mildly curious, mildly distracted. *Paranoid schizophrenic?* He said it in the same tone of voice you might say, *Canadian?*

What was she, paranoid schizophrenic? What was she? Paranoid schizophrenic?

I wondered if I could slap him. I'd been lifting weights. I pictured his head flying down the hallway like a bowling ball, like in *Alice in Wonderland.*

Downtown Orlando was deserted except for homeless people pushing shopping carts under the highway bridges, where cardboard dwellings leaned against the steep banks of concrete and the sides of the ramps. I drove fast, turning left on a red. I turned on WDIZ. Bad Company. Again. All the words came back. I sang hard and loud and well, and I longed for a cigarette; I never smoked.

I got off on Fairbanks, then realized it was way too soon. It was easy to get lost in Orlando. It's set slantwise, so north is east. I pulled into a Publix near the highway. Inside, I bought a *Vogue* and a four-pack of baby wine bottles. I drove the back streets in the general direction of my mother's house. If I didn't think about where I was going, I'd get there. If I started thinking, trying, I'd end up in Aloma, Bithlo, Narcoossee.

In my mom's driveway, I leaned over the steering wheel, hooking my chin on it. Her house was pitch-dark. It looked vacant.

I opened one of the little screw-top wine bottles and sipped the greasy merlot. Each time I thought of Keith's words, *war zone* and *mental institution,* I felt a pinch. I finished off the first bottle.

I knocked softly, then harder, on the front door. No lights came on and I didn't hear a sound. Then the garage door churned upward halfway and I ducked under it, my suitcase banging my shins.

"You are in the nick of time," my mother said, not unkindly.

"It's so hot in here!" I said.

She darted into the kitchen. "It's late October!" she yelled. "Okay to heat a home in winter, last time I checked!"

I went to the guest room. It was hot and stuffy, and the closed-room smell was overpowering. I'd never be able to sleep. I sat on the bed.

Against the wall, on the floor, were unframed oil portraits of my brother and me.

In my portrait—I was about five or six—I wore a silvery-white princess dress with a big blue silk sash. My brother was in a little blue jumpsuit. We looked well groomed and loved and suburban, almost rich, like children from a book. She had never framed them or hung them. They were propped here temporarily, for my visit, for my benefit. She knew I coveted them. She didn't hang art on walls: she propped it on the floor and covered it with pillowcases. She didn't like to ruin good plaster, she said.

I moved the portraits to the dresser, then closed the door and took off my pretty skirt. It was damp from the nervous sweat of a long day. I took off my strappy top and my excellent pink bra and my sexy agonizing sandals. I hid the remaining wine bottles in the drawer of the little dresser that nested between the beds. I pulled back the drapes. Bedsheets were tacked to the walls, covering the windows. I pushed them aside. I used some of the clothespins to hold back the fabric. I lifted the blinds. Dust flew like smoke. I sneezed and sneezed.

"Bless you, oh goodness, bless you! You okay in there, darling?" my mother called sweetly from just outside the door. "Are you hungry? Can I feed you? I have so much food! I was expecting to feed so many people, and now it's just you!"

I pulled and pulled but the window wouldn't open. I ran my hands around the sides, feeling for an obstruction. And then I saw. Little holes had been drilled into the metal frames and there were nails in each hole, securing the windows.

I pulled the nails out and opened the windows all the way. The air was jasmine and gardenias, that familiar perfume. I breathed in deep. I tried to remember. Had she always nailed the windows shut? Yes. It was just how we lived. Bare lightbulbs. Sponge baths in the garage. Walking around on our knees. Windows nailed shut.

Paranoid schizophrenic.

That could not be. Schizophrenics were like Dave's first wife. They were locked away, they were on meds, they were *crazy, crazy people.* My mom was peculiar. It was not possible for me to be thirty-eight years old and not to have known my mother was a paranoid schizophrenic.

....

I lay back in the tepid bath. A black smear in the shape of a wolf's head gloomed on the ceiling above the tub. The salts I'd chipped out of their ancient glass decanter lay on the surface of the water, chunky little islands floating around my body. I would look at the hot-water heater in the morning.

I closed my eyes and sank lower in the deep old tub. I wondered how you would know if someone was crazy. Not just *peculiar, quirky, wacky, safety-conscious, different,* but truly insane.

My mother screamed.

"Who did this? Who did this? Who opened this window? Who has been in here?" Her voice was coming closer.

I jumped out of the tub and wrapped myself in a towel and went into the hallway.

She had covered her face with her palms and she was looking at me through her fingers. I felt enormous, pink, and steamy.

"Who opened a window? Who did it?" She turned and faced the wall.

I had seen her like this before, many times. How had I forgotten? How had I brought Dave's boys here? What had I been thinking? What had I been *not* thinking?

"I opened it," I said. "I had to. I had to get air." I followed her into the room. The window was shut tight, the air perfectly still.

"What in the name of heaven is going on in this room!"

she cried. She put her hands to her throat. She was shaking, shivering. I realized I'd seen all this before.

"Mom," I said, looking at her across the bedroom. She was plastered up against the wall, pressing her palms back into it. "Why are the windows nailed shut? What if there was a fire? I had to get out?"

She rolled her head around, as if my words were taxing every bit of patience she had left. "Heather, please, please put on some clothes. Common decency dictates. This is unreal. My God. My *purse*." She left the room, closing the door firmly.

I crept out to the living room and called Dave. He was happy to hear my voice, I could tell. His voice beamed and ambled and embraced me. Had he been drinking? Too much?

"Dave," I interrupted. "I have to ask you something and I just want you to tell me, okay? Simple and straightforward."

"I'll do my best, sweetheart."

"If you just had one way to tell, how would you know if a person was crazy? What's the one defining characteristic? How do you know?" I knew he would know.

Dave said there probably wasn't one thing.

"But if there was."

"Well, sweetheart . . ." He was talking too slowly. I got the sense he was holding back. He knew; why didn't he want me to know?

"Just tell me."

"They see things that aren't there and hear things no one else hears."

I felt immense relief. Keith was an idiot. I knew my mother. This was not her. I would ask her, and she would say of course she didn't see things that weren't there or hear things no one else heard. I said good-bye to Dave.

"Who was that you were talking to?" my mother said fiercely. We were in the hallway. For a tiny person she was taking up a lot of room, like a live downed wire. She put her arms around herself.

I knew what she'd say to this question. I knew, absolutely, she would say *no.* Did I even need to ask?

"Have you brushed your teeth? They are so important."

"Mom," I said. I was guessing she'd be too insulted to answer. Which would be a good kind of answer. I made myself say it, the question Dave had given me: "Have you ever seen anything that wasn't there or heard voices or things other people don't hear?"

Her hands flew to her mouth, as though I'd socked her there.

She said: "You just want to lock me up. I know you. That's all you've ever wanted."

She turned and ran down the hall and locked herself in her dark bedroom and I didn't hear a sound.

Dave picked up on the second ring. I told him what she'd said. "It's the wrong answer,." I said. "It's the wrong answer."

He said to get a hotel room. "You can't stay there now."

I packed and loaded the suitcase into the car and flew across Orlando.

Seven

I think everyone has one day like this, and some people have more than one. It's the day of the accident, the midlife crisis, the breakdown, the meltdown, the walkout, the sellout, the giving up, giving away, or giving in. The day you stop drinking, or the day you start. The day you know things will never be the same again.

I'd left my mother a note on the kitchen table; I'd double-underlined *I love you.* I drew the little pig holding a balloon on a string that we always drew on our letters to each other. I drove toward the airport, stopping at my father's house. His back door was wide open. I walked past Donny, sacked out in the same position he'd been in when I was here with the boys, which seemed, now, long ago. I passed the large framed portrait of my father in his silver Afro, centered on a black and red Indian rug. I walked past my old bedroom, where what sounded like the same porn movie bleated and hummed, a woman, or more than one, moaning *uh uh uh* from behind the closed door.

I found Fred in his wheelchair, smoking, at the edge of the swimming pool. It was four in the morning. I sat on the edge of a planter filled with sand and beer bottles and plastic plant baskets, frizzled with foliage long dead. I asked him straight-out: Was my mother mentally ill? Had she ever been?

"Hell, no," he said. He was so close to the edge of the pool. Was his brake on?

"You can tell me," I said.

"I can't hear you," he said.

"I wasn't talking," I said. "I'm waiting for you to tell me about Mom."

"Wah no," he said intently, frustrated. "I don't. No, no, no." He smelled of pee and gin and smoke.

"Whatever I say or anyone says, you say no. It's a reflex."

"No," he said. "No."

I laughed. He didn't. Wasn't he freezing out here in shorts? His skin was so thin. The pool smelled green. The thick water was low.

"Was there ever something wrong with Mom?" I paused. "She was never in an institution, ever?"

His expression didn't change. Ash dropped on my inner arm, stung. I blew it off.

"Was there some kind of breakdown?" I wondered how much he knew. Did he know that after he left she couldn't leave the house for months? I was eleven, my brother was nine, so Mom must have been forty-five years old, unemployed. Did he know she made us walk around on our knees? Did he know about the so-called safety drills? How to swim for the surface if Suzy went off a bridge. How to get out of the house in case of a fire. We'd roll around in blankets, then scuttle toward the front door, patting the walls, patting the doors before opening them. It was fun, we didn't care. Anytime an adult got down on the floor to show you something, you got excited, you said "Yes, yes, yes." We were small children. We were for fire, we were for apocalyptic afternoons. Now I stood, leaning over him, bent at the waist, hands on the wheels of the chair. We were right at the edge. "Dad. I have to know. Was Mom ever in a mental institution or diagnosed as mentally ill?"

"Aw, come on," he said. "Shit." He looked at me, confused, surprised, as though his feelings were hurt.

We were right at the edge. Wind rustled in the palm trees, and in the mercury vapor lights their bright orange nuts glowed like eyes. I'd forgotten that sound, that gentle scratching sound the fronds make that could drive you crazy.

"She's not crazy," he said. "Peculiar." His eyes were blinking fast, fast, fast.

I palmed at the furnace of smoke between our faces. He had a cigarette between his fingers, another going in the ashtray on his thigh.

"Well, she nails her windows shut. Has she always done that?"

"No. Why?" he said, loud, flat, his eyes a blend of curiosity and irritation. "Wah." He leaned forward. This was my father: leaning forward, drink in hand, wondering what, sure of himself, about to say no, annoyed for no reason at all and for every reason, leaning hard into his next chance to expound.

I pulled up an old plastic chair and perched on the edge of

its damp seat. I got out my notebook. "What about when I was born? Was she okay after? Was she ever hospitalized?"

"No," he said. "What for?"

"She was gone at least twice. I know she was gone. Because we stayed with the Hahns, those people you knew from work."

"No," Fred said. From inside, Donny's snoring rolled out, like rocks tumbling downhill. "Him!" Fred yelled. "Him! Sleep! He sleeping for *three days now.*" He raised his arm and shook his fist into the sky.

"Rip Van Winkle," I said. None of the Sellers brothers worked. They were dead or unemployed.

"Rip Van Winkle," Fred said, nodding sagely. "He has to go. I want him *out.*"

"But Fred, you begged him to move in with you. Remember?"

Another eruption of *no*s. The lights in a window across the street flicked on.

I took his hand, caught his eyes with mine. "Did she really have leg surgeries? She was in the hospital. Remember?" I felt like a child impersonating a detective, a vague middle-aged version of Harriet the Spy. "What for—really?"

Fred's mouth was open; he was staring at me, uncomprehending.

It came to me that she hadn't kicked us out until after I'd told her the story of Dave's wife. Was having him in her house—someone who knew mental illness—too risky? She'd been excited about us up until that moment. That's when everything had changed.

Fred was crying now. My brother had been colicky and my

mother had struggled with that, but that was all, he said. She was a good mother. She loved you.

"So, where would she go when she disappeared for days at a time? What was *that* about? Did she do that when y'all were first married?"

"Where would she go." Fred laughed, but without smiling; it was more like coughs of resignation, micro-explosions of despair. He nodded at the glass. *Refill this.* I took the glass and held it in my hands. It was cold and hot. He said, "I was real disappointed you didn't come with those boys last night. I had extra chairs brought down from the Moose. And a mess of smelt. I was waiting. Waiting for you. Waited *up.*" He underlined the words with his good hand, with the empty glass. He looked sincerely sad and he kept looking that way. It hurt under my ribs, in my muscles, in my lungs, to see that look on his face, his eyes, his forehead, everything dropped.

I told him I was sorry. "We had to see Mom," I said. "Remember?"

"You did not. You did not. You did not say that. You did not." He banged the flat of his hand on the armrest.

I went inside and pulled the jug of gin from the counter, where it sat with four brother bottles, the largest size, the kind with built-in glass handles, bottom-shelf. Donny erupted into a wheezefest and I startled, spilling.

I watched my father through the kitchen window as I washed my hands. His tiny bird legs, the yellow-gold hair flanging out and shimmering in the dawn light, his jaw shivering. He looked so lost and desperately in love with the world at once.

Back outside, I flew through more questions. What about

covering up the television with blankets every night? Had she always done that? Was there mental illness in either family? What had her mother been like? What about her sister? I reminded him Aunt Katy would not leave her bedroom, then the house, the whole house. He didn't know what I was talking about. She was peculiar, he kept saying, but she was a good person. "Sweet. Sweet person."

"Fred," I said. "Is there something about Mom you aren't telling me? I'm begging."

"Of course I am not telling you something," he said. He wasn't smiling. "I'm not telling you anything. If I told you something, I'd have to kill you. Classified!"

I laughed. He grinned wide; his giant, glorious teeth gleaming in the intense light that came from the kitchen. I saw he was crying, really crying.

I leaned forward and put my palms on his knees. I breathed in the smoke.

"Fred!" I said. I slapped his knee. "Well, what? What is it?"

"She's peculiar. I'll grant you that." He scooped his head in a giant nod. "The rest? Not telling." He shut his lips tight, pulled them into his mouth.

I paused at the gate to the pool. He looked so bad. I said, "Just tell me what you know. What can it hurt? What's the big secret about Mom?"

My father closed his eyes. "To my grave," he said. He put his hand on his heart. With the cigarette.

I slung my purse on my shoulder and got my car keys out. "What if my plane goes down? What if something happens between now and when you will tell me?"

He winced and swallowed, and then he swallowed some more. He looked at me—right into me. He blinked his giant black liquid eyes. He said, "Then you will die a peaceful sleep."

I turned in the rental car, then ran for the terminal.

I smelled like my father, coated with cigarette smoke and gin fumes. I moved as one moves in a nightmare, running but not getting anywhere. My legs weren't working in sync with real time or with each other. I lurched past the gates, my bag banging my calves, my shins, my ankles.

No one was at check-in at C47. The waiting area was empty. The doors were closed. Did I have the wrong date? The wrong gate? Was I in the wrong terminal altogether? I double-checked the gate. Then I read the marquee message as it bannered by. *Gate change Grand Rapids gate change. A12*. And a delay.

The closer I got to A12, the more my mother began to seem like Mom again, and the madder I got at Keith Landreu. She was not insane. She was difficult, quirky, kind, mysterious, eccentric, "peculiar." If my mother was a paranoid schizophrenic, Fred would have known. I would have known. *Someone* would have noticed and said something. Relatives would have taken my brother and me and raised us. (I'd always wanted my aunt Adele, a gorgeous redhead with a yellow convertible, to do this very thing.) Authorities would have intervened. There would have been doctors, medication, checkups, social services, tons of evidence. It would have been impossible for her to get away with paranoid schizophrenia; it wasn't a very subtle illness. Was it? You couldn't be a paranoid schizophrenic and raise two kids and keep it a secret. It wasn't like low blood sugar.

I was so distracted that I took the wrong tram. I tried to stay calm; I had hours to find my gate. I had just oriented myself in the right direction, down the correct corridor, when who should come lumbering up, out of breath, looking frantic and pissed-off, but Keith Landreu.

"Frick," Keith said, reading something on the bank of the monitors. I stood there, unable to speak or scoot away. "Fucking A." He looked right at me, for help, for someone to blame.

He wasn't Keith. He didn't have Keith's voice.

This happened, I knew, to everyone. When we were upset, we saw the people on our mind in everyone else. I knew it was common, like déjà vu, but still, whenever it happened—whenever I mistook someone for someone else—it made me feel haunted, lunatic. I often said hi to people, just in case I knew them. "Do you know him?" a friend would say, and I never knew how to respond. *Maybe?*

Faux Keith lumbered on his way. And I stood there, breathing as though I'd been chased, in the middle of a busy corridor of the Orlando International Airport.

On the plane, I pressed my face hard to the glass. I said a prayer for my dad as we bellied over his house. I could see his car. With one arm, one leg, and a rusty red knob bolted to the steering wheel, gin between his legs, he was still a better driver than I was. He never got lost. He never got caught. He knew all the shortcuts and two-tracks.

I watched Orlando turn into a tiny toy town, and then Florida became a patch of squares of sodden green and tan, pocked with blue lakes and gray rivers. Then we were above the clouds, which looked like a silver-white floor that would hold us if we fell, and I slept.

One

In my new third grade, no one looked familiar, not even the teacher. I wasn't sure I was even in the right classroom. Already, I had attended six different schools. I was the perpetual new girl, trying to figure out who everyone was. I was shy and unresponsive. When I was called up to write cursive letters on the board, I wanted to, desperately. I loved letters. But I could not make myself get out of my seat.

My mother wanted me to work on the expression on my face. I always looked so sad when she picked me up. The word she would use, she said, was *bereft.* She wanted me to try at least to look happy. She was worried the school would call and report her for mistreatment of a child. "Maybe you can offer to help the teacher. A teacher can be a friend. The best way to find a friend is to be a friend," she said in a singsong voice that didn't sound like her at all.

My third-grade teacher, Miss Tolbert, was not a friend kind of teacher. She wore tiny suits, smoked Virginia Slims at recess, and snacked on Butterfingers in the afternoon. She despised me because I couldn't talk in class. When I was called on, I knew what to say but the words wouldn't come out of my mouth.

During recess, I hung around Miss Tolbert while everyone else ran around screaming their heads off. I communicated with Miss Tolbert telepathically. *How old are you? Do you have a boyfriend? I know you have Butterfingers in your desk drawer but I won't tell!* She never answered. She wasn't even trying to receive my subliminal communications.

I wasn't worried about not fitting in with the other kids. I was worried about how I didn't fit in my family. When I watched other kids playing, I wasn't wishing for friends. I was wondering which ones had mothers who would adopt an extra girl.

The summer after third grade, my father seemed to be around a lot more. He was no longer away on business for months at a time. On weekends he grilled shrimp and steaks on the back patio, tossing me little bits of raw meat, for which I begged. My mother laughed and sang bouncy songs from the 1930s, from her childhood, and made gleeful faces and little waving motions with her hands, like rainbows. We went to Missouri, all of us, and my father drove us all to Nashville to an accountants' convention, where activities were organized for families. My mother began to talk about wanting another baby. At this, my father's face would turn dark, and dinners would end abruptly. Still, we were back to being a family. It seemed as though we'd been through something unpleasant and mysterious and now we were back on track.

And there was hope for me being a normal girl. Mysie Fenton, who lived down the street, invited me on an overnight trip to her grandparents' beach condo in Smyrna. And I was allowed to go. Mysie's parents were Christian Scientists and she couldn't have any medicine of any kind, ever. My mother respected them for marching to their own drummer. We did not take medicine, but we were not part of a religious movement. We were allowed to have half a baby aspirin in an emergency.

Mysie and I swam all day, and in the afternoon her mother made us lie down and rest but we could talk. As we lay on the shag carpet, propped up on our elbows, touching, we examined her copies of *Teen Beat.* She wanted to talk about which Cassidy was our favorite, about the Osmonds, and about Leif Garrett and how he liked pink, and might wear lipstick—just for photographs. What did I think? Did he? Was I really looking? Was I getting bored? Mysie already had boobs. She wore a mesh bra-vest, like a little half tank top. It did not obscure the boobs. In fact, it made me look at them more.

I didn't have a favorite singer. What was the point of choosing one? They were all exactly the same: blond shaggy boys in white shirts open way low. I wanted to go outside and body-surf and count bird flocks; I had a theory I liked to test, that they were always an odd number. But to be polite, I told her I just could not decide which boy I liked. I liked them all the same, I said. Her mother said it was good I wasn't so boy-crazy;

Mysie should try to be more like me. I loved Mrs. Fenton. I thought she was brilliant and kind and wise.

But I am *boy-crazy,* I wanted to say. *I'm completely boy-crazy. I just can't tell any of those star boys apart.* I didn't want to like odd boys; it was just that they were the ones I could tell apart from the others. I kept quiet, though. I wanted to keep my membership as a near-Fenton. But the more time we spent looking at those magazines, the more I hated the Cassidy boys, and Leif, and their ridiculous pouts and bubbles of thought and blow-dried hair. Mysie kissed the pages. I restrained myself from eating them.

Miraculously, I was asked back. Mysie's mother called and asked me to put my mother on. My mother, in a fake-friendly voice, made all the arrangements with Mrs. Fenton, but when she hung up she was livid. "What have I said over and over and over again about not answering the phone? We never know who it is going to be. And the phones aren't safe. We have to keep that kind of communication to a minimum." I was to walk down to the Fentons' and politely tell Mysie that we had chores to catch up on and I wouldn't be able to go after all. I was hysterical, but finally I went. Mysie and her mother came to the door in matching aqua shifts. I told them my family was going camping, but thank you for the invitation and feel free to invite me again.

"Oh, so special and adventurous. Camping where?" Mrs. Fenton said. I panicked. Where did anyone camp? Why couldn't I think? Camping, camping, camping. I had no idea. I ground my teeth, turned, and ran home, windmilling my arms, pretending that I wasn't really a lunatic and a terrible liar.

....

That same summer, when things came so close to normal, my entire family went to a pool party at the Ahearns'. My father knew them from work, a very nice, conscientious, Catholic family with good values, my mother said. She put on a blue knit pantsuit and a watch. She packed towels and made a cake, as though we visited people all the time.

It was exotic and wonderful to be all in the same car together. As we sped across Orlando, my mother gripped the handle on the glove box with one hand and the armrest inside her door with the other and closed her eyes. *Let me walk,* she begged. *Just let me out of this death trap.* My father told her to shut up. My brother and I hunkered down in the way back. My mother cautioned me to work on my expression. I had the pout again. The despairing pout.

The three Ahearn girls were lined up on the stoop in front of their house. My father and Mr. Ahearn went out back with beers. I followed my mother inside. Mrs. Ahearn and my mother sat in the kitchen, wallpapered with black kettles and cooking pots, and they talked and talked. My mother was not herself, but in a good way. She talked fast, with exclamation points. Mrs. Ahearn told me to go play with the other kids. I slunk down onto the floor, behind my mother's chair. My mother said that the Ahearns had the nicest noses. Perfect aquiline noses. The Ahearn girls were going to grow up to be beautiful women.

"How can you tell?" I said. I was hanging in the doorway

now, leaning into the kitchen from the foyer. "How can you tell they will be beautiful women?"

"How could you *not* tell?" the new version of my mother said. She looked at Mrs. Ahearn with pity, as though she were sorry I'd said such a rude blind thing. The bone structure, my mother said. She couldn't explain it. They just had the right kind of bones, and perfect noses. I asked my mother what kind of nose I had.

"Honey," she said. "Please. You have a fine nose. Weren't you asked to go play, nicely?"

What kind, though? I needled. I knew she would have to be nice in front of Mrs. Ahearn. How come I hadn't known noses came in styles?

"I think someone is fishing for compliments," my mother said.

I got tears in my eyes. I wasn't fishing. I just wanted to know if I had the right kind of nose to become a beautiful woman. It was looking like no.

My mother got up from her chair and said please excuse her. She grabbed my shoulder hard and steered me to the front door. "We are guests in this house," she hissed. "Go play with the children."

I didn't want to go play with those kids. I was sobbing, shaking. I could see myself in the hallway mirror. My mother was standing across from me, leaning over, hands on her hips. "Please just tell me what nose," I said. "What kind?"

"Button," she said. "I'd say closest to button."

"A cute little button nose?" I said. I stepped toward her and put my arms around her waist. She pulled back.

"Well," my mother said, appraising me, hard. "Your nose isn't your strongest feature, honey, I'm sorry to say."

What was my strongest feature?

I had nice hair, she said. She was kneeling down before me. She had given in to niceness. "Now, honey, please. Please do as you have been asked! I'm begging you," she pressed. "I'll be right there, Margot," she called to the kitchen, in a fake, *I'm so embarrassed* way.

I spent most of the party in the backseat of the car. At some point my mother joined me, slumped against the door of the passenger seat. Other neighbors had arrived, and they weren't quality people.

"You can't stand people having fun," my father said when he finally came out to the car. He was wearing a towel around his shoulders, no shirt. It wasn't our towel. He drove home with a beer in one hand, steering with the other. My mother said he shouldn't drive with a beer, it wasn't safe. He yelled at her. "Why are you so goddamned averse to having a good time, to happiness?" He sounded perplexed and furious, like stripes.

I hung over the edge of the seat, begging them to stop fighting. "You are as bad as she is," he said. Then he took the beer and poured what was left into my mother's lap. He held the can way up high, and the stream of beer looked like pee. My mother didn't move until he was done. Then she snapped out of it. "Thanks," she said. "Thank you for cooling me off." She made sweet faces. "I was really hot and now, thanks to you, I am all refreshed. You are a wonderful, thoughtful person." She leaned over and kissed him on the cheek. "You are a swell guy, real swell guy." The car smelled like beer, like pee, like sour bread. Soon enough, my brother and my father started fighting, and my father pulled over, and my mother screamed, and I screamed for it all to stop, and that was the unequivocal end to our stint as a happy normal family.

Two

"You're going to cry," Molly said. I was in my early thirties, and Molly was an ex-boyfriend's sister with whom I'd kept in touch, off and on, for years. We sat on the green carpet in her living room. Recently she had put all her Super 8 movies onto videotape, and she said there were great ones of me, playing with her babies. I didn't think I would cry. I thought it would be fun. Politely, I watched as unfamiliar babies played to the sounds of Windham Hill. I spotted younger versions of my boyfriend, always smoking a cigarette, his long yellow hair pasted to the sides of his head, his yellow long board under his arm, wearing the red flowered bathing suit I had mended more than once. I remembered that bathing suit of his, how it had felt in my fingers, stiff and sexy on him. I figured one woman for a younger Molly, the others her friends. Strangers frolicked on the beach, kids played in a baby pool. People held up giant submarine sandwiches to the camera, grinning. I didn't cry. I didn't feel anything. I waited. Maybe the part with me was coming up later.

I looked at Molly. She was sniffling on the sofa. When the tape ended she said, "You looked so cute with short hair. Do you think about cutting it again like that? And God, that body of yours."

After that, I avoided situations where people might ask me to watch family videotapes or look through photographs. I was unable to shake the idea that something was radically wrong, but I tried not to think about it. I hoped it wouldn't happen again.

I thought: *So many people look the same, everyone dresses the same.* I thought: *I am not paying enough attention.* I thought: *I'm fucked up, an introvert, a narcissist. I'm dumb, socially awkward, a misfit, self-defeating, self-absorbed.* In the years after college, it had gotten harder and harder to make friends. I was mostly alone. In my heart of hearts, I knew what the problem was. I was mentally ill.

⁂

On the flight back to Michigan, I went over and over all that had happened in Florida, feeling increasingly foolish. My mother hadn't ever been diagnosed, as far as I knew. I never saw her take a pill—she refused to take so much as an aspirin. When she broke her arm, she wouldn't go to the hospital—she lay in the garage for two days, she told me months later, rather than face a doctor. True, she'd been in the hospital at least once in the past that I knew of, and for mysterious reasons: "her legs." Still, the mentally ill whom I was aware of cycled between group homes, the streets, and hospitals. A mother couldn't be crazy and her daughter *not know.* I'd confronted my mother and upset my father because of a high school boyfriend's offhand remark, his cruel theory. None of it made sense. But it also did.

When I landed in Michigan, I drove straight from the airport to the nearest bookstore. I settled down on the floor in the psychology section and read.

One in a hundred people developed schizophrenia, and this was true across cultures, all over the world. The disease ran in families. A parent afflicted with schizophrenia produced children with drastically greater odds of developing the disease: one out of ten children of schizophrenics had the illness. It always got worse, never better; it was difficult to treat, and incurable.

Schizophrenia wasn't one thing, though. Schizophrenia was a group of things, a cluster of disorders affecting thinking, emotion, perception, and action. There were a lot of kinds, sizes, and shapes; sufferers tended to have wardrobes of schizophrenic disorders. The illness cycled, symptoms going into remission, then coming back, often worse than before. When some symptoms receded, others came to the fore. Some schizophrenics did quite well for long periods of time.

My mother had cycles. I'd never really thought of her habits in that way. Some of the time she was like any mother, baking four-layer cakes, taking trips to Jetty Park, buying me sandals, putting up the Christmas tree. Then suddenly she would pack us up: we had to move, we had to get out. In the middle of the night. What about school? Not to worry. She was a teacher. She would teach us. We could live in the back of Suzy for a bit.

Until she found some work. Sometimes she took off for days and days on her own. I was scared and proud to be in the house by myself. When she was gone, I felt like a character in a book. When she was gone, time slowed down into a force that felt endlessly absorptive, like a vacuum.

Most of the time, her reasons made sense—as much sense as adult reasons ever make to a child. I had to wear strange used clothes because we were not rich. Trends were for sheep, fools. We had to move because she was dead set against the divorce, the bank was foreclosing. The wrong food contained toxins that killed people; people had died from eating food they thought was perfectly safe. I couldn't argue. Her bizarre habits were swirled into the days with no obvious pattern; she happened like life, in hours, in years.

Maybe it wasn't just that I had gone back and forth, between her house and my father's house. Maybe she, too, had gone back and forth: okay, not okay.

I set the book down, embarrassed. Wasn't I just being melodramatic? This was what people always did. They read about disorders, and suddenly everything applied to everyone. I was keeping a score sheet in my head, two columns. She has it. She doesn't. She has it. She doesn't.

I opened up an introductory psychology textbook to the section on schizophrenia. It opened dramatically: "Schizophrenia is without a doubt the most dreaded psychological disorder. If depression is the common cold of psychological disorders, schizophrenia is the cancer." *The cancer.* I thought of my mother: a thin, terrorized specter in the hallway.

What exactly made schizophrenia *schizophrenia*, and not

something else? The book said that what separated schizophrenia from the other disorders was strange thinking. This made me angry and, like Dave, distrustful of diagnosis. I *loved* strange thinking. My work as a teacher of creative writing was to lead students to *strange* their thinking. The example of strange thinking in the book was disturbing to me: "One man begged for 'a little more allegro in the treatment.'"

"Imagine trying to communicate with this person," the book stated. I was imagining that, and it seemed nice, like a nice thing to do. Who wouldn't want more allegro in the treatment? I wanted more allegro in everything. Could I imagine trying to communicate with this person? Yes! Communicating with an allegro-wanter felt like my life's work, the goal of poetry, of writing. What I couldn't imagine was happily communicating with a judgmental bystander.

My mother, however, would never approve of "a little more allegro" in anything.

The next key characteristic of schizophrenia was the tendency toward "word salad." There was an example, a rambling block quotation that strung together a grandmother's death, sunlight, dinner, and cats that didn't exist, interspersed with inappropriate laughter. Again not my mother. Again more like me. "Word salad" was the exact name of a writing exercise I gave my students at the beginning of the year. In a piece of writing, those moves from death to dinner could be crucial, heartbreaking.

I opened a fat gray volume titled *Schizophrenia.* I found a chart that listed the warning signs of the disease: birth complications, separation from parents, withdrawn behavior, emotional unpredictability, poor peer relations, solo play. One could also consider this the recipe for becoming an artist, a writer.

I was just about to call it a day—all this was doing was calling my own identity into question—when a quote by John Ashbery caught my eye. "The lure of the work is strong," he wrote about art by mental patients, "but so is the terror of the unanswerable riddle it proposes." I wrote that down in my journal. I read it over. *The lure of the work is strong, but so is the terror of the unanswerable riddle it proposes.* It didn't seem to be saying very much. Art by madmen was spooky? Still, I found the poet's interest cool and reassuring. I turned the page and there were samples of schizophrenic artwork, two drawings and a painting.

I'd forgotten all about the collection of drawings I'd discovered in my mother's closet when I was about nine, the paper yellow and brittle, cracking. They looked exactly like these. The drawings were of skulls. The skulls seemed on the verge of falling apart, as if whatever was inside was in the process of bursting out; craniums crackled with electricity and breakage. The irises were laced with elaborate jagged lines, *crazed.* Eyeballs sprang out of their sockets. Most of the skulls were mounted on spinal columns, the vertebrae singed, twisted, tilted, the bones way too far apart. The lines were thick and soft and crude, but there was an enormous amount of detail. I brought them to my mother and she said, "Put those back where you found them and do not root around in my things." But I wouldn't let it go. Finally, we went through them all together. My mother explained they were done by her sister, Katy, who'd been a talented artist, who should have gone to college but instead, right after high school, had married her sweetheart, also uneducated. Willard, my uncle. The high school janitor. My mother shook her head. Katy had made a huge mistake, not nurturing her talent. "You have her fingers," my mother said. "You have the hands of an artist as well." Don't make her mistake, my mother said. Get your education. Don't get pregnant, don't get pregnant, don't get pregnant.

I loved those drawings. I wanted us to have them on our walls. My mother forbade us to look at them. Whenever I was home alone, I would get them out and puzzle over what it was those skull heads knew that I did not know; they had such an air of secret insight, a glee in their own great otherness, such certainty. They could see without a doubt that I was a fool and due for a fall. And they seemed to say, *You know it, don't you.*

But I'd never known my aunt. Katy hadn't been able to leave her house, then her bedroom, in years. She'd died of emphysema, but no one had ever said that she was also mentally ill. My mother hadn't gone to her funeral. She hadn't gone to their mother's funeral, either. I'd never spoken to any of the relatives on that side of the family, at my mother's insistence. When I'd asked for their addresses to send them graduation announcements she'd said no, we can't do that. They'll think we are just asking for money. Yes, that was the point, I thought. But I followed her wishes. I didn't want her angry at me. I didn't want her to cut me off as she had them.

The big textbook fell open to another page, and there she was. A photograph was captioned *The schizophrenic look:* piles of formal but frenzied curls, low over the forehead. A pretty face, but a face covered with urgency, sheeted, closed, absolutely not okay. It looked *exactly* like my mother. I pored over the photograph. My mother had "the look." I sat there, knowing this and not knowing it, both at the same time. As I always had.

I scanned through the index, looking for references to "children of schizophrenics." I found a reference with "children" and "schizophrenia" that turned out to be a discussion of the diagnosis of schizophrenia in childhood; it was becoming more common, though still controversial. The next two references were equally unhelpful: long discussions of the controversy surrounding the "icebox mother," a long-standing theory that cold mothers created schizophrenic children, currently disputed in the medical community. Was my mother an icebox mother? This was the problem with all this stuff. Everything seemed like it *could* fit, and nothing did. She wasn't icy, really. She was more like all the kitchen appliances going at once.

Flipping through pages, I landed on a section about schizophrenics and faces. Schizophrenics made strange faces, faces that didn't fit the situation.

This was my mother, no question about it. She made all kinds of faces; it was part of the way she communicated, punctuating her sentences with moues and quick grins and exaggerated expressions of surprise, *Aha!* If you walked by her eating at the table alone, her face looked like it was controlled by a radio dial twisted by an invisible hand, passing through expressions like radio frequencies, holding each for a second or two. She looked as if she were having an ongoing conversation with herself.

In childhood, I'd rankled whenever my father or any of his relatives said my gestures and expressions reminded them of my mother. I *looked* like the Sellers side, they all said, but I *seemed* like my mother. No, I said vigorously, I couldn't see it. I couldn't see that I was like her at all. She was fair, blue-eyed. I was dark, auburn-haired. She'd visited me in college several times. "Your movements are just like hers!" friends had said. "No, no, no," I'd said. "No."

The passage explained that schizophrenics had trouble reading emotions. They couldn't tell what someone was thinking by their facial expression. They couldn't utilize social cues. Irony was not available to them. I skimmed along until two words brought me to a complete standstill: *face recognition.*

I put my finger on the words and closed the book over my hand. I closed my eyes. The book was talking about emotions on faces, but the phrase itself, *face recognition*, made it easy to conflate the two concepts: reading emotion and identifying faces. It was as if I'd shaken a kaleidoscope. It was all the same pieces, but suddenly a long sequence of misunderstandings, from when I was very young to just the night before, sprang into light, lined up, crystallized.

It was as though all along I had been someone else, and now I had a glimpse of who was who.

That night was to be my last with Dave and the boys for a long time. I had to return to upstate New York, where a stint as a visiting professor would run through to spring. I told Dave the whole story twice, in his arms. He smelled like popcorn and fresh laundry. He listened to all the details and then said yes, maybe there was a face thing. It explained a lot, he said.

Across the room, in his dresser, Dave had his list of goals for the year. I knew the list by heart: *(1) Be kinder. (2) Run faster. (3) Be more loving. (4) Pray more. (5) Volunteer. (6) Find a great house for me, Heather, the boys and . . . ? (7) Buy a great van.* I hadn't known him even a year, but I told Dave, in that moment, that I wanted to marry him. He never yelled at his kids. He was patient and gentle and thoughtful. He never criticized me. He had only kind words for my parents. He held me and heard me. He loved me, and for the first time in my life, I was sleeping through the night. The guns, Libertarian websites, the stockpile of silver, the generator—these were differences of style, not deal-breakers.

"I want us to get married," I said again in the morning.

He wanted me to think about it. He wanted me to be sure. I told him I wouldn't ever be sure but we could at least try it. "We can always get a divorce," I said, laughing. I was kidding. But I could see I hurt his feelings.

"I'm going to miss you guys," I said. "A lot." I leaned into the boys' bedroom. They were playing a video game and didn't move. They didn't look at me or say anything. Their thumbs rolled over the little plastic buttons. I walked over, knelt down on the nest of comforters, among pizza boxes, empty Coke bottles, a bag of Doritos. I rubbed Jacob's head. "You're coming to see me soon. There's Nintendo. In the house." They didn't take their eyes off the screen.

Down in the driveway, I loaded my stuff and the dog into my car. Dave sat in the passenger seat to say good-bye. "Don't think about your mother too much," he cautioned. "Think about some other things, too, okay?"

"Why did I take a job in another state again?" I said.

"You like to move," he said. "You love being new. I want to be with you, honey. Don't worry. We have plenty of time."

I pulled out in my little car, watching him wave, and I wondered: If he walked down the street tomorrow in my little town in upstate New York, would I know it was he? Would I recognize this man? The man waving at me now, in my rearview mirror, was Dave. I knew this: I had just been standing there, next to him, in his embrace. But when I looked at him, I realized I had to say to myself: It's him.

My new existence, twelve hours east of Dave and the boys, was like hiding from my life and coming into my life at the same time. Already, I was struggling to identify my new friends. In the classroom, students sat in the same seats and in small sections—twelve in a course—and the key to recognizing them was to memorize the pattern. But the women in my running group were difficult to tell apart. I couldn't distinguish Bonnie from Betsey from Linda: it was always cold when we ran, and all that was exposed was our faces. Once, I commented on how hard it was to tell which was which, and Bonnie said, "Yeah, we get that a lot." As in Michigan, I tended to avoid situations where I would run into people I was supposed to know. I shopped late at night. I skipped nearly every campus event. I made plans to attend readings or concerts or meetings, but when the hour drew near, I couldn't overcome the urge to get into my big bed with a book.

My house was on campus, and the master bedroom was large, with a complicated roofline. My bed was like the bed in a fairy tale, high off the floor and tucked under the eaves. Tucked into this cozy nest, I called Dave on the telephone every night. I needed to talk about Sarah, my mother, and face recognition, over and over and over. What was paranoid schizophrenia, exactly? How did it get diagnosed? I was trying to get an outline, a shape for it.

Dave spoke the way a sofa would speak: slow, wide, comfortable, each word cushioned with space around it, upholstered. "Well, sweetheart, I'm not a psychiatrist," he'd say carefully. Had they used the word *schizophrenic* around Sarah? I wondered. Dave said no. The diagnosis was so final, conclusive: it meant the end of hope for normal life. "You're always going to find people will be slow to say that word or phrase out loud or in print. Sarah had been in the hospital when she was a teenage girl, but people probably wanted to give her the benefit of the doubt: this was a young girl who was upset, who had emotional issues. No one repeated the diagnosis aloud. They found ways to not buy into it. Not to be difficult, but for the sake of their daughter, out of hope. If you hadn't known about it before, seen it before in someone else, you'd have said she was going through a rough patch, maybe going through it a little rougher than most people, but give her a couple of months to herself, let her have some therapy and rest, and it will all be fine."

Most people thought Sarah was difficult, peculiar. "My mother," Dave said, "thought Sarah was a pain."

That word again. *Peculiar.* A code word we use when we don't even know we're using code.

Did he know before he married her? Had anyone ever said anything to him? Dave paused for a long time and then he said, "Rumors swirled around." But people didn't talk about mental breakdown. They worried. They worried they had caused it, contributed to it, or failed to prevent it. And their worry was diluted by the long stretches of fairly normal-looking life, ordered by all the desires humans have—for children, for dresses, for shrubs to plant along the back of the property line. There was always so much else to talk about.

In any case, Dave believed this avoidance of diagnosis was as it should be. Why would you go around telling everyone, *Look out! Don't let her have kids! She's going to snap!* Sarah's parents loved their daughter and wanted her to have a normal life. Illness was a theory, something separate from the girl herself, a story made of her life. "Arguably, in a freedom-loving society, you are going to default to letting someone go off on their own."

So her parents didn't tell Dave about her hospitalizations. I knew my mother had dropped out of college for mysterious reasons. If it had been for a breakdown, it was understandable that she would have wanted to keep that information from my father. From me. From everyone.

I loved my mother and wanted her to have a normal life; I wanted people to think the best of her. I wanted them to think the best of me. I wanted my love for her to be right, not wrong. I obsessively thought about my mother. How could I diagnose her using a checklist in a book? How, when she fit the criteria perfectly, could I not? Most of all, I worried about my own ability to see things and know things: if she were a paranoid schizophrenic, how could I have fooled myself? Could I ever know for sure?

I called Dave and called him and called him and called him. I called him in the middle of the day, at work. He was unfailingly patient and kind. He seemed smarter than any doctor, any therapist. I worried about relying on him too much, but he said we were good. We were figuring it out.

One night, after tossing and turning at three a.m., I pulled on my running pants, found a scarf, hat, and gloves, and put on my coat over my pajamas. In the hall mirror, I looked like a mental patient. The dogs barked with joy.

I got the leashes but didn't hook them up, and we walked around the block, loose. The streets of tiny Canton, New York, were deserted. My face was hard and my toes were numb. Streetlights flickered and buzzed, straining, it seemed, in the cold.

My neighbor Mrs. Knapp was watching television on her stiff velvet sofa, her chimney emitting a perfect constant S of smoke, as in a painting. A cheesy painting. It was like she was having ideas in there and they were coming out. Across the street I could see the backs of the heads of my colleagues Bob and Sarah, watching a black-and-white movie. I couldn't believe so many people were up at three a.m. I couldn't imagine myself in such a window, such a life, sitting so still, dishes done and put away, just the right amount of light to see by, to feel cozy by. I willed myself not to cry: the tears would freeze my eyelids shut.

At the bottom of Jay Street, I walked down the hill and cut over to the golf course, covered in a foot of crisp snow. Every once in a while the snow crust would break and the dogs would fall into a little crevasse of their own making, then clamber out and trot along sturdily, as though they'd never break through again.

I imagined my mom down in her house, in Florida, in her too-large flannel nightgown, the windows nailed shut, the air dusty and close. She wasn't that bad. She was never as bad as Sarah. I couldn't imagine telling anyone my mother was a paranoid schizophrenic. She bought groceries, baked cookies, kept up her yard, planted shrubs and small trees. Lately, she'd been going to an exercise class at the YMCA.

It would devastate her if I said these words out loud. She would never speak to me again. I tried saying it to myself: "My mother is mentally ill." It was like walking out on ice in the dark. I could only go a little ways, and then I skittered back to land. No, no, no, no. It was crazy! It was so melodramatic. She was my little mother, papery and difficult, like good stationery. I didn't see how to be who I'd been all this time and also believe in those two words. *Paranoid schizophrenic.* It felt like saying "My mother is a hairy spider, and I am her spawn." Freakish, larger than life, monstrous.

I could see it. *My mother is paranoid schizophrenic.* I could see the surface and the shape of it. But I couldn't be in it. My mother was *my mother.* I walked and walked and walked and tried to get the two things to line up: my mother was really, really crazy, and I hadn't known it. I herded the dogs back to my house on the hill. I looked up at the light coming from my capacious bedroom upstairs under the eaves, the windows revealing only part of what was inside. I remembered how when you are a little kid and you look at your house, you can't figure out which window corresponds to what room. I couldn't match up my experience of life with my mother with what it looked like from the outside.

For Christmas I went back to Michigan and played Nintendo and drank wine and snuggled into life with Dave and the boys. We house-hunted halfheartedly, talking in greater detail about construction techniques and roofing applications than about our relationship or the future. We barely talked about my mother. But back in Canton for the winter term, I resumed calling Dave every night, like a hotline. I asked him about different things my mother had done: not letting food touch other food; not letting me go to school activities, join a sport, march in band; not leaving the house after dark; not going to malls; not answering the phone. Were these examples?

Dave explained two things to me: portals and tampering. His understanding was that schizophrenics couldn't tolerate anything that was a conduit for the voices and the visions. The voices and visions tended to come in through framed things: a window or anything that was a kind of window; mirrors, photographs, paintings. Anything that emitted energy: radio, television, telephones. Sex was a portal. Death was a portal.

This could explain why my mother devised elaborate schemes for me to call home. Let it ring once, then call back, let it ring twice. Why she refused to go to her mother's funeral, sleep with my father, get a microwave, go to restaurants, go to weddings. Church. Church was one giant portal. "It's just too alive," Dave said. Statues, crowds, tombstones. Too much energy. Too much comes through.

Schizophrenics, he said, always had a reason for what they did. To us, their actions looked crazy, but if you took the time to piece it together, to go through the steps they went through, you could see they had a well-thought-out plan. The goal itself would likely never make sense to us, but the steps they were taking were the right ones to get them down that particular path.

Tampering was another schizophrenic safety cap. Tedious food rituals, the ban on restaurants, hiding food in closets. Not going to other people's houses or having people come over. Dave explained they didn't do these things to be difficult or weird. They had to do them. It was all for our safety. Other mothers would be careless, uninformed. They would bring food in from unchecked sources. They wouldn't lock doors, they would leave windows open: all manner of difficulty and threat would be running rampant through these homes. My mother took her mothering seriously; she did not want harm to come to us. She was trying to keep us alive.

"I don't know if it's insanity, really," Dave said. "It's just a real different world from our world."

When I was ten, Fred purchased a beautiful painting at the Winter Park Sidewalk Art Festival and hung it in our living room. My mother hated it. Too black, she said. I loved it, this beautiful abstract painting with a black background, subtle wisps of white that were to me cars and commuters and clouds, the energy of a good city, moving quickly. And buildings, black on black. There were pieces of red too. I visited the red places, splotches (planets) and streaks (bad moods, crime, be careful) and lines (open all night, go, go faster). I could stare at that painting for an entire afternoon; it was like reading a novel.

My mother said the black, the red, did not fit in with her décor at all. She was Early American. We had a table from Ethan Allen. She hated the painting. She hated that my father spent money on it. She hated that she wasn't consulted. She hated contemporary. She hated art on the walls. She hated anything on any wall anywhere. First she draped the painting with a sheet. Then she took the painting down. She bought a tube of yellow ochre oil paint and slowly, over a period of weeks, she changed the red parts to mustard. Then she started covering all the black, the ground, leaving jagged islands around the white wisps. She ended up painting the entire canvas yellow ochre. It took three tubes. I was beside myself. It was as though she'd painted over a living person. And for her, I now realized, it was *just like that.* The painting was too alive for her.

Dave was the only sane person I ever met who understood mental illness from the point of view of the mentally ill.

Because of his marriage, he'd been forced to pitch a tent in the land of the insane. He'd camped there, he'd passed through, he understood the culture. I'd been born inside those borders, deep in that country, but I did not belong there. Of course, I didn't know this then; I didn't know there were other lands. Paranoid schizophrenia wasn't my address, but for a long time it was where the mail came.

When Dave came to visit me for Valentine's Day, we went to Ottawa, stayed at the Château Laurier, took photos of ourselves eating breakfast, swimming. We made plans to get married as soon as possible: that April, on the boys' spring break.

I called my mother, the first time we'd spoken since Orlando. I told her Dave and I had very happy news: we wanted to invite her to our wedding.

There was a long silence. She took a deep breath. "I can't even believe you are considering this. When I think back to what went on in this house—oh my gosh in heaven, I am getting upset now. Heather. I'm getting very upset!" I tried to understand what she'd just said.

"Please don't be upset," I repeated gently. After this long spell of thinking about my mother as someone who suffered from schizophrenia, and keeping in mind all that I understood about the disease, I knew that my news was less likely to provoke a tender mother-daughter moment than a dangerous schism that would make us even more distant. Still, I needed to be the daughter who invited her mother to her wedding, and part of me had believed she would come. It was my *wedding.*

"No," she said. "I am upset. There's more. As long as we are talking."

"Okay," I said.

"I want the money you owe me back as well. I hate to bring that up. I know Dave is only hourly and deep in debt because he had all those medical bills from that other person. But I really do have to ask. It's time. Way overdue time, in point of fact."

"Mom," I said. I told her there was no money; I didn't owe her any money.

"Heather," she said. "I will always love you, but the damage you've done is irreparable. You've taken so much. These things add up. I think I have reached my limit with you."

I told her I understood. And I did.

She was pulling back, to preserve herself. She had to bring out the big guns. I was going into someone else's house and not coming back out. A wedding invitation wasn't what she had been waiting for. It was what she had been dreading. Me, out in the world: it wasn't safe—for me or for her.

I could be kind to her, but I was done colluding.

I was starting a new life.

Dave and the boys drove out in the van. The town was covered with snow. I pinned two-dollar carnation boutonnieres on David Junior and Jacob, and we got married at the courthouse, in a tiny dank paneled basement room. The orange curtains on the little casement windows were askew; they reminded me of the curtains in my father's house. The women from my running group were there, in their running clothes and headbands—hard to tell apart. I wore sandals and, over my thin white dress, a coat. The judge, a runner, said, "For better or worse, for faster or slower," and Dave cried and I cried and the boys looked hot and uncomfortable and pleased to be on their spring break, but not pleased to be in a tiny courthouse basement in a forsaken town on the St. Lawrence Seaway. Then we went across the street and got bagels. It seemed perfect to me.

Three

My sophomore year of high school, Fred allowed two drifters to move in with us, in the house he'd bought on Gondola, out by the airport. It had three bedrooms and a funny little swimming pool in the front yard. He was working at Martin Marietta—as a tax advisor, he said—but he was often home at three in the afternoon. Then, after dinner, he'd take off and be gone all night. I'd been living with him off and on.

The men had tried to come in my bedroom at night. They stole my jewelry, my cash. I had to put my dresser in front of the door and hide in there. I said he had to make a choice, them or me.

He said there was no reason not to be nice to his friends, no reason at all. He said, "You're turning into your mother."

So it was back to my mother's. She said this was it. No more back-and-forth. She forbade me to talk to Keith Landreu on the telephone, but I talked to him every day after school, for hours and hours. She forbade me to see him, but he snuck into our house in the afternoons while she was out job-hunting, and I snuck into his house at night. Then came the day he walked past me at school, his lips tightly pressed together, and looked right through me. I froze in the flow of kids; I couldn't believe that look on his face: closed, over, done, stay away. Just the day before, we'd been naming our children and decorating our apartment in London. I wanted to be dead. For days, I couldn't stop crying.

I missed my father's cooking. I missed the little pool in the front yard. I called him after school and started going there for dinner again. As soon as the drifters moved on, I moved back in.

One afternoon a white Cadillac nosed into the driveway, slowly, like it was being filmed. An arm came out the window, waved, and a woman poked her head out. "I have heard *sooo* much about you, Heather," she said, smiling at me so hard it hurt to look at her. "Oh Lordy, I am so happy to finally, finally meet you!" She had a little feathery cap of black hair. She popped out of her giant sleek car, leaving the engine running. She came over in her high-heel black patent leather strappy sandals and hugged me hard and long. "I've got some things for you. Look at you! You are so beautiful! And I've heard how smart you are. Your daddy worships you." She took me by the shoulders and looked deep into my eyes. "You don't have to like me," she said. "Just don't be overtly evil and we're going to be fine, deal? Oh, I just want to visit! You are so damn dear." I didn't want to but I laughed, a burst of relief coming out of me against my will.

"Okay, all right, then, let's get this stuff inside. I never know what your daddy is going to have over here and what he isn't gonna have, but that's okay! I bring what I need!" She was rooting around in her backseat. Her car stereo was playing John Denver. She turned, holding a basket, and set it on the hood and came over and hugged me again. "I'm going to fall in love with ya! I know I am!" Her boobs pressed into me. Her perfume was something famous. She handed me a present, wrapped.

"Is this for Fred?" I said. But really, I knew who it was for. I knew I was going to love whatever it was. I was thinking already what it would be like if I lived in her house. If she and Fred got married.

"Oh, we're gonna have so much *fuuuuuuun*," she said. She clicked off her car at last, tossed her keys into her purse, slung it over her shoulder, and said, "Okay! Look at you! Just look at you now! I bet the boys are going wild. I love your eye shadow. You look just like your mom, don't you?"

"No," I said. I couldn't see that I looked like anyone in my family. "Fred hates it," I said. "He calls it goop."

"We love goop," she said. "We can't help it, can we, now? Can we help we love goop and pretties?" And she skittered into the house, calling my father's name. I didn't even know I loved goop. I did, though. So much.

Ruby Redding was gorgeous and kind. She had giant breasts that shot straight out of her chest, high and pointed—the Grand Tetons, my new boyfriend, Wayne, called them. She had a flat stomach, thin hips, and a wardrobe of shiny high heels—black, silver, white, gold, bronze, hot pink. She wore either black straight-leg pants or fuchsia straight-leg pants, with bright flowered low-cut silky tops. She wore bright shiny beaded necklaces, at least three or four. Always, she wore her gold necklace, which was a mounded hunk of gold—her "nugget," she called it: it was all of her ex-husband's gifts melted down. He was a bastard. But Ruby had taken her bad old days, she said, and made them into something she really loved. That could be a good thing for me to know, she said. That bad can be converted into something really beautiful. "All that pain was worth a thing or two."

"Worth a thing or two," Fred said, laughing in a mocking way, questioning her with his eyebrows. "That makes no sense."

Ruby taught me to two-step, make tender biscuits, play cards, curl my hair, and give myself a pedicure. She brought me pretty new blouses that I never wore: they were too slippery, too secretary. She brought me her old maxi dresses and high heels and her old beaded necklaces from the fifties, which I wore all the time, with shorts and tank tops, with sundresses, with my bathing suits. I twisted them around my ankles and hooked them into my hair. In Ruby's things, and a pair of sunglasses, I felt like a movie star, and would whisper in the mirror, *You look like a million bucks,* winking and setting my jaw. She handed me her daughter's old hippie caftans, ironed, and told me my daddy was the best thing that had ever happened to her, if only he didn't drink so much, if only he wasn't married. For a long time, I thought she meant to my mother. It was from Ruby I learned my father truly had divorced my mother and had married another woman, Bella, who'd been in the circus and had a fat and unfortunate son. She said the reason women liked my dad so much was that he talked. There were two kinds of men: Strong silent types were common and were silent because they had nothing to say. Talking men, on the other hand, were fun: they loved women, dancing, having fun, cooking, snuggling, and this is the kind of man you wanted.

I gave Fred over to Ruby. Because she loved him so much, I could relax, I found some space, I was no longer crucial to his very survival. In this space, I found I could despise him, his habits. At the same time, I found I could love him. This kind and easy woman made him safe, less strange and dangerous. And those dresses in the closet: how easy it was to pretend they were hers.

Ruby and I had our best talks while we did the dishes. "Now, I know your daddy thinks you just need to stay here, live with him, take care of him, but don't you worry about that, Heather, you need to go to college. Don't you ever tell him I said this to you. He would kill me dead. You're the light of his life, but you have to stretch your wings. I want that for you. I want it so much."

She said she'd take care of ol' Freddy the Frog. I should focus on my life, and live it. "This is your turn! This is your whole life ahead of you!" College was where I would find a good man to marry. Not Wayne. Don't marry that boy, she said.

Wayne was acquired soon after Keith Landreu ceased acknowledging my existence.

Wayne wore floral bell-bottoms, dashikis, and beaded headbands. He was famous at school because his mother had given birth to him when she was sixteen years old and he had a bizarre medical condition that was causing him to go bald and grow a thick, wiry red beard.

Wayne just gave me rides, I told Ruby. "He gives you a lot more than rides, honey," she declaimed. "I just don't think he is on par with you. I don't think he's your caliber. I hate a man who honks his horn for a woman. He should be coming to the door."

Wayne refused to come to the front door to get me. He thought Fred was a drunk who harassed me, who was weak. Wayne idled in the driveway and peeled out every time he picked me up, laying rubber up and down our street. My father hated him.

Ruby shook her little cap of black feathered hair. She wasn't kidding. She wanted me to hold out for the very best. "You've got something special in you, Heather," she said, and the way she said it, I almost believed her. She'd tear up, and then I would too. Then Fred would barge in and say it was time for inspection, and things would click back to crazy-normal, just like her words had never been spoken.

Many nights my mother came down there and parked in the driveway, taking notes on our comings and goings in a little spiral notebook. It was hard to concentrate with her out there; sometimes Fred would go yell at her. Sometimes I went out and sat in the truck with her. She would talk about how much she loved Fred, how horrible a mother she was, how badly she wanted to get us all back together. If she could undo her mistakes. If I could undo mine. She went on and on about what she believed I'd done. All my lovers. The money I had stolen. How I had driven the family apart, brought us irreparable harm. I knew I hadn't done anything, but I felt guilty anyway. I told her she was a good mother. I told her that living with Fred wasn't easy and that I missed her, wished I could be with her. She didn't think we should say anything negative about my father. He was a brilliant, brilliant man. The smartest man she'd ever met. He loved us. No, the problem was her. And her problem was me.

One night the four of us were playing hearts, Fred and Wayne and Ruby and me. Fred and Wayne were laughing together, like old pals. I had won the last two hands but couldn't shoot the moon.

"Hold your cards, I can see everything," Wayne said. "You'da got shot by now if this were a real game."

Fred liked this talk; he banged on the table, *yeah yeah yeah.*

"It's your turn. Go!" I said. He blew smoke in my face and that's when I heard the front door creak open. "Is someone in the house?" I said.

"I'm concen-mo-trating here," Fred said. He whacked the back of his hand toward me, staring hard at his cards.

Ruby called out, "Hello, hello, hello!" and she and Wayne and I all looked at each other across the table.

I got up from the table and went into the kitchen.

"Mom," I whispered. Her hair was in a kerchief and she had on her winter coat, though it was hot enough for shorts and bare feet. She was rooting through Ruby's purse, a white leather handbag perched on top of the dishwasher.

"Who dat?" Fred hollered.

"Your turn, dude," I heard Wayne say.

"Heather?" Ruby called.

I grabbed my mother's shoulders. I whispered, hard, "You can't go through people's purses!" This wasn't the first time this had happened. My mother had snuck in before, taken other women's purses. I had looked the other way, happy that my mother was causing problems for my father's livestock. "Quit messing with my stable," he would say to my mother. He had threatened to call the police on her. "Go right ahead! Go right ahead, buster!" she'd fire back.

I tried to take Ruby's purse from her, but she pulled it to her chest like a football.

Fred and Ruby and Wayne came into the kitchen.

"Oh my gosh in heaven," my mother said.

Ruby said, "Is that my bag, hon?" She took a step forward.

"Don't push me, don't push me," my mother said, sidling out the door.

Fred was banging on the counter with both hands, laughing. "Lordy, Lordy, Lordy, hold on, now. Hold on," he gasped.

I followed my mother. She climbed into Suzy, locked the door, put her seat belt on, and curled tightly over the steering wheel. I tapped and tapped. She glared at me, but she opened the door. I climbed in.

"Mom," I said.

"Yes, honey. Gosh, it's been a long, long day! Has it been for you too?" She sounded clear and sweet and strange.

Slowly, slowly, I inched my hand across the bench seat. I wanted to get Ruby her purse back without hurting my mother's feelings, without making her feel foolish.

"Mom," I said. My hand was spidering inches from her thigh. "Mom. We're just friends. We were just playing hearts. It's not fun or anything." I could feel the heat coming off her thigh. The engine was running. "Please be okay," I said.

"Oh, Heather." She turned to me, hard, flashing. "He hates me, he despises me, and so do you. I sit alone, night after night, all I can think of is your health and safety."

My hand was back under my leg. My father was yelling louder.

She said, "I'm not this kind of a person. I am a person who *respects*. But I don't even know you anymore. Or your father." She was shaking. "I am pushed to my limit. I am on the brink."

The purse seemed like a bomb. I couldn't touch it. Carefully, I got out of the truck. My mother drove away, chugging slowly around the corner, hitting the curb. I watched her disappear. Somehow, it seemed like it was all my fault. I stood in the scrubby crabgrass yard and looked at the sky. Then I walked down to the lake. Maybe I would be kidnapped. Maybe it wouldn't be that bad. We'd become friends. I'd write home.

I never found out how Ruby got her purse back. No mention was made of any of it.

That winter, Fred took me to dinner at Gary's Duck Inn to celebrate some big news. We sat for a long time in the parking lot while he cried, tears and mucus and sobs, a huge old messy cry. "Just don't leave me, punkin," he said. "Please don't leave your ol' daddy. Stay with your daddy. Please, please, please."

He threw his head onto my shoulder. "I don't want you to grow up. That's my problem. Don't leave Orlando. Promise?"

I promised. I pulled closer to the door. I had one hand on the handle. "What's the big announcement? What is going on? Do you have cancer again?" As I spoke, a group of sloppy-looking men in cheesy suits burst out of the swinging doors of the restaurant. "We don't have to eat here," I said. "We could just get subs or Rossi's or something."

"No, we're going to have a nice dinner. It's our last dinner together for a long time." He wiped his nose and face and wiped his hands on his pants, but the moment he touched his pants, he was sobbing again. I stroked his thin shoulder. I felt so bad for him. I had a theory about his drinking, his sadness, his hollering, his bras and panty hose. I knew his father had beaten his mother to pieces. My uncle Donny had told me she'd been hospitalized for a broken collarbone more than once. My father had left home when he was fourteen, moved in with the manager of the movie theater where he sold popcorn, changed the reels. I had decided he wore feminine things not because he was gay but because he wanted to stay soft.

"Are you sick?" I said.

"No," he said. He laughed through his tears. "Not the horse pistol." He was in perfect health, he said. He hit the dashboard with his hands. He was going to live to be a hundred. "Let's go eat," he said.

I walked in before him and asked the hostess for a table for two.

"Get us a good table. A nice table," he said, too loudly. She moved her grease pencil around in the hostess stand. *Where can I stow this loud man?* she must have been thinking. *Where can I hide these terrifying people?*

He lowered his hand by my leg and burned my pants with his cigarette. I brushed the ashes to the floor and went to the bathroom. I patted my pants with wet paper towels. There was a perfect round hole where my leg showed through. The skin looked fine, but every time the pants rubbed, cold air came in, and it burned. I held my hand over the hole, limping, and the hostess led me to our booth. My father had peeled back the little curtains that separated our booth from the next one, and he was talking to the family there, telling them about German wine, the *Reezlings,* the only thing worth drinking.

I tried to draw him back to our table. I buttered his roll. I jiggled his drink. What was the big news?

"Order." He banged me on the head with the menu.

"Fish in the bag," I said, refusing to open the menu or to pick it up from where it had fallen next to me.

"No," he said. "Try something else." He named the other dishes I should order. The red snapper. The sirloin. The surf and turf. He called out each one as though it had been invented moments earlier, was brand-new. The waitress tapped her pen on her black leatherette pad.

I told her fish *en papillote, por favor.*

No, no, no, no, he said. He argued. I ordered a glass of Chablis. He grabbed my hands and squeezed them, finally. "You don't know how to have fun. That's your problem."

"Tell me," I begged when the waitress left.

He slammed both hands down on the table. "The old man

is going to Europe. I'm taking an opportunity to inspect Germany. For two months. How do you think that sounds, huh?"

"I have school," I said. But I was thinking I could learn more in Germany. I wouldn't have to be with Fred all the time. Then I could stay on, as an au pair, learn German, possibly go to school in France, study art. Ballet. I wished he'd told me sooner. But I would support it. I wanted to go. "It sounds good, Daddy," I said.

"You're not going," he said. "Freddy's going to Germany. Solo." He made wing motions with his arm. He drained his cocktail. And added: Donny would be coming down in a couple weeks to take care of me. He smacked the table again, hard, with his flat hands. He had tears in his eyes. He motioned for the waitress.

I didn't say anything. Fred was going to Germany. Who knew why or how that would work? Ruby wouldn't marry Fred until he quit running around with other women; maybe she would let me live with her. Maybe she wouldn't—the hurricane that was my mother made it hard for anyone to take me on. I knew it was a crazy thing to do, and I felt sorry for myself in advance. But I had to hope for my mother. I had to turn myself into the girl who could fit with her. Fred sat there, his mouth slung open, a wild, vacated look in his eye. His hands were coming across the table like liquid, aiming for my arms. I drew back. I knew I could do it. I could work my way back into her.

Four

Married, I moved back to Michigan in May, and I stretched myself between two homes and, in a larger sense, two lives. The boys were continually late for school. My roof leaked. My computer died. Dave had a cold and the dogs had hot spots and Jacob had a D– in English. Junior was called "Fish" at school, because he refused to take a shower. Every day the boys' cell phones rang and I saw them carefully check the incoming calls in the greasy, tiny windows. "It's her," Jacob would say. "Mom again," Junior would say. They would shake their heads and put the phones away and I wondered how they felt, how their skin felt, what they remembered of her. She called the boys hundreds of times a day. Dave had cautioned them not to give her their numbers. Their visits with her had to be supervised. Dave had shown me a photograph of her and warned me not to let her in my house if she came by. She wasn't supposed to come near him. But would I recognize her if she did show up?

My own mother wasn't speaking to me. If I called, she hung up. If I called right back, the line was busy; it would be busy for days. I quit calling. I'd never gone this long without talking to my mother. It was freeing and ungrounding at the same time. I was not myself.

Mother's Day, I woke up at Dave's apartment, Junior standing over the bed. "Okay, close your eyes, close your eyes, close your eyes." He blindfolded me. I let him lead me down the hallway. Dave said, "Be gentle, be gentle with her, now." He thanked me for going along with it. The boys had been conferencing all week.

"Okay, okay, okay," said Junior. "Jacob, hit it!"

I opened my eyes and I was in the doorway to the living room. Pieces of purple tissue paper were taped over the doorway, a quilt of paper. Through the purple tissue paper, I could see Jacob standing by the light switch. Dave was in his running shorts with the camera, at the other doorway.

"Burst through!" Junior said. "Burst through to the side, you can go now, you can do it!" He gave me a shove. And I did burst—into tears.

New dishes—silver, gray, with blue flowers, the sweetest dishes and all of their cousins, every possible piece—covered the table. Every square inch. Saucers, cups, serving dishes, a hundred pieces of china.

Junior had saved up from his grocery store job and purchased the set. "Even the little gravy boat!" He rocked it, swam it over the table. "Don't cry!" he said, and he shook me by the shoulders.

"Gentle, son, gentle there, big fella." Dave pulled him back.

Jacob burst through the purple paper, over and over, until it was shreds.

....

We never used those dishes, or any dishes.

Evenings unfurled and Dave nibbled on chips and salsa, standing by the fridge. The boys were always MIA. I complained. They couldn't just be mooching other people's dinners every night. I wanted to cook for us. I worried. I kept telling Dave we needed to know where the boys were. I wanted him to help me do this. But Dave didn't believe in ordering the boys around, imposing routine where it had never existed. We never ate dinner together. We never even sat down at the table. For weeks, the dishes stayed on display, the twelve settings mashed together, stacked on the table. And then at some point Dave boxed them up and put them away. I kept the gravy boat. I used it down at my house, for flowers.

We still spent evenings and weekends house-hunting. But our social life wasn't social, it was just life. Dave didn't have close friends or any hobbies or groups; he said his focus was us, me and the boys. I'd been in upstate New York for too long; I'd drifted from my Michigan friends. They didn't approve of Dave anyway. I felt uncomfortable taking him to college events: his beliefs were so different from everyone else's. He was gentle but opinionated, and his voice carried. "You just want to be a mother," one friend said to me. "You don't have anything in common with that man." Quietly, I stopped speaking to her. When another friend found out he was in the NRA, she shrieked. What was I thinking? "Don't you want to know people from a variety of backgrounds? Isn't that what liberal is, by definition?" I said. I felt sick inside. "No," she said. "Not really." Dave always spoke highly of my friends. I didn't tell him of their criticism, my susceptibility to it.

That summer, Dave and I drove around the county and walked through old schoolhouses, fixer-uppers on the back rivers, ranches by cemeteries and highways. We skipped vinyl-sided developments; we sought out the fringe. Could we live on a houseboat? Could we live in two trailers, out in the country? Could we afford a new house, three levels, each of us with a zone of our own? The process felt like us getting ready for life together.

We were so wide open to every possibility that we actually had no vision at all.

"Anything good?" Jacob would ask, paging through the blue notebook in which I had collected all the real estate flyers, annotated and hole-punched. I gave all the houses nicknames. Peachy. Scruffy I. Scruffy II. The Bird Nest. Summer peaked. The Fourth of July passed. One night Junior slapped the notebook shut and tossed it across the living room floor. He was in his grocery store shirt, a black polo; his little name tag read *David D.* He said, "You guys aren't ever going to buy a house." He said it plainly, confidently, stating a fact. He sighed, hoisted himself up, and went out the door. I didn't see him the rest of that week. He was spending time with friends, Dave said.

I thought he should spend more time with us. I thought there should be a curfew, I thought there should be rules. I thought, now that we were married, that what I thought should count.

"They're fine," Dave said. "I'm not going to be a police. You're the one with the busy schedule. Not us."

Many nights that summer I slept at my own house. One morning I woke up alone, made tea, and let out the dogs. Out back, a utility guy in a tan Carhartt jumpsuit was examining my roof, holding a long pincer on a stick.

"Good morning, sweetheart," he said. He said it like a radio announcer, like he said it every day. Like it was fun for him to say.

I jumped back into my house and slammed the door. I had the phone in my hands, ready to call 911.

"It's just me," he called to the back door. "It's me, sweetheart."

"What are you doing?" I yelled.

"I'm just looking at that branch up there. On your roof. Potentially causing a problem." He was talking really slow, as though to a wild animal or a dementia patient. As though I were on a ledge, about to drop.

No matter that I knew it was Dave, it didn't *look* like Dave. I felt irritated at Dave, and tricked by Dave, and frustrated because this—this not recognizing him—wasn't his fault at all.

I turned my back on him. I went back up to the kitchen and got my tea and walked out the front door and over to the park and sat under the giant tulip tree. I was being a bitch. Ever since I'd gotten married, I'd been in a bad mood.

⁘

August. Dave was in his bedroom, ironing his shirts, watching *Rambo*.

The dinner hour had passed; no one had eaten. Again I was on the bottom bunk bed between the boys. "Show me again," I said to Jacob. He needed to shower tonight. He was so dirty and so cute. He was like a giant Newfoundland puppy or a character from *The Lord of the Rings* with his long blond hair and giant, pawlike hands and feet.

"Press A." Junior reached for the controller. He was mad we hadn't found a house yet. I was playing Nintendo to cheer him up. I had to plan my syllabi for the upcoming semester and turn them in. But Nintendo was so much more fun.

"She has to learn," Jacob said gently, and he took the controller from Junior and pressed it back into my palms. I was surprised to see Jake was a natural teacher. Softly he said, "You wake up. You're on a beach. What would you do in real life?"

I stared at the screen. There was my guy, a little blur of blue light, a red shirt, and my yellow head. Standing on a beach. The ocean, an abyss. What would I do in real life? I looked at Jacob. "What would I do? I would worry."

"You would start walking. So walk."

"Press A," Junior said. "You always press A. A. A. A. A." He reached over, pressed the button.

The beach was beige and endless.

"You notice a cave," Jacob said. "You're going to want to go in it."

I didn't notice a cave until Jacob said so. I didn't want to go in it. I was claustrophobic. Plus, I was walking down the beach, without a care in the world. When I saw the cave, I thought: *Keep walking, no sudden moves.* I thought: *Cave man.* I thought: *Run, flee, swim, die.*

"Oh God," Junior said. "I can't watch." He extracted himself from the bed and loped away.

Jacob pressed my thumb down with his giant index finger. My guy appeared in the mouth of the cave. Jacob said, "You go in the cave. You see a shield. What does that make you want to do?"

"Worry whose it is."

"Press A," Junior yelled from the living room. "Always. It's going to be press A. Press A!"

"Unnecessary yelling!" Dave yelled from his bedroom.

I held the controller and stared at my guy in the cave.

"Press A," Jacob said. "On the shield. You can do it." He grinned. He took the controller. Now my guy was on the shield. They were one with each other.

"You know that you want the shield and your task is to go find the sword."

"How do you know that?" I said.

Jacob explained: "You *always* need weapons. If you don't have weapons, that is going to be the first thing you need always, okay?"

I picked up the shield.

"I'd run now," Jacob said. "Go, go, go. Leave."

"Am I in danger?"

"No," Jacob said. He rubbed his eyes with his fists. "It's just that this part is boring. It gets so much better."

"Mostly, you'll run into non-playable characters," Junior said, leaning in.

"Like life," I said.

"The rest of the game is going to be finding people and talking to them," Jacob said. "People are going to tell you things. They're going to make finding the mission more complicated."

"The little dude is right," Junior said. "I hate to say it. You know I do. But he is."

And so I went where I hadn't been before, with only a vague idea of what I was supposed to find.

Meanwhile, that summer the librarian at my university introduced me to PsycLIT, a search engine for specialized articles and papers on a sweeping range of medical conditions. I searched with the key words *recognition, schizophrenia, faces, emotion, offspring, right left confusion, face, memory.* I found dozens of articles, but nothing I read suggested that a schizophrenic parent would produce a child unable to recognize people by face. When I figured out how to access PsycLIT from my office on campus, I drove down to school late at night, working in the dark at my little desk in 308 Lubbers Hall. I typed in *vision, children, schizophrenic mothers, children of schizophrenics, offspring of schizophrenics,* and I searched *faces, families, mentally ill.* Writing the searches was like writing poetry: Which combination of words would be magical? Which words would open the door? What door would it be? I kept playing with the words, trying to find the article I needed, the one that would say, *Yes, children of schizophrenics had this sliver of the illness, it manifested in this terrible face confusion.*

One night I was skimming along, and there it was: *face recognition; also prosopagnosia.* I knew, intuitively, this was what I was looking for.

The article was about stroke victims who were perfectly normal in all ways except for one: they could no longer recognize even close friends and family members by face. The disorder was called face blindness. It was extraordinarily rare. Fewer than a hundred cases had been reported in all of history. I read the article, full text, on screen. I did a search for all of that author's work. I typed in *face recognition, prosopagnosia, face blindness.* For the first time, I left the word *schizophrenia* out of the search. And I found dozens of articles.

Prosopagnosia comes from *prosopon*, Greek for "face," and *agnosia*, as in *agnostic*, "doubt." I was, without a doubt, a face doubter. The condition was caused by a blow to the head, a stroke, a trauma. Sufferers recognized people, just never by the internal features of the face. They used voice, gait, jewelry, and context. Common sense. They compensated. Many could function well. Others became withdrawn, housebound, even suicidal.

I kept studying articles I'd retrieved from the library, trying to understand what face blindness was, how it worked, and most important, how it was related to my mother's condition. It had to be related somehow. My theory went like this: The schizophrenic brain was essentially created by massive wiring problems that resulted in a person's interpreting reality in ways that seem bizarre to us but made perfect sense to him. Face blindness was similar. A wiring mishap created all these misperceptions on a much, much milder scale. I was certain face blindness would be common in the offspring of schizophrenics. I didn't have mental illness. But face blindness was my mother's legacy, the shadow of her biology. It was how I was related to her. I knew this in my bones.

When I began my search, like most people, I hadn't understood the basic differences between vision and perception. I believed I saw what I saw, heard what I heard. I believed in direct input theory: an object was in the world, and when we looked at it, the image appeared directly in our head, as if on a television set.

As I read, I learned the brain didn't use direct input. *Perception* and *vision* aren't the same thing at all. Vision itself is simple, like a camera: it captures images. Vision parts—lenses, retinas, irises—are simple parts, so simple that some aspects of vision can be improved with straightforward medical intervention to repair or enhance them. Vision merely captures images. Vision doesn't happen in the brain. It happens before information gets to the brain. But we don't see or hear until the brain takes over. That's perception. Perception is what our brains do with those raw "seen" images. Perception is what scientists call "the black box." Study perception, and you step into the mysteries of consciousness and knowing itself. Perception really doesn't have a lot to do with vision. In fact, most of the wires that connect the brain to the retina hook up to memory functions.

Perceiving is a sophisticated dance of remembering: it's not an eye thing but a memory thing. When we "see" something, we don't necessarily identify it anew. Mostly, memory "fills in" the image. Old impressions give meaning to what we see; we never start from scratch. The famous example used to teach this concept is that of a dog running behind a picket fence. You don't ever see the whole dog, but your brain remembers what dogs look like and how objects are divided and obscured behind fences. Perception is knowing that at the end of the fence, a whole dog will emerge. While you are seeing a sliced dog, you perceive a whole dog is back there. You remember how fences work, how dogs work. Perception overrides vision: you see what you know, not the other way around.

If I truly had prosopagnosia, my *vision* for faces would be perfectly fine. And I knew I had perfect vision, 20/20; I didn't even need reading glasses. When I looked at a face, or anything else, I didn't see a blurry image or anything weird. I just saw a face. But perception dictated and dominated vision. Something was wrong with how my memory archived faces, it seemed, if it archived them at all. I could see faces. I couldn't remember them at all, ever, not even for a second. That's why I couldn't easily tell people apart.

I wondered when I had gotten it. Did I have it my whole life? It was so hard to tell. The articles stressed head injury as the cause. One night I made a list of the blows to my head:

Wayne's rough wrestling, my father's drunken swinging, the time he clocked me with an iron skillet. It was hard to escape childhood without scars. Car accidents. My most serious car accident had caused a severe concussion and memory loss, and left scars along my cheekbones, above my lip. But I had had problems recognizing people long before that. Maybe something had happened to my head that I didn't remember, would never know about.

I didn't believe a blow to the head had caused my recognition problem, I believed I'd been born with it. But there was no way to know; things had been so chaotic in the household. I'd been overexposed to stressful weirdness and underexposed to friendships, neighbors, television, movies. I hadn't really noticed anything was wrong until I was in high school, when I went to the same school, finally, for a couple years in a row. That's when I realized: I really don't know these people. I thought this was a sign of mental illness.

Now I believed face blindness was a distant cousin of schizophrenia; it was how I was related to my mother. Face blindness didn't tip me over into mental illness. But it could have. I believed that a similar neurobiology must underlie both conditions. My mother had had to come up with bizarre, elaborate theories to explain her experience of her own mind. I'd had to do the same thing. But while she believed she was very, very sane and everyone else was crazy, I was certain I was mentally ill. In fact, she was and I wasn't. We both were perfectly wrong, and perfect for each other.

I found more and more articles; none of them mentioned schizophrenia. The disorder wasn't a mental illness at all.

In the early research, the extremely rare cases of face blindness were always traced to a stroke, or a blow to the head. But recently, scientists had discovered congenital or developmental cases. Face blindness was much more complex—and perhaps even more common—than originally thought. Scientists weren't sure what the exact problem was in these developmental cases, where a person just seemed to have face blindness from birth, but it was becoming more clear that the mechanism that allows one human to know another by face is sophisticated, involving many steps. Faces, it turns out, are processed in a special way, not like any other object humans come across.

But prosopagnosics read faces as they read any object—car, house, gun, horse—by looking at the parts. Tiny individual distinctions are lost. For face-blind people, a given human face looks more or less like all other human faces. They aren't able to organize fine distinctions in mouths, noses, cheekbones, eyes. The special processor, the face processor, isn't installed. Face-blind people perceive faces using the standard object processor.

Late one night, I wrote to the authors of several of the articles, and I e-mailed two famous scientists who'd written about face blindness and perception: Antonio Damasio and Steven Pinker. I asked my burning questions: How might face recognition relate to paranoid schizophrenia? There had to be a connection between the two disorders. Are there any research studies I could be part of? Sending these e-mails, I felt myself part of the world, connected by a thread.

Our house-hunting dwindled. But one Saturday afternoon Dave and I were driving around town when we came upon a For Sale sign. I picked up the little flyer. It was out of our price range. I tried the doorknob. It opened. Dave said, "Don't go in."

The house had a tiny slice of lake view, though it wasn't really lake anymore, more marshy sluice. I took off my shoes and headed up the stairs, spidering up the stringy beige carpet. This was a great house. I could feel it.

Dave stood in the doorway. "Don't go up there," he warned. I turned on the stairs. He looked so thin down there in my living room. He was staring at the ceiling, frowning. He would never live in this great house with me. I knew. It was too fancy. It was too much.

Upstairs, I grazed through the bedrooms, arranging furniture, making the boys' rooms perfect, in spite of the low ceilings and chemical smells. I imagined them growing older, out of these rooms, into the basement. I expanded my writing studio. The slice of sluice lined up with my desk chair. The boys had friends over and I brought up popcorn, Cokes, fabulous snacks. I fast-forwarded. The boys grew up and moved out to live on their own. The room became a nursery. My babies, my babies, I could still have babies. I nursed at the window, looking for the tiny tongue of lake. This wasn't the season for it.

Downstairs, Dave had rapped on the walls. He was thinking: hollow, cheap. He was thinking: $180 a square foot. He was thinking: housing bubble. Against his taps, my home sounded like a coffin. He hated the black appliances. He hated having neighbors. He was right. The house was overpriced. We shouldn't spend so much. It was, after all, looking more and more like it was going to be all my money. Dave was having issues with his credit, the bankruptcy history behind him.

We went to the Blue Moon and I ate expensive soup and he had two beers. He held my head in his lap all the way home. "We're good, we're good," he kept saying. "It's okay, it's okay." I had the strong feeling it wasn't okay. I had nurtured the idea of a real family for so long that I wanted everything to fit just right. The dinners felt crucial. This house felt imperative. Why didn't we feel like a family in spite of these things? Why didn't we feel *right*?

Days passed, then weeks. I didn't hear back from any of my queries to the scientists or the government's Rare Neurological Disorders offices. I hunted on PsycLIT, finding related articles almost every night. My list of key words grew as I harvested the new vocabulary from each new article: *face perception, self-perception, face processing, lateral dominance.* I found information on mothers and faces. Nine-minute-old babies showed a strong preference for looking at faces and facelike patterns, compared with eggs, blocks, or random patterns. Given a smiley face on a circle and a circle in a random pattern with those same lines, those same two dots, babies would always prefer to stare at the smiley face. A few days after birth, a baby knew its mother's face from other faces and, soon, strange faces from familiar ones. There was a developmental dip: adolescents got much worse at recognizing people, then they improved again. Babies born with cataracts, who couldn't undergo the intricate operation to correct their vision until they were six to eight months old, all grew up to be face blind. Similarly, people blinded in childhood who had rare, risky corneal transplants as adults found that when they got sight, they lacked, among other things, the ability to determine who a person is by face. The basic face recognition system is installed before birth, it seemed, but during these crucial six months, it has to be employed, tested, used, in order to become the sophisticated working system most people require.

I also learned that schizophrenics had trouble making eye contact. Normal mothers typically stared into their babies' faces for hours and hours, transfixed. This was how the baby learned, in part, to read faces. My mother always avoided direct eye contact. Could her behavior, rather than her genes, have been the cause of my condition?

I thought of Dave's theories: portals, tampering. Faces were a window. Maybe, as with paintings and portals, too much came through them. Maybe my mother had to avert her eyes from my gaze. Maybe my face recognition software never got used during the crucial window. Or maybe she had dropped me on my head accidentally and, *boom*, the face light went out. I waited anxiously for the scientists to write me back. I wanted them to tell me: *There are more people like you. Come to our lab,* I wanted them to say. *We will fix this. It won't hurt one bit.* I wanted diagnosis. I wanted certainty.

....

One night, Dave and I were sitting at my kitchen table, drinking wine and listening to Hank Williams. He asked me to close my eyes and describe my mother's face. I couldn't. It wasn't as though she didn't have a face; I just couldn't conjure any visual images. I saw her from the side, her shoulders, the outline of her body, her thin bones, her way of hunkering into herself. "I can see her," I told Dave. "But I can't see her face. It's like it's there but just out of reach. Nothing looks missing, it's not foggy, it's just that I can't get any specific details. It's really hard to explain. It's like the idea of her face. Like if you tried to picture the Grand Canyon, you have an idea what it looks like, but what you picture probably isn't the actual landscape.

"Can you picture your mom's face?" I said. "What do you see, exactly?"

"I can see her face now. I can see her face when I was a kid. Just like she's there."

"Wow," I said. "I can't do that."

"Wow," he said. "Try yourself."

I closed my eyes. I couldn't imagine my face. I could feel myself looking out of it, but when it came to looking at myself, I drew a blank.

I tried him. I looked at Dave's face and then I closed my eyes. I couldn't see his glasses or his facial hair. With my eyes still closed, I brushed my hand along his jaw, his nose. I thought this would cause something to light up, switch on. Nothing. "I know you have a goatee, because we have talked about it. But if I weren't feeling it right now, I'm not sure if I would be able to accurately say if you had a beard or not. I have no idea if you have a mustache or not," I said. I rubbed my fingers under his nose. "Oh," I said. "You do."

And then—with summer ending and school approaching—we found our house. A gray split-level on Elm Street. We loved it equally; it wasn't too expensive. It was just a couple blocks over from the house I lived in, and up the street from Dave's apartment. It was practically in our own backyard. The elms, save for two, were long gone from disease, but the street had been replanted with locusts and sycamores and maples.

It had a finished basement for the boys, with a workshop for Dave, a newer furnace, an upstairs bedroom for my office. A giant garage for all Dave's antiques and projects, the skis, the bikes, Junior's hovercraft project and tae kwon do boards, the cement blocks that had piled up in Dave's living room. It had a fireplace, a creek in the backyard. A Sub-Zero fridge. I envisioned dinner parties, pizza night, the boys standing in the kitchen with the fridge door open, draining the jug of SunnyD. There were cork floors in the cozy dining room. I envisioned dancing.

Dave and I looked through the house a second time; it was the farthest we'd ever gone with a house. This was it. All the houses and months and doubt and not knowing, solved. We told the real estate agent we wanted the house. I wrote him a check for one thousand dollars. Earnest money. After he left, Dave and I walked up Elm Street, tramping over the packed snow, grooved crusty by the plow's tractor tires. This would be our cute, clean, plowed street. This would be our sun. These would be our neighbors. A handsome, prosperous man shoveled his walk in perfect even stripes, scraping it to the bone; his sidewalk gleamed like a wet tongue. A golden retriever barked once—*Hello!*—from atop the snow pile. Two little white-blond boys in black parkas whacked each other with sticks. It looked exactly right: houses and neighbors and order like in a dream, a child's drawing of a street in winter, one you'd hang on the fridge.

Dave said softly, in his gentle easy way, "The man coming toward us, you know him. He works in your department. The rock-hound guy. We saw him . . . at the geology show? . . . The one at the civic center?"

"I don't think so," I said. "Rick Jones?" Rick was craggy, more friendly-seeming. I felt I would know if we were passing someone who worked in my department. Even after all those articles, my brain signal was loud and clear: I had never seen this person. He was a stranger.

"Yeah, honey, it is. You want to say hello."

As he passed us, the man said, "Hi, Heather, Dave."

Dave squeezed my hand.

How was I going to spend the rest of my life not knowing who people were? I was sick of relying on Dave. I was tired, angry, sick of doing my best to pretend I knew. "How do you do that?" I lunged up and kissed him on the cheek and we stopped walking and hugged. In the middle of the sidewalk on Elm Street, in winter, on that dead-quiet afternoon, we were hugging, I was hanging on to him, and he was holding me. It didn't feel like dancing. It felt like tipping over.

Five

My mother said fine, I could live with her while Fred went to Germany. But, she emphasized, there would be rent, and it was temporary. I had to be out when I graduated high school. On the day of. If not before. This was twenty months away.

Well, college, I said.

You aren't really college material, she said. Not anymore. "The fun ride is over. You want to act like an adult? You can take on the responsibilities. No rights without responsibility! That's what I have always stressed with you children. Always." Her voice grew loud when she made these speeches, loud and cheerfully dogged, just as it did when she talked about the evils of communism, or the trap of credit cards, or the shameful mediocrity of products made in places like Thailand, the Philippines, or, worst of all, *Taiwan.*

After one of these tirades, I asked her point-blank: "So, why did you even have kids?"

And she slapped me, across the cheek with the back of her hand, dripping wet from soapy dishwater, hard, so hard my teeth felt loose and bruised. I bit my tongue. My mouth tasted like blood, but there was no blood. I wished there were blood. She had used her whole arm, and moved so fast—it was such a direct, quick, unhistrionic thing for my mother to do—that it had taken me absolutely by surprise. And then she'd walked out of the room, almost like a dancer.

I carried on for hours, slumped on the floor in the corner of the kitchen, wailing so she could hear me, so I could hear myself. But I was impressed. I wanted her to know she'd been effective, that she'd gotten to me. And at the bottom of my despair was a cold calm stone: I'd deserved that slap. And inside that calm, cool knowing, a deeper knowing: this mother I had was not a person who'd really wanted children.

There was some kind of animal—bigger than a squirrel, maybe a muskrat, a possum, or coon—trapped in my bedroom. We were handling the matter by not opening the door. "I've got many other problems besides that," my mother claimed. "And I do not have money for professional extermination."

Every night, the thing circled the walls, and I thought I heard it wailing. It was dying, it had to get out.

I didn't open the door.

My mother didn't care if I was paid or not, as long as I was working. I signed up to be a candy striper. At the hospital, I took great pride in going directly where I had been told not to go, 5B, the indigent ward. I dropped off cigarettes and magazines, envisioning myself as a girl Robin Hood. I kept waiting for some great doctor to hire me or marry me or cite me for my good work, in a lavish public ceremony.

One day two candy stripers stopped me in the hallway. They wore their pink-and-white candy-striper pinafores. The little white hats. The white hose, white shoes.

"Fine, don't say hi, Heather." The girl frowned at me in an exaggerated way.

"You always act like you don't know us," the other one said.

"Heather, you are such a snob."

They were tormenting me, trying to trick me, or else they had me mixed up with someone else. I turned in the opposite direction, feeling stupendously stupid. After a few long purposeful strides, I turned back. From behind, I could see that they walked a certain way, and I recognized them instantly. They were Christy Summers and Lauren Martin, girls who went to my school, girls who lived three streets down from my mother's house. They were best friends: nerdy, unpopular, nice girls, girls I'd known for years, girls I liked and wanted to be friends with. They walked down the wide corridor so certain, sure of where they were going, sure as stalks.

Why, when I was out in public, did I act so much like my mother? Why did I treat everyone like a stranger, like the enemy? Why couldn't I be friendly, social? I didn't want to be like her, not at all. But I wasn't becoming my own person. I had no favorites, no preferences, nothing that individuated me, or collected me into circles. Other people seemed to know exactly what they liked: Mounds or Almond Joy, board shorts or cord shorts, school spirit or pot smoke, baseball players or football players, school or hating school, *The Dukes of Hazzard* or *CHiPs*, *Fantasy Island* or *The Love Boat*. I adored and feared and despised and felt uncertain about all of these things, equally, all the time. I didn't even know if I liked the Beatles or the Stones.

Part of me was secretly glad I was this way. Instead of participating, I listened and watched. I dissolved into uncertainty. I turned invisible. It was socially crippling and completely nerve-wracking, but I felt that not knowing things about myself was a special talent, something good and useful, my sole superpower.

To get myself through the year, I began to cultivate an amalgamated Nancy Drew/*Great Gatsby* college fantasy: I would live in an old-fashioned dormitory, have my own room, my own bed, my own thoughts, library within walking distance. All day people would talk about books and ideas, ideas just barely touched on in high school, like communism, France, schwa *e*, impasto. I imagined a boyfriend with oatmeal linen pants and horn-rimmed glasses and a nice, old-fashioned slow sedan from the 1940s or 1950s; we would walk holding hands and go to soda shops, and I would wear plaid skirts and glasses and carry piles of books secured with a rubber strap. His mother would live in a mansion; I would glide down her hallways in white floaty dresses.

Come summer, I started lifeguarding at the YMCA on Saturdays. Sitting in the high chair under the red umbrella, I calculated the money I was making per minute, how much I would need for first-semester tuition, room deposit, the food plan. Between calculations, I blew my whistle: *No running, no running, no running.* It got to where the job was so boring, you wished for someone to start drowning. I never spoke. The other lifeguards didn't chat with me, and boys didn't linger at the foot of my chair, staring up at me from behind Ray-Bans. I was working. This wasn't my social hour. I aligned myself with the pool director, a darkly tanned woman in her sixties with short, straight white hair, pool-blue eyes, and a military manner. I was hoping she would say, publicly, that I was a model lifeguard and the others should try to be more like me. At the end of summer, she said they didn't need me back next year.

My mother during this time was working temp jobs for Kelly Services. No one really wanted her, she said. She could tell when she walked in: she was despised. I took this at face value; it sounded like the real world was a lot like school. She read detective novels from the library at dinner and shouted at the characters and I read the encyclopedias and shushed her. We did the dishes together.

The animal in my bedroom at some point must have died; neither one of us would open my bedroom door. Now the house seemed to be dormant, asleep in a kind of rigid, forgotten stupor. The furniture was covered in white sheets. Most of the bulbs were missing from the lights and lamps. We hunkered down, using only the kitchen, her bathroom. We shared her bed.

She didn't talk to me so much as lecture me. "You think these boys you are seeking out like you? No. Do they have your best interests in mind? No. They are thinking about *their* interests. I know about the boys who come by here after school, Heather. I get calls. I have sources. I've read your so-called diary.

"If you get pregnant, you are out. Oh You Tee out, in a skinny minute, don't even think you have a place to stay here, because you don't. Nosirree Bob, don't even think about it. Don't even let such a thought darken your door. You want rights? You've got responsibilities. Consider that. Reflect on that.

"And I'm onto you."

She smelled like talcum powder and lotion and something else, something metallic, like wet iron. When I tried to give her a hug, she gripped my arms, hard, and pushed them down. She darted away, throwing the dish towel at me, the front door slamming behind her. It was like I was the one living with a mercurial teen. I felt world-weary and magnanimous. I put dishes away. I cleaned out her fridge, a museum of frightening former food items.

I babysat. The time I spent in the homes of other families, alone with their children, were the choicest hours of my life. I read books at the library on how to babysit; I memorized games from 1950s party guides so I would be prepared to entertain any number of children. I skimmed books on child development written for teachers and psychologists. I imagined various dilemmas arising, and how I would handle them capably:

a neighborhood fight, a hurricane, food poisoning, the parents not coming back.

I loved the children and I also loved the moms. Mrs. Anderson, the painter, with her sprawling ancient plantation home, white columns peeling, the screened sleeping porches where I taught her daughters to sew doll clothes, where we had tea parties and dressed up as angels and princesses. Mrs. Ripple, the nurse with a perfect lacquered hive of ash-blond hair, whose husband was a dentist and whose kitchen and bathrooms gleamed like surgical theaters. In her tidy, color-coded home, I felt like a tropical butterfly, a little messy, but in a good way, an antidote, a tiny hurricane working for the force of good.

I kept my money in a shoe box, under the bathroom sink, back behind the towels. I checked and re-counted it every day.

The Madigans' house sat up on the hill, the windows shining clean, the gold drapes drawn back. The house was smiling. I showed up at half an hour before I was due. Mrs. Madigan had tennis, lunch at the club, then golf. In her white tennis skirt and pretty top, her sunglasses on top of her head, she took me straight to the fridge. Leftovers were in labeled glass containers. Chicken curry. Spaghetti. Mushroom beef. Any of this was for me. Any of it.

As soon as I got there, Jay said to his mother, "Can you please go?" Jay was almost three. He cried when she came home.

While Jay napped, I lay on the cool blue satin bedspread in the guest room, pretending my husband was coming home. What would I make? Beef Stroganoff? Or lemon fish with white rice? The shelves were lined with novels that came from Book-of-the-Month. Kurt Vonnegut, *Go Ask Alice*, Saul Bellow, Norman Mailer, Truman Capote. Some I read, and some I sort of read.

At bath time, we always had bubbles and songs, and long, drawn-out plays where Jay played bubble-bearded pirates and baseball players and told me exactly what to say. I drifted through the hours, watching, carried along on a gentle warm tide of three-year-old energy, surreal and sweet and mind-numbing, unmalleable. I imagined this was what it was like being on drugs. Night after night, Jay told me about the brother he was expecting, George, and what we would do the next time I came, and how he would play football in college and I would come and watch him. In Jay's dresser drawers were tiny ironed University of Florida T-shirts, pajamas, even underwear printed with the grinning gator. In his closet, UF jackets and tops and footballs and seat cushions. His mother had been a cheerleader there; his father had played football. Jay was going to UF. He was going to be the quarterback. He was going to UF, would become a fireman, and then, he said, he was going to marry his mom. He was three, but he knew all this. I was almost seventeen, and I had no idea what I was going to do after graduation.

Eventually, school started. Wayne and I skipped a lot: the beach was fifty minutes away, fewer when the Torino was running well. I felt smug and smarter than everybody else. When it rained, or even when it was sunny, we went to the downtown public library. (*We're not sheep!*) I had taken to the psychology section, searching out the contours of my mind and my mother's. I found a checklist that seemed to describe my mother: *dementia praecox*. I'd never heard of it before. I didn't think she was demented. But *praecox*—which sounded like *peacocks*—maybe it meant someone who acted demented, showed her feathers in a crazy way, a showy way—that fit. The checklist was very specific. These people were always afraid someone was trying to break into the house. They believed they were being followed. They had many moods, all intense, happy one minute, terrified or enraged the next; then it was as though nothing had happened. *Dementia praecox,* I wrote in my journal, and I underlined it.

I found myself a few entries below. My condition was much worse: dysthymia, a chronic sense of unhappiness. It was more common in women than men, you could start having it in childhood, there was no cure. I wrote all this down too. I put down an equals sign and then my name.

I didn't really believe this was me and my mother. I was exaggerating us. Dementia praecox was a kind of psychosis; my mother wasn't psychotic. Psychotic was ax-murdering. I'd seen *Psycho* (or most of it, until my mother stormed down the aisle of the movie theater and loudly ordered me to leave). I didn't think she was insane, I thought she was a pain in the ass.

I looked for my father in the book too. I did not find him, his habits. But with these parents, I wasn't even sure exactly what I was looking for.

Sometimes, when I came home from school, my mother was hidden in her closet, under blankets, and she wouldn't move or speak. It was as though she were dead. I would sit with her, but she would recoil, like a cornered animal. I knew she wanted me to go away, not to see her like this. I would ride my bike up and down the streets of our neighborhood. Wayne turned out to have another girlfriend; he seemed somewhat pleased to confess his cheating. I missed Keith Landreu so much my heart hurt.

I don't know when exactly Fred came back from Germany. He didn't call or come by, but I tracked him down. I could not live in my mother's house. When I told Fred she was too strict, he said, "She has ruined both you kids. That woman has ruined everything she comes into contact with." Which wasn't really true, I thought, but I said yes, yes, yes. I moved back in with him.

The first day back in his house, things were very strange. The radio was on, not the television. Fred was not drinking. He was on the roof, sweeping off branches and leaves and loose gravel. He edged part of the front lawn. He sawed down dead palm fronds and had me drive all the stuff out to the dump. This went on for three days. He ate two bags of Oreo cookies and grazed on Lorna Doones and doughnut holes.

I pieced together a story: Instead of firing him outright, Martin Marietta, where he'd worked off and on, had sent him to a plant in Germany because of his drinking problem. Things had not gotten any better. When he came back, they must have given him an ultimatum: thirty days of rehab or he would lose his job. It was his second stint in rehab, he told me by the pool on the night of the fourth day of my living back with him. I had chemically adjusted the pool: the water was clear and blue and sparkling. I was floating on a raft in my purple bikini, drinking an Old Milwaukee. He was drinking pure gin from a tumbler. "Some messed-up people in there," he said. "Real bad. Real bad." He shook his head. I wanted to know how bad, how were they messed up, what had he seen? When had all this happened? How did he get there?

"Classified." He laughed and coughed and laughed. He banged on the table.

It was good to see him again. I didn't really want to know the details.

Ruby was back. We all went to dinner—Ruby and Fred, me and Wayne—at an old restaurant in Wekiva Springs, on the river. Wayne and I had never really broken up, despite his cheating on me: I just didn't have the strength or energy to start a big conversation. Plus, I needed him to drive me around, and I needed someone to call when Fred was out of control. Eventually, I would go off to college and then we'd be done. Wayne was adamantly against college; he bragged that he went to the school of hard knocks. This always cracked Fred up. I'd heard him say the same thing of his own education, though he had an MBA, had attended Northwestern.

We watched the raccoons with their cute little paws and bandit faces claw food off garbage can lids. Fred ordered a bottle of wine in a pale green fish bottle. He quickly emptied the bottle and made the fish swim above our glasses. The waitress brought a cake. Everyone sang. I wished to be rich and go to college. I blew out the candles.

Fred wanted to dance by the table. I said no, no, no, but he dragged me up out of my chair. There was no music. He hung on me. His nails had the usual polish; under his shirt, the standard bra. I looked at Wayne and Ruby, who were staring off into space, slanted, a few steps left of center themselves. I pretended it was fun to be out in a restaurant, to be doing things my mother would disapprove of. Ruby and Fred ordered more drinks and I tucked my feet up into Wayne's lap and he rubbed them and made as many hard-on and woody references as he could, all of which I pretended not to understand.

My father made a long toast to me. "She will never abandon her daddy, isn't that right, girl child?" He was standing, staggering, slurring, and people were watching.

"That's right!" I said, and I pulled him down into his chair and he wept.

Fred went to the men's room or the bar or the car. He was gone a long time. Wayne had gone somewhere too. He liked to talk to women and he liked me to see him doing it. I didn't care. I couldn't even pretend to care. Ruby smoked Virginia Slims that came out of a pink leather case. Her lighter was a Zippo, silver, expensive, and it snapped into flame with a sweet click.

I was sitting on my chair sideways, watching the little raccoons, ready to go home, go to bed.

"Your daddy shore is something special," she said.

I said, "He is something," and she nodded and nodded, but it wasn't so much like agreement, it was more like her head was loose. It was too sad to see. I felt like my father was a bad influence on Ruby. I wanted to get out of there. I wanted it to be just me and Ruby. If it was just us and my birthday, we could have gone together to New Orleans, gone shopping, to a nice restaurant, and to bed, early, nice, normal. I told her I was going to round everybody up so we could get going, and she said, "Oh, you'd better probably not. He has to think it's his own idea."

"Well, it's my birthday," I said. I excused myself and wandered around looking for the restrooms. There was a man leaning on the pay phone but not using it, tilted, smoking a cigarette in the shadows. He looked crazy, large, and unreal, like a man coated in something. I slid past him and pressed open the door to the women's room. I felt something grab my bottom through my dress, a hard squeeze.

I turned around slowly, scared to make a scene. Where he had touched me felt on fire. I was dreading everything that would come next.

"It's your old daddy! It's your old daddy!" he hollered, grinning, grabbing me, shaking me, and I saw the teeth, the wide, white false teeth. "Happy birthday, number-one girl chile. Happy—" he slurred, lurching toward me, wanting to hug, or dance. I put my hands up: *Stop, stay back.* I didn't smile. "You scared the shit out of me," I said. "What are you doing?"

"Classified!" he said. He leaned against the wall, coughing, coughing.

I stormed into the women's room, locked the stall. I couldn't pee. I was too scared, all tight inside. If I had thought about it all, which I did not, I would have said I didn't recognize him, because I didn't love him enough. I was embarrassed by him and I didn't want to know him in public. I believed my father was right: I was like my mother. Difficult on purpose, deliberately obtuse, only happy if I was miserable and making other people miserable. Not knowing people—it was such a *her* thing to do, maddening and obstructive and attention-grabbing and thoroughly weird.

Six

We'd found the perfect house, the house with levels. Dave took the day off work and we went to my bank. Dave was the loan officer's name too. Bank Dave was shiny and superbly neat, and his pale stocky hands flashed over his calculator like a professional dealer's over playing cards. He told my Dave it would be cheaper and easier if everything was, at least for the application process, in my name, because my Dave had some cleaning up to do. My Dave had no savings, none at all. He needed to clear out some debts, write some clarifying letters, tidy up old business. Then we needed to get an inspection and send Bank Dave a copy of the report.

I wanted to tell Bank Dave that Dave was a good man who'd stood behind a sick and troubled woman and then cared for their children, all on his own. This was why his credit score history wasn't perfect. He had good reasons.

I also wanted to call everything off, right then and there. I wanted to stop, and regroup, and think this all through. But paperwork has a momentum of its own, and I signed and signed and opened my folder and signed.

"Stop," I said as we left the office. "We can take the stairs."

"You okay?" Dave said.

Was *he* okay?

"It's big," he said. "It's just big. And all the old stuff. I'm of course going to be thinking about all that. I'm sorry about all that, Heather. I wish so badly I had more to offer you."

"They're here," I said. "The stairs." I worried that when I pressed the door open, alarms would ring throughout the bank, throughout the whole downtown.

I told myself once we had this house it was going to be easier. We would be together and we would get better at things: money, dinner, trust. But I was anxious, I worried, I consistently felt something bad was going to happen. Soon after we signed the loan application, a woman came to Dave's house. Dave was at work. The boys were in their bedroom playing Legend of Zelda on the GameCube. I was cooking dinner, which I would likely eat by myself, though I'd set the little round office table for four. My first thought when the doorbell rang was: *This is Sarah.* When I opened the door, the woman took three steps back. She had a serious briefcase and no coat. She looked alongside the house, like she was expecting someone to be escaping.

She asked for David. She used his full name. I wondered if I was supposed to know her.

"Which one?" I said.

She gave me a look that said, *Don't get smart with me.* I told her there were two, a senior and a junior. "I am the wife," I said. I felt I was incriminating myself.

She said she was the process server. Again she looked down the driveway. I was trying to remember if I knew what a process server was. What was the process? What *was* "being served"?

She let me sign for Dave. The envelope was from a law office. It was, she said, an outstanding balance. It could be for anything, I thought, and I went inside, weirdly calm. I'd been waiting for something bad to happen. Had I been hoping for a reason, any reason, to leave? I knew Dave had spent a few nights in jail. I knew he'd had to be very careful or he'd lose his driver's license permanently. It was so hard to square these facts about Dave with the kind, gentle man I slept with at night. Why hadn't he told me about lawyer debt? What was it for? I was terrified to buy a house with this man. I sensed I would be the one paying this lawyer bill. I was disappointed at how ungenerous I felt. I felt I was in over my head. I felt like I didn't love Dave enough, and that feeling was sickening. I felt like a deserter.

I set the envelope on the sock pile on his dresser. I turned off the noodles and told the boys they could eat whenever they wanted to, everything was ready. I slipped out and drove home, and then I tossed and turned all night.

I thought about leaving all the time. But I pressed forward. I asked Dave to drink less. He said he was fine, it was fine, I was worrying way too much. I arranged for the house inspection.

And at the same time I arranged to meet my old boyfriend, Dick, for lunch. Dick was not a Dave fan. Since meeting Dave, I'd hung an American flag on my porch, taken archery lessons, and discontinued exclusive NPR listening. I had questioned mindless Bush-bashing. I had questioned the two-party system. Dick felt Dave was not the right man for me; he had told me this on more than one occasion. Dick believed I was turning into a conservative. Dick felt Dave had led me to isolate myself from my friends and from my real self. But Dick was also bright and sensible and he knew me and he cared. And I needed somebody to be honest, brutally honest, about my marriage.

He sailed up to the table at the New Holland Brewery. "Hello, there, Heather, you look beautiful. As always." He slid into the booth and put his folded hands on the table like we were at a summit.

Dick was tall, distinguished, white-haired, in a crisp black leather jacket. He believed he looked like Alan Alda, something I was entirely unable to confirm. There were half a dozen men in our town who looked just like him: tall, white-haired, aging well. Dave and I had joked about the ubiquitous Dick look-alikes. I leaned across the table and gave his cheek a brushy kiss. He smelled good, like cigars and office furniture and toothpaste. He was sixty now. He smelled organized, *effective.*

After we ordered, I said, "I need to know if I should leave Dave or try harder."

"Leave Dave?" he said, aghast.

I told him about the legal notices, the bankruptcies, the process server. I hadn't known how much debt there was. What if there was more to come, more of the past yet to be revealed? Everything was going to be in my name.

Dick rested his hands on mine. He looked at me hard. I braced myself for the big *I told you so.* "Heather Laurie," he said. "You have to stay with this." Dave was a good guy, he said. Sure, his politics were a bit questionable, but he loved me, I obviously loved him, there were the boys, and I had married him. I couldn't cut and run so soon. I had to stick it out. For better or worse. "You took vows," he said. He made a wincing face. His hands were still folded on the table, but now his index fingers were pointing at me, like a church steeple.

When the sandwiches came, we ate. After a bit, Dick said, "Let me ask you something a minute. See Marlene?"

"What?" I scanned the restaurant, happy for a topic change. I didn't see anyone I knew. I took his pickle without asking.

"Marlene," Dick said. "Marlene is right there, you see her."

"No."

"Heather."

"What?"

"You are looking right at Marlene Cappatosto. The woman who waved over here a second ago? Why do you pretend you don't see her? She thinks you *hate* her. Why do you always snub Marlene? She has mentioned this to me several times. She'll see you and say hi and you walk past her as though you do not know her at all."

I thought of all the articles I had read. How complex recognition was. How was I going to explain it? People would think I was mentally ill. "I haven't ever seen her and known it was her and not said hello," I said. "I wouldn't do that." I couldn't imagine how to explain face blindness without sounding like a complete wacko.

"She's a nice person," Dick said.

I shifted around in the booth. "I have a thing. It's a thing. I can't always recognize people."

He gave me a strange look. He said, "Oh, you do not." He frowned in a pursed way. "You knew who I was." He notched his face, as in *Checkmate*. "You always think you have something. Remember the Lyme disease? Remember that? Remember when you thought you had Ménière's? And the whole dengue fever thing?" He laughed.

I tried to explain. It was true, I had overreacted to mosquito bites and what was probably seasonal allergies. But sometimes I knew people. Sometimes I didn't. Often, I didn't *know* if I knew them or not. It was a real thing. Very rare, from what I had been reading, and most often caused by a stroke in midlife, but I had it. I knew who he was because he came up in clothes I knew to be his, and he sat down at my booth: he acted like someone who knew me. I wasn't stupid, I figured it out. But not the same way he did. I couldn't recognize the human face. I often said hello, I told him, to other men in town, thinking they were him. "A lot of men look like you," I said. "This happens to me all the time."

Dick shook his head. "No," he said. "I've never heard of anything like that before. Come on," he said. He put down fifteen bucks, excused himself, took his coat from the back of his chair, and went and sat with Marlene and the other women.

I always forgot why Dick and I broke up, and then I always remembered.

....

A cop car trolled behind us on our way to the final inspection. As always, Dave drove extremely slowly. The boys, on their scooters, outpaced us.

"Your seat belt," I said to Dave. I was tapping his arm with my fingers, not nicely. I was like a crow. With my feet, I was trying to get the beer bottles under the passenger seat. Dave had been drinking in the car on the way home from work. We'd had our worst fight yet: he was on my car insurance and I wanted him to get his own. I vowed to stay calm, not to bring this up now.

"I can see the fear in your eyes. You don't want to live with us."

"It's a cop," I said. "These bottles are driving me crazy." When had things gotten this bad? Why was he drinking? And why did I join him late at night, nearly every night?

"It's okay," he said.

"You know it isn't. How can you drink in the car? You can't. You can't do this." Beer bottles were rolling around loose on the backseat floor. I had pushed them under my seat and they'd come out the other side. "We can't move in together if you drink like this." I meant something much wiser. I meant this to come out in a loving *We're a team, I'm in this with you* way. The cop turned down a side street, but I did not relax.

We pulled into the driveway of the perfect gray house. My split-level. The boys circled the car on their scooters. Dave cut the engine. He took my hand. He said he was sorry in a soft voice. In a different voice, he said he didn't know what the drinking was about. He said, "I have to do something about it. I don't know what it is. No one in my family has this. No one I even know."

I got out of the car and went inside, where the realtor was beaming with his clipboard. "Isn't this a wonderful time?" he said. "Isn't this an exciting day?" I sent the boys around back to explore the creek, the tree house, the shed.

The inspector was upstairs inspecting. Dave had been on the roof and seen something he didn't like in the chimney; now he was trying to get the working fireplace to light. I leaned over him. I was worried on all sides.

"I do not get it," Dave said. "I hate to think the guy is lying, but this thing hasn't been used in . . . I don't know how long. I don't get it. I think it's broken. This is just not a working fireplace." Dave's head was in the fireplace itself and his body was on the hearth. From where I stood, the man had no head. I sat on the hearth and patted his leg. I felt sick.

"Easily fixed, no doubt," the realtor said. "We can give the seller a list of everything you need fixed before closing; that's typical—supertypical."

The inspector yelled, "I've hit the mother lode! You're gonna wanna see this!"

We found the inspector on the pull-down stairs that led up into the attic, his upper half swallowed by that space. We each took a turn peering in. Every cranny of the attic was insulated with spray-injected foam. There was controversy, apparently, whether or not it posed a toxic threat.

"Whoa," Dave said. "Excessive."

"What do you think about this stuff?" I asked the inspector.

"They went all out," he said. "Whoever put it in, they went whole hog with it. That's for sure."

"We have to think. We were not expecting this," I said. The realtor shook his head.

"We didn't say no. We just have to think. I'm not sure. I'm just not sure."

Reeling, I retreated downstairs. I discovered that the doors to the garage and the half-bath were split, splintered. I knew this kind of damage, intimately. It was damage done in anger, fury. I called for Dave.

Keys jangled, and a man burst in.

"What the fuck are you doing in my house?"

I shook all over. I leaned against the wall, inching toward the bathroom, where Dave and the inspector now stood. Was I supposed to know this man? Had I seen him before?

"We're allowed to be here." I said this to the floor with great confidence. I looked up, looked him in the eyes. He was like a person on fire. He was thrumming with rage. And then I knew: I could live with Dave and his drinking, I could live without dinners, I could live with a town full of Republicans, I could live with the lunar stuffing between the walls, but I couldn't live in a house where this man had lived. I said to the man's shoes, "We will never buy your house!"

The inspector said, "VanderSluis? We went to high school together? Mike Van Lente. Hey, how's it going?"

"You're inspecting now, I heard that. You got laid off? Why are you in my house? Isn't the realtor supposed to be here?"

I slid out of the vestibule and ran up the stairs, through the kitchen, out the front door. I ran to the car and got in fast, like I was being chased. I had recognized that man's face. He had the look, the male version of my mother's face. I knew that I could not live in this house where he had lived. Rage felt soaked into the walls. This house would never smile on us; inside of it, we would only be unlucky, uneasy, and unkind.

The boys found me in the car, hopped in the back. I rubbed my face, refused to cry in front of them. "So, what's happening?" Jacob said softly, nervously, slowly. I heard his feet clinking the beer bottles on the floor of the backseat.

"We're not getting it," Junior said. He breathed out dramatically. "I knew it." He slammed his body back onto his own seat. Then he got out and slammed the door so hard it bounced back open. He ran down the street.

Jacob said to me, after a bit, "Whatever. You know that's David." Then he leaned over the seat. He said, "I'm going to go, though, okay, Heather? I need to do some things and stuff. . . ."

Then he took off down the sidewalk, sliding around on the snow, catching his brother at the corner. I watched them hitting each other, reenacting the drama that had played out in the vestibule, that was playing out between me and their father, under the surface. Through the windshield, the house looked dark, closed and empty, but not the right kind of empty, not the kind I wanted so much to fill.

The house fell through. The status quo prevailed. Married but not living as married. A family that wasn't functioning like a family. Fine and not at all fine.

....

A giant manila envelope came in the mail. Wisconsin postmark. No return address. It was a letter from my cousin Patty, Katy's daughter. Enclosed were photocopies of Katy's skeleton drawings, and family recipes. I had forgotten I had written Patty back when I first contacted the scientists about schizophrenia and face blindness. She was the only one who had answered.

> *Let me answer your questions one at a time. No, no one in the family has mental illness as far as I know. Aunt Florence had a severe paranoid reaction in Europe and had to come right back home, but do not bring this up to anyone—she doesn't want anyone to know, especially your mother. I was in a mental ward for six months due to a breakdown brought on by exhaustion after I had my two children and working so much. My mother (Katy) died of agoraphobia and emphysema—she couldn't leave her bedroom the last three years of her life. People always said your mother was peculiar, but there was no mental illness in the family.*

To the contrary, it sounded like every female member of the family suffered some form of mental illness, and childbirth was a specific trigger. The sheaves of drawings were the same kind hidden in my mother's bedroom closet, the ones she'd forbidden us to look at. There was one of a snake eating a blood-drippy heart, the snake wrapped in other snakes. Dave asked me to put the drawings away. He was worried that spending time with them would upset me. But I liked them. I liked the boldness and weirdness. I liked being in the presence of the strange, dark, unstoppable creative impulse.

I was in the tub with a glass of wine when the phone rang. I wrapped myself in a towel and answered.

"Your mother is very hurt, very hurt, Heather, by your saying you do not love her, and you must make amends, you really must. She's your one and only mother!"

I didn't recognize the voice at all. Had I ever heard it before? It was old and forceful, midwestern, Germanic, terrifying. I pretended to know whose it was.

"Love is a two-way street, and she's your one and only mother. My circle is praying for the two of you to heal. It would be wonderful if you and me and your mom could go to church all together when we are up there. I can't get her to go down here! She thinks she's sinned too much! Oh, Heather! So much healing. So much—"

"Who *are* you?" I said finally. My voice sounded polite and afraid.

It was Bernie. She was visiting my mother in Orlando, and they were driving up to see me. They would arrive Monday. Hadn't I gotten the letter?

They'd gone to kindergarten together, my mother explained when she got on the phone. Bernie, she said, was her best friend. She'd talked about her thousands of times. They were looking forward to Michigan and nice cool weather. Wasn't she lucky to have such a good friend? My mother's voice was loud and clear, high and fake, like she was acting in a bad play. Or being held hostage.

"How do you two know each other again?" I asked.

"Bernie is my best friend!" she yelled dramatically, and I could tell she had an audience.

"Have I met her?"

"You were very little. I think very small."

I asked my mom if it was hard to talk right now.

"*You* are so perceptive! I'm so proud of my beautiful daughter! I can hardly believe I'll be seeing you in a couple of days!"

When I suggested a hotel, my mother said that would be impossible: Bernie was a minister's wife and could only stay in homes, because that's what she was used to; plus, she was on a tight budget. But we would pay, I said. No, my mother said. It wasn't possible. They wouldn't be any trouble. Her voice was loud and strained, taut with forced cheerfulness.

When we were little, my mother regularly gave us emergency words, *white dog* or *pineapple.* If we were ever in trouble, we were to work them into a conversation with her, staying on the line as long as we could. Our captors would not know, would not suspect, but she would get help. I wanted, now, to ask my mother if she needed rescue, if she wanted to use a code word, if she remembered the secret system.

"Angel," I wanted to whisper into the phone now. *"Purple cucumber. Schmatzhagen."*

The last time my mother had visited me in Michigan, I had just moved in, classes had just begun. I was nervous and new. I'd left her alone in my house with a painting project to keep her occupied, and strict instructions: Don't take the dog out, don't go anywhere, don't engage the neighbors in conversation; just stay inside. I'd be back a little after four. When I came home, I found she'd taken down every painting, everything I had on the walls: the Haitian blue woman, the 1950s Virgin Mary print, the Renoir reproduction in its lacy gilt frame, the painting of fish taking other fish for a walk on leashes underwater. She'd put the paintings behind the sofa and pressed two furnace filters against them. She'd tacked sheets over my bedroom windows. I'd found the trash full of food: she'd thrown away my tube of garlic paste, canned coconut soup, couscous, jars of condiments, chutneys and pastes and olives and sun-dried tomatoes.

Back then, I'd felt censored, over-mothered, oppressed. We'd fought bitterly; she'd left early. Now I understood that these actions were her way of keeping me safe, leaching out the bad energy. But I didn't want her coming up here, going through my papers, taking my savings bonds and bank statements for "safekeeping." I didn't want her cutting the buttons off my dresses. I didn't want her running around in my fragile new marriage. Most of all, I didn't want her scaring my stepsons again.

"If you don't want us, just say, Heather. I'm not going to come where I'm not wanted. I very much want to see you. If you feel otherwise, please, just say. The trip is an expensive one for me. Please. Just say how you feel." This was her natural voice.

"I can't wait to see you!" I said, and I hung up the phone, desperate childish schemes running through my head: I could leave town, I could stay down at Dave's. She and Bernie could stay at Dave's while he and the boys stayed here. I could go to a hotel. They could just stay in a hotel. How bad could it be? A couple of days.

That weekend I got out extra blankets and put them on the sofa. I made up the twin bed in the guest room with fresh sheets. I found soap, new soap. I made a grocery list. School was starting in a few days. I tried to get my syllabi organized for classes, but I couldn't think what books I'd ordered. I couldn't imagine students reading those books, whatever they were, and me talking about them. To what end?

The evening before school started, the last Sunday in August, was a cool night with a warm breeze. I was walking down College Avenue, carrying my quinoa salad in a yellow Pyrex bowl draped with a blue linen towel. I wanted to feel effective and Martha Stewart–ish. I wanted to feel participatory and welcoming. I was on my way to a potluck dinner for new women faculty. I did not want to go. I wanted to go to parties but I hated going to parties. I had no idea why. As I crossed the street, a strange old station wagon pulled in the spot beside me. A man got out and smiled a dopey smile. I stepped back and looked at the guy, trying to figure out if this was someone I knew. He wasn't looking at me as though he knew me, or otherwise. It took him a while to speak.

"Hey, sweetheart." He opened his arms wide. He was holding a tall boy in his hand. In a paper bag. I knew the outline of a tall boy.

"Did I scare you?" Dave said. It was Dave, it was Dave, it was Dave. Of course it was Dave. I shifted my salad to my other hip.

"Whose car is this?" I looked inside, holding my salad as

one would a toddler. There were empty beer bottles on the floor, the seat. Dave, Dave, Dave.

"Well, sweetheart, I accidentally bought a car on eBay," he said. "Ended up high bidder." He laughed and shook his head. "Great car, though. Great car. Single owner, old lady. Low miles. I've been looking for one just like it." He sounded warm and fuzzy, fluffy, hell-bent on happiness.

"My mother is on her way up. I'm late for a school thing. Welcome new women faculty. I told you about it." I wanted to say a lot more.

"Well, sweetheart." He frowned, but in a deliberate way. It was not a convincing frown.

"Why are you drinking?" I said. I sounded mean as a rat.

He looked into my eyes. He said in a kind voice, thoughtful, flannel, "That's a hard one to piece together. As I have said before . . ."

"Things have to be pieced together," I said.

I was approaching the apartment where the potluck was being held, wondering how long I would have to stay to not be weird or rude, when a woman came toward me, saying hello.

"Hi, I'm Heather. I'm in the English Department," I said. "Are you looking for Jenn's? I think this is it."

"Yes, of course, I know," she said. "I'm Jane Small. In History. Our offices are down the hall from each other? In Lubbers? This is my fifth year here. We have met." She smiled. "Many times."

I opened the door and followed her up the stairs. I didn't really believe her. Jane Small? I didn't think so. That was not my idea of Jane Small at all, not even close. I thought Jane was a much thicker-boned person, older, less happy.

Inside, I beelined for the kitchen and concentrated on helping Jenn lay out the plates. She had beautiful plates. I said hello to Beth Trembley, who turned out to be Janis Gibbs from History. They looked a lot alike. I filled my little plastic glass with some wine. I scanned the room. Jenn's home was the upstairs of a house, an apartment. It was nice. She had a pretty scarf over her television set. I knew people did this to add color where there would otherwise be black plastic, a blank screen. It made me nervous, though. I moved from the television to where a woman was standing alone by the stairs. She looked nervous, afraid, and I knew she must be new. New woman faculty member. I went up to her. "Hi, I'm Heather," I said. "Welcome to Hope."

She said, loudly, her voice stiff, "I'm Jane! Jane Small from History, we have worked together for years. I am just down the hall from you." On the word "hall" she pointed her arm out. She held it out there. I got the idea the arm was saying *Go away* and *Why can't you get this?* She said, loudly, dropping the arm at last: "You know me."

The party stopped on the loud words, in the way a party like this always does. Something was said, something with sharp edges, and it rose over everything else, and it rested on top of the party for a moment, like a sheet of aluminum.

And then it fell. The party readjusted itself, and the chatter rose again and wove around the room, women's voices, Three Mo' Tenors on the stereo, Jenn in the kitchen calling, in her voice like silver water, "Almost ready, folks! Almost ready!"

I stared at Jane. She looked nothing like the woman I had met on the sidewalk. She had on a jacket outside? Or maybe she had changed her hair?

I slipped out of Jenn's apartment before dinner; I didn't say good-bye. On my way home, I walked past Dave's apartment. I looked up in the windows. There was Jacob in the dining room with his sword, frozen in a stance, the weapon over his head, shining. He looked so serious and straightforward, like he was going to carve the place to pieces. I almost wished he would.

I felt perched on the edge of my own life. I'd been fooling myself. I had no idea what I was doing. I felt as though not one of us—Dave, Junior, Jacob, me—knew what the hell was going on and what made sense.

And so, finally, I called for help.

One

In the corner of the therapist's office was a beige file cabinet. On top of it, a pebbly fountain whirred. I wondered what was in those drawers. Probably files, notes on all the other patients. Reading files, lying back on the couch. I would love that. It would help me, finding out about other people's secrets.

"Welcome," he said. He sounded so serious, way too serious.

He was so close, I could feel the heat off his pants on my bare legs. Sweat ran down my body, beaded under my thighs, soaked my palms, my feet. I'd been so anxious to get to the therapist's office, and now that I was in it, I couldn't think how to begin. I wanted to leave. I wiped my hands on my denim skirt. I felt frizzy and frantic.

Peter Helder, Jr., was calm and dry. Sandy hair, sand-washed silk shirt, slacks dry as drapes. When he'd leaned into the waiting room to call my name, I hadn't wanted to follow him; he looked so polished and professional and tall, like a manicured tree. Where would he go that I could possibly go?

He leaned over, even closer. "Welcome," he said. "I'm glad you are here." He was hovering in the airspace over my knees. He was like a vulture. A handsome gold vulture.

"What's most pressing?" he said.

I looked at the sofa. I wanted to lie down on it and close my eyes. I wanted him to just do the therapy to me, suck it out of me while I slept. I wanted a complete overhaul. I wanted new limbs. I wanted a new neck to hold up a whole new head. I wanted to be hypnotized, brainwashed, monitored, imploded, reconstituted, turned invisible, turned inside out, and cured. I wanted my organs replaced with all new organs, no scars. I wanted him to hover over me and infuse the stew of me with clear insights and shiny bits. I wanted all this change to happen while I lay semi-dozing, in a state of beauty and receptivity, quietly thrumming, on the couch. But it wasn't a lie-down kind of a couch. It was a forward-facing, upright, massive ship of a thing—a sofa for adults, for work, for serious conversation, maybe for reading John Steinbeck or drafting torts. There had never been a free association on this sofa in its entire life.

He leaned in even closer.

I showed my sweaty palms.

"Well," he said, smiling. "We know you're alive."

A lump of speech blurbed out. I told him about Dave drinking in the car, how we'd gotten married in upstate New York but we didn't live together, how Dave didn't want to ever have dinner together, how I didn't want to blame everything on Dave, how I was wondering if I should leave him, how I wanted to figure out what I was doing wrong.

But the thing that had really brought me to this sofa was my mother's visit. I didn't want her to come. I needed some help with her visit. So we wouldn't have problems, as we'd had in the past. I told him I thought she might be a paranoid schizophrenic.

He waited to see if there was more. There was so much more. I told him about the incident—almost a year ago now—when I'd asked her if she heard or saw things that weren't there, and she answered: "You just want to lock me up."

"That's the wrong answer, right?" I said. "Do you think she's a paranoid schizophrenic? I'm not one hundred percent sure."

"It's an unexpected answer," he said. "Unusual answer." I waited for him to go on, to explain. But he was very quiet. He was staring into me, hard. I closed my eyes. He must have realized I did not really want to hear an answer. I was not ready to explore the implications of a mother with paranoid schizophrenia. I opened my eyes and took a breath and my voice was high and fast; I sounded like a forced-friendly version of myself. "I feel so bad that I don't want her to come and visit. I want to be able to handle these things better. I do love my mother. She's very old."

He took in a long breath. "Yeah, this isn't a good time for you to have a mom visit," he said. "You can tell her now isn't a good time."

I was surprised to hear him say this. I thought therapy was all about working on difficult relationships with family members, learning to get along with your mother. I thought it was all about the mother.

"I can't tell my mother not to come and visit me." Again I heard my voice as forced, girlish, breathy, too high.

"You can," he said. "It's one sentence. She will feel some pain. Your marriage is in crisis. You tell her that you and Dave are dealing with some issues. Now is not a good time."

I looked at his wall. He had a metal sign, cut-out letters, bolted to the putty-colored wall. It said IMAGINE. I looked at the clock. This was weird therapy. Wasn't there supposed to be a checklist of questions? How many schools I'd attended, if there was a history of substance abuse, how old I was when my parents got divorced? Somehow, forty minutes had passed. I wanted to tell him the sign was not a good thing. A word on a wall, never good. I could never come back here. "But I can't tell my mom not to come," I said. "It would kill her."

"It won't kill her."

"What would I say exactly? How would I say it?" I didn't like this therapist at all. He was for rich people, for dry people, for shiny, normal, well-funded people. This was terrible, terrible New Age therapy. I would interview three therapists, good ones, and find the right one for me. A woman. I needed a woman and a checklist. I needed things to proceed in an orderly fashion.

"You tell her you love her and you do want to spend time with her. You tell the truth. You and Dave are going through a difficult period in your marriage and it just isn't a good time for a visit," he said. He was using a low, serious voice, the kind of tone we'd been urged to employ in dog training school, firm, low, clear, one straight line. "There's a lot to sort out before your mom comes and stays in your house. She may never stay in your house again." He looked at me, kind of checking me over, to see, I suspected, if I could handle the truth. He cocked his head. "You might not ever know—you might not get a clear diagnosis regarding your mother. You can still take a clear position."

I shook my head. "I just want advice on how to not let her get to me. When she's here. I want her to have these grandkids." It was so easy to romanticize this notion in my mind, to see my mom and her dear friend Bernie with me and the boys and Dave, at the beach, at the all-you-can-eat buffet, taking photographs at the Old Windmill. "She's not young. She's not getting younger!"

Helder shook his head. "The adult speaks. The child who wants to please her mother, who never wants to do anything to make Mom unhappy, she has to be kept in the backseat. She can't have the car keys." He paused. "The reality is you and Dave live in two separate houses. The semester is starting. Fuck. It's so much. A mentally ill guest would be a very challenging thing for anyone to take on, in any circumstance. Very hard."

I looked at the clock. I wiped my hands on my skirt. How, I asked, could I have gone my whole life not knowing about my mother? How could I have not known what Keith knew when he saw our house?

"It's your mom," Helder said. "Because it's Mom." He sounded firm and knowing and clear. "When a child has an alcoholic father, he sees him drink all day long but he doesn't have a label, a concept. You just know that at night, when the tires make a certain sound in the driveway and the doors slam a certain way, with a certain sound, you just know you need to hide."

I was in my father's house as he talked, and I could see the Fairmont in the driveway, slanted, and Fred reeling through the rooms. I was in my closet.

"She was your mother," he said, and I snapped back into the present. He said "mother" like a boy would say it, like a priest would say it, and everything, in that moment, in his office, made sense. "You don't have to have clarity," he said, "to take a clear position."

I wrote this down though it made no sense to me.

"You're shaking," he said. He looked worried and sad and urgent. He wanted me to call her after the session, cancel her visit, and then call him back.

When I'd first moved to Holland, Michigan, nine years earlier, October's long, dark, cold, wet days made me fat. I craved potatoes and milk and dough. I knew no one. I had no friends. At the one and only department dinner I attended, people talked about their churches, the new chaplain, and their former churches. When I called Ter Haar Floor Specialists to redo my upstairs bedroom, they said they gave the quote only to the husband. I called another company, same thing. I ate a container of Chunky Monkey almost every evening. I'd watch four episodes of *Friends* back-to-back, eating ice cream, then call up ex-boyfriends from previous lives. After Florida, I'd moved to Texas, and in San Antonio I'd changed apartments five times, for reasons that always seemed reasonable at the time: it was closer to work, it was quieter, it was farther from work, there were more people around. I thought I liked moving. I thought I liked the prospect of a fresh start. But in Michigan, I felt worse than I had ever felt in my life. I couldn't sleep, but I never felt like I really woke up, either. I ate and ate, but food tasted plain and strange and thick. I burst into tears between classes. I wore shapeless flowered flannel shifts and felt like a slow wool ship as I lugged my books to school and back in tights and clogs. Then it started snowing, beautiful and terrible, and I couldn't get warm. I couldn't figure out how to make new friends; I simply never "ran into" people and it was hard to start conversations in a friendly way. Many people in the Midwest looked the same: pale, bland, corn-fed, sturdy, plain. Same with the roads. I'd never lived on the grid before. I was constantly lost. Suddenly 163rd became 47th and then inexplicably 120th, and on all sides were identical desolate muck farms. I was going downhill fast in a flat, flat world. I applied for teaching positions in Altoona, Riverside, somewhere in Arizona. I read the job ads for teaching English in Egypt, in Dubai.

In the phone book, I'd found Pine Rest counseling services, and for a few weeks, on Friday afternoons, I'd seen a woman named Christine. Stultified by the lack of sunlight and the midwesterners' close-knit reserve, which struck me as hard, rude, and unforgiving, I wanted drugs. I wanted to know what was wrong with my life and how I could get things together. Christine wanted me to exercise, to join Holland Area Newcomers, join anything, maybe a winter walking club, and then see.

I didn't join things. I didn't go to things. Why not? Christine wanted to know. I wasn't sure. I was busy. Very busy. "I'm not a joiner," I said. "I'm a professor."

She said she knew many professors who were active in the community. She knew a professor in a book club and another in a dinner club. There was a professor in my very department, she said, who ran a quilting club.

I couldn't imagine these were intelligent professors.

It wasn't the place, she said. It was me. "You're going to move again, and guess who you're going to find when you get there?"

I stared at her. I was hungry for cake.

"You!" she said, pointing at me triumphantly.

In the third session, Christine was eager to talk about why I pretended not to know her at the grocery store and the fabric store. She understood patients wanting to keep a distance, but I had looked right at her and acted as if I had never seen her before. When she'd said hello, I'd turned away. Why? We could talk about ways to interact when we ran into each other. I didn't have to pretend.

I thought she was deranged. "I never saw you at the store," I said. "I've never seen you outside the office." There was no doubt in my mind. If I'd seen her, I would have known. I would have said hello. I was a friendly southerner.

"Why are you saying you didn't, Heather? We both know you did. Twice. You looked right at me, Heather. If you would prefer I pretend not to know you when we run into each other in public, I can do that. Let's talk about it. Let's dialogue openly."

"I didn't see you, Christine. I've never run into you." My depression had a hostile cranky marbling, which I enjoyed more than I could have admitted.

I never went back. This was not therapy. It was argument.

After my first session with Helder, I decided I wouldn't see him again. He was a good man. But IMAGINE was not for me. I would assure my mother that she was welcome. Dave would help me handle her. Maybe she could even stay at the apartment; the boys could stay down with me. It would be good to be together. My new therapist would help me communicate better with my family. When I thought about it, though, what I liked best about the session was that Helder said *fuck*. A good, hard word, a word with a life of its own, a fearless word. A rent in the dry elegance. *Fuck*.

"We are on our way!" It was my mother and she was whispering hard, breathy and excited. She was so excited to see me. She was calling from a pay phone. She wasn't quite sure where.

Peter Helder, Jr., therapy vulture, flashed before me, shaking his head. *The adult drives the car.*

"Well, Mom, it sounds like a lot. It sounds like too much. You don't have to do this. You know," I said, "I can come down later this fall. I can visit you." As I spoke, I sensed this would be the end of our lives as we knew them. I was surprised at what was coming out of my mouth.

"What do you mean? What's wrong?" She sounded sharp and guarded. "We are on our way, Heather. What's happening?"

The words came out on their own. I told her I was afraid I couldn't show her a good time because I was absolutely overwhelmed with work.

The line went dead.

When the phone rang again, the voice on the other end was strong as iron.

"I'm praying for you."

It was the middle of the night.

"You are hurting your mother. How can you tell her you do not love her? How can you say a thing like that to your dear sweet mother? She loves you so much, Heather. She wants to heal this rift. It is time to heal this rift. She thinks you don't want her to come! I need you to talk to her, she's right here. She's very upset."

"Where are y'all?" It was quiet on the line. I was afraid they were down the street, that they'd come over anyway.

"You need to have a relationship with your *mother*, Heather Laurie Sellers." The way she said the word "mother" scared me.

"Bernie," I said, very calmly, in the voice I used for students who talked too much. "I am not sure my mom is up to making this big of a trip. She is very fragile. And I am not able to take off work to have company right now. I am going through a difficult time."

It was all like a dream. Not bad, not good.

In the morning, I called Peter Helder, Jr. I needed to come in.

Two

I started driving a car when I was twelve. Fred, tumbler of straight gin in hand, would yell at me for turning left on red and for driving on the wrong side of the road, but he continued to put me behind the wheel and gave a lot of verbal direction and physical correction, grabbing the wheel, torturing my elbow. I hated driving. Often I had the sensation I was in the wrong lane, headed in the wrong direction, as though somehow everything was reversed. Even after I got my license, I had trouble figuring out which way to go, which side of the road to drive on, and how to get from one point to another. One warm spring day, when I swung out of the Winn-Dixie parking lot and onto the wrong side of Orange Avenue, my father had had enough. It was time for me to get my head examined.

I was thrilled. Finally. All my life, I'd wanted my head examined. My whole family believed I had mental problems and I wanted to see a neurologist very much. I wanted the doctor to say: *She shouldn't have to drive.* I wanted him to say: *You people are ruining her!* I wanted a long, complex surgery with a recovery in Europe, like in a book. No visitors. I wanted him to explain to me how I could get into a great college up East. These desires felt only vaguely unrealistic; I was in high school.

At the neurologist's, Fred didn't want to wait for me in the lobby. He didn't even want to come inside the office and meet the doctor. I sensed the reason he had decided to take me to a doctor at all was that my mother had been down to the house every night that week, laying into him about what a bad idea it was.

The neurologist was waxy, shiny, and kindly, and his hands were thick and freezing cold. He ran a little serrated wheel up and down my shins. He banged on my knees with a rubber arrowhead attached to a hammer. He held out fingers. I held out my fingers to match his. He asked me questions: Who was the president? What day was it? Press on his hand with my foot. Other foot. Lift my right hand, right, left, left, right. I giggled and he took it very seriously and wrote everything down. I thought it was going too well, I was doing too well, it was going to look like nothing was wrong. *I'm not this great!* I wanted to say. *Really, I'm a wreck, help!* But I couldn't speak up. I smiled and tried to look brilliant. He left without saying anything. I thought he would be back so I could tell him the whole story. But he never came back.

When my dad finally picked me up out front, there was a man in the front seat, in my seat—his buddy Joe Plaster, he said. I climbed in the back with the gin bottles and made a big deal about kicking them to the side, so they would know I knew just what they were up to. "I just paid forty-five bucks.

How was it?" my father said. He shook his head. "A buck a minute."

Joe shook his head. "A buck a minute. What us assholes are doing wrong, that's what I want to know," he said.

Driving around, skipping work, drinking all day, I wanted to say. *For starters.*

"So?" my father said as we sped down Orange Avenue, through a red light. He swung his hand back, swiped me on the side of the cheek, trying to knock some words out. "Well," he said. "Invite some of your friends over for dinner tonight. Let's have a backyard barbecue. I have a mess a catfish. Make hush puppies." He was all lit up, smiling at me in the rearview mirror. I was staring at my knees. Why had they jumped? Reflexes. I had good reflexes. I was despairing over my knees. I'd blown my one chance for diagnosis.

"Poobah commandeth. We're having a party. C'mon, now. Don't be like your mother. Don't get like her, now. You two are just completely averse to fun, that's your problem. Smile, now! Get with the program!"

"I'm not giving the United States government, or anyone else, personal information of any kind," my mother said. But she had to, or I would not be eligible for financial aid. I'd listed my mother as my primary guardian, thinking I'd have a better shot at a need-based scholarship that way. But Social Security number, bank information, a copy of her last tax return—these were required items.

My mother set her mouth in a long thin line. "Please don't ask me again. You know my views." She turned the sheaf of forms facedown and put the saltshaker on top. "Florida State University?" she said. She put on her reading glasses and stared at me hard, leaning back in the chair with her legs spread open, like a seasoned cowhand. "You? With your grades and your behavior? You need to get a job. Save up. And *grow up.*"

"Can I just please have your Social Security number?" I said. "I'm going to need it for other things too. They have to have it."

Over her dead body. She took pleasure in saying the words *dead body*, like it was a victory—a hundred-pound woman against the entire U.S. government.

"I feel like you're against me," I said. "Just really against anything I want. I thought you wanted us to go to college. You'd saved up. You and Daddy."

"There is nothing I support more than my children—within reason! You are the reason I go on! I would have killed myself long ago if it wasn't for my two precious, beautiful, wonderful children. I would not even be here. I do not know why I am even here, really. I don't. Does that sound terrible?"

The next morning, all the forms were gone. She denied throwing them away. I gathered a new set of forms and they sat on Fred's kitchen counter for weeks. He had said he would help. My mother was a fool, he said. She had money to help me. Plenty, he said. He should know: she'd got it from him. He said I must put her as the primary parent. Her address should be my address. It was in my interest to do it that way. He refused to give me copies of his tax returns. He refused to fill out the financial aid forms. I rooted around in his office, a frightening little room off the garage where porn magazines were stacked several feet high, covered in filmy dust. Theoretically, in addition to working as an accountant for Martin Marietta, he ran a tax consulting and filing business and this was the headquarters. As long as I had known him, only two or three people had brought their taxes to him. Their paperwork had disappeared into the maw, mixed in with piles of bills and printouts from Martin Marietta and bank statements and credit card receipts and insurance and legal paperwork and those gross magazines. I rifled through the mess but couldn't find anything I needed. I suspected my father hadn't been filing tax returns.

As the spring semester wore on and the weather got hotter and steamier, the kids from nice families talked about where they were going to college. In the halls, between classes, the rest of us watched them, hating and pretending. Someone was going to Clemson. A few others to the University of South Florida. Most people were going to the University of Florida. Sara Simko, in her capacity as student council rep, accosted me every day after second period. I had changed my route, but she figured it out and cornered me in the rear stairwell.

"You have not signed up for graduation and it's a decision you will regret for the rest of your life," she said. "I will walk down with you right now if you want me to. I will. Let's!" She was like a little mother, with that sweet, perky, bossy voice of hers, her bangs curled and sprayed against her forehead in a tight, matronly C. I was touched that she worried about me. She had to wear a back and neck brace because of scoliosis and

I worried about her too. I flipped my hair around, shifted my purse onto my other hip.

"I'm cool," I kept saying. "It's all cool." I wanted her to keep talking. I wanted her to tell me what to wear to the ceremony. I wanted her to fix my hair. Not like hers, but nice, and I knew she could. I wanted her to drag me down to the office, to invite me to go to graduation with her and her family, to move in with her family. I wanted her friendship.

"Heather Laurie Sellers," she said, and she stamped her little feet in her little mauve suede flats. She had tears in her eyes. I wanted to have tears in my eyes. The bell rang.

Wayne started hounding me too. I had to go, he said. *We* had to go. Yeah, it was a dorky sheep-mentality mindless waste of time, a sick ritual: most of our classmates had already peaked. They would lead, he said, lives of soulless desperation. But we had to do it. We had to do it *stoned.*

I did not want to do anything stoned. I was having a hard enough time going from point A to point B straight. Of course I wanted to go to high school graduation. But how? If I went to graduation, I would have to invite my parents. It was too stressful. I liked them inside; I liked them one at a time; I liked them asleep. As long as I didn't think too much about who they were, I loved them.

My mother presented me with tiny little slivers of newspaper ads: secretary, product hostess, telemarketer. I threw them all away. My father kept urging me to apply to Valencia Community College. He himself was thinking of teaching out there.

"I'll probably have to fail you," he said. He thought this was very funny.

Ruby said she couldn't see him as an instructor, exactly. Maybe an administrator? A consultant? Teachers, she said, required patience. Heather-Feather, she said, would make a great teacher.

"What subject are you thinking of teaching?" I asked gingerly. We were playing hearts after dinner at his dining room table, the way we did every night.

"Life!" he said. "The philosophy of life according to Fred P. should be a required course. A prerequisite for all learning. For all educable peoples."

"That's a class I have to take," Ruby said. She laughed in a nice way. She fingered her gold-nugget necklace and dropped it between her breasts.

"Yes!" Fred hollered. "Hell, yes!" and he slammed both palms on the table. Then he leered at Ruby. "Where did that nugget go? Where did it go? Can't see it no more!"

The kids who were going to Valencia were regular kids. They smoked. They wanted to stay in Orlando. They liked Orlando. They liked Bob Seger and longnecks and drawings of pot leaves and surfboards and Camaros and Styx and the laser show at the planetarium. I wanted a school where I could study philosophy. Psychology. Art history. I wanted a bicycle, not a car. I wanted a bookish boyfriend, not a stoner. I wanted to go to school up North. Up North seemed more intelligent and sober and elegant. But I really had only one very basic requirement: I had to leave Orlando.

"I have the feeling you might be prone to BS a little in front of a class," I said. "No offense."

"'BS'?" Fred yelled. "*All* BS!" He laughed long and hard until he started coughing and choking. "*All* BS." And it started again. "It's college," he said. "It's *all* BS. Best preparation for life there is."

"You are whip-smart, cute as a button, and flunkin' three classes, honey bunch." My guidance counselor was like a broad from the 1940s: redheaded, plucky, talking fast. "I got one question: Why are you with that Wayne Goggins? I'm sorry, but he looks like a forty-year-old man!" She was a spaz, a nut, but I was happy to have landed her and not one of the other two guidance counselors, the gigantic gruesome PE teacher or bearded, wizened Ichabod Crane.

"I do not like what I have been seeing," she continued. I'd been called into her office before, when Wayne had interrupted my fifth-period PE class, slung me over his shoulder, screaming at the top of my lungs, dumped me in his car, and peeled out of the parking lot. There'd been other incidents. I knew she thought Wayne was a bad influence. I knew she thought I should stand up for myself. She cited other problems: how my grades had dropped into the toilet since I'd started seeing Wayne, how I didn't seem to have any girlfriends. I wasn't in any clubs. She asked me if he was isolating me.

I couldn't speak. I *isolate me,* I wanted to tell her. I wanted to tell her about my parents. I wanted to tell her I had no idea why I had no friends. The school was huge. I never felt like I saw anyone I knew.

"That's not love, hon." She leaned way over her desk and peered up into my face. She was shaking her head very slowly back and forth, her tongue moving in the opposite direction, hitting the inside corner of her mouth, a little windshield wiper. "That is not love. You live with your father?"

I felt myself turn red under my curtains of hair, and I burst into a full-body sweat. In my halter and tight pink jeans, I was sticking to the hard wood chair in her office. Above my head, an air conditioner squeaked and hummed in the window; I guessed you would get used to the racket after a while. I wished I was wearing something less trashy, more studious, more college-y, more like my dream. Something more like the real me.

"It's temporary," I said. My father's house was out-of-district.

"Did you know you have had friends come in here, worried about you because of that boy?" she said.

"Sara Simko," I said. "She's like my little mother." I rolled my eyes.

She smiled. "I've seen the carrying on, Heather. I've seen and heard plenty. These things go in one direction." She made a kind of sputtering, farting noise and lowered her hand from way up in the air down to her desk with a thud. I guessed the hand was me. She handed me a business card: Katherine Weckerlie, MSW. "Think of this as guidance homework, hon," she said. She wanted me to see this counselor, she said. It could really help. I had to get a permission slip signed by my mother, take it to the first session.

She opened my file. My permanent record. "Look at these test scores. Stunning. Your grades—you've missed a lot of school. But my letter explains some of the background situation, I think. Here is the form you need to fill out." She handed me a yellow form. She typed away at a letter in progress in her typewriter. She said, "I'll send the letter to the college you choose."

I had no idea what she knew of my family, our lives. I had no idea what else was in my permanent record. If my mother knew a counselor had used the words "background situation" with respect to our lives, she would have forced me to change schools again. Or she might have left town, attempted to start over, get anonymous again. So I smiled, nodded, and kept my mouth shut. To even think about any of this, I feared, would make the good parts stop working. *Don't think, close your eyes, don't hope for the best.*

I glanced over the application form she'd handed me. It was one page, two sides. At the top, with boxes next to them, were all the colleges in the state system. Florida State University. The University of Central Florida. The University of Florida.

"Thanks," I said. I wasn't sure what box to check. I wasn't sure what address to put, my mother's or my father's. I'd have to take my time with this form.

"No," she said. "No, no, no." She finished typing and whooshed the letter out of her machine. "Check a box."

My hands were sweating. She handed me a pen and I wiped my hands on my pants and took it. In fourth grade, we had moved up to Tallahassee for part of a year, all four of us. It wasn't clear why. We lived in a little apartment. Tallahassee had all four seasons, and hills, very "up North" and college-y. The kids all had gorgeous Georgia accents. My mother said I had to stop talking like those Georgia kids. I couldn't stop. I contracted some bizarre illness and couldn't go to school. I had a fever, hallucinations, rashes. My mother left me home during the day. I do not know where she went. One day I was better. She let me go back to school. Then my mother moved us back to Orlando and Fred stayed behind in Tallahassee.

Florida State University was in Tallahassee. I checked it. Because I'd lived there. Because it wasn't where everyone else was going. Because it was where Sara Simko was going. I had the strong feeling I had just changed the course of my life forever, and at the same time an equally strong feeling that nothing would change, ever.

Our time was up. "Good luck, Heather," the counselor said. She put her hand on my shoulder. In my heels, I was taller than her by more than a head. "Be smart, girl," she said. "Be smart."

I stepped out into the hot general school office. A line of kids I didn't know waited on the bench for their turns—we all had to have our relentless futures approved. I hid the packet of forms in my notebook. Most of my classmates already had their acceptances.

Instead of going back to class, I walked down to the lake and lay on the grass and fell asleep wondering. I tried to remember what the sky had looked like up in Tallahassee. It seemed like it had been a different kind of sky, higher and smaller than our

Orlando sky. But I had been just a little kid then. I lay there wondering, pretending hard not to hope. I could be a stewardess. If worse came to worst, I could completely lower myself and abandon all hope. There was a lot of that in Orlando.

I thought about the neurologist visit a lot that spring. I waited and waited for Fred to say something about the results of the tests. I waited for the neurologist to call. I was sure he needed to send me to a specialist. In May, a few frayed-at-the-edges kids were still waiting for their college acceptance letters. I was waiting to see what was wrong with me.

Then everyone was waiting for final report cards. I didn't care at all about my grades: I was making either an A or an F in each class; I knew that there was nothing in between.

I quit asking Fred if he'd heard word. He seemed to not remember that we'd gone to the neurologist, and sometimes I wondered if I had just dreamed it. But I remembered the little wheel on my knee, the little rubber mallet, the questions about the day, the president, where we were. I went through Fred's mail. I thought about calling the office myself, but I couldn't remember the man's name. For the life of me, I could not remember. I looked under *Neurology* in the phone book, but no name looked familiar.

Three

In my second and third sessions, Peter Helder, Jr., wanted to know if I had discussed divorce with Dave. Had I approached the subject, since we were separated?

"We're not separated," I said. "Not really."

"You don't live together," he said. "You are separated. You are estranged from Dave. Essentially, the marriage is non-relational."

Yes, yes, yes. I had talked *around* the subject of divorce with Dave. I had asked him if *he* thought we were separated. I had asked him what he thought about divorce. I had even asked him if he thought it was possible to get a divorce without hiring lawyers. Amicable? I said. The only time people ever used the word *amicable* was with *divorce*. I had said *amicable* a dozen times. Whenever I got near the subject, he looked haunted, or terrified, or furious. He would get a stony look on his face and then he would say he loved me, he didn't want trouble, and he believed we had it real good.

"We just got married," I said to Helder. "It's been such a

short time. I have to try. Most of the problems are on my end: I brought so much baggage to this!" I'd be turning forty soon. There wasn't time to find a whole other husband, start completely over. "We're not officially separated," I said. I proposed bringing Dave into therapy. I wanted to work on the problems. I wanted to read a helpful book on marriage and do sex homework and learn communication skills. Like normal unhappy couples.

Helder said we weren't in a homework situation. We didn't even live together. "I think you're hiding behind Dave. Dave is your defense."

I didn't understand. Helder talked about codependence. A term I'd heard for years and thought I'd understood and wisely dismissed. I'd suspected there was something silly about codependence: Wasn't there a book on this topic that was generally mocked? But as Helder talked, I realized I didn't understand codependence at all, I never had. I needed Dave to be weak so I could be weak? I needed Dave to be weak so I could be strong? I tried to take notes as Helder talked on and on, but I couldn't complete sentences. The page in my notebook from that third session read:

The most important thing . . .

Ambivalence doesn't have . . .

Neutral ambivalence

Until you . . .

When I looked back at my notes in order to see what it was I was learning, and I found these fragments, I was surprised and stymied. Why didn't I write down the important things? What were the missing parts of the sentences? Why couldn't I remember?

Helder said I needed to speak from a clear position, take a stand. He said I could tell Dave that I was through trying to change him. "I am pursuing divorce to protect me from my desire to change you." He said I needed to say aloud to Dave: "You have abdicated your responsibility as an adult."

I could never say these things to Dave, hurt him this way. Helder said this was a feeling state, a child part of self, a girl who felt she wanted someone to fix things, wanted someone to know her and understand. "This is a feeling," he said. "Not a position." He said Dave was a really good man who had a lot of trouble committing to people, life, himself, relationships. We weren't a good match. He understood my family and that made him super-compelling, super-comfortable. For me to be in a relationship that did fit would be very uncomfortable.

Helder wanted me to divide myself into one hundred parts. Like a senate. And then take a poll. How many senators thought the Dave relationship was going somewhere? How many saw a future?

I froze. I saw my senators; that part was easy. But they all looked very serious and stern and foreboding. I was scared to ask them for their opinions. "Vote?" I said to Helder.

"If my wife told me she was thinking about divorce, I would be galvanized into action," Helder said. "If my wife said, 'Pete, I have some serious issues and I am thinking about leaving this marriage,' I would be on the move," Helder said. "That would get my attention. Dave seems to be shut down. Not really engaged in this relationship."

But he was so kind. So patient. He'd helped me so much.

"And you can honor that," Helder said. I was crying by then. He called that grief. But I said no. No, it was hope, it was hope and I wanted to try. I would bring Dave to counseling.

Libertarians, Helder said, didn't come to therapy, and when they did, they didn't do well. They had a very structured worldview, one that wasn't up for discussion. On that note, we have to end.

I leaned forward but didn't stand up. "I came to therapy to talk about my mother," I said. "Not really my marriage."

He stood up and brushed his sweater. He said I was learning to talk about my life more objectively so that it felt like a part of my life and not a part of myself.

"Wait." I got my notebook back out of my purse. I didn't care I was making him late for the next session. I wrote down the sentence *I am trying to learn to talk about all this more objectively so that it feels like a part of my life and not a part of myself.*

Then, with my hand on the doorknob, I told him Dave had bought a project at Goodwill, a Viking ship made by a kid, a giant and flimsy thing, thinking Jacob could use it at some point at school, to turn in. It was an abdication, wasn't it? "Jacob might not even have a Viking unit! But he should do the work himself."

"This is a doorknob moment," Helder said, "like when the patient says, leaving the office, 'I slept with him.' Then they walk out!"

"That too," I said.

He smiled and handed me my receipt. "See you next week," he said. He was friendly and closed for business.

In the parking lot, in my car, I read over my notes. I tried to remember what words might go in the blanks. *Internal world re-created in external world,* I remembered from another session. My pages of fragments: this notebook was me. Some beginnings. Some attempts. Gathering glimpses at all the little pieces. No complete thoughts, no wholes.

I started my car and eased out of the lot. I was going to be in therapy for a long, long time. I wasn't even a sentence yet. But I had some syllables, some new sounds. The first halves of the sentences I was accumulating were solid. I trusted them.

From therapy, I drove directly to my classroom on campus. I went from a room where I knew nothing, not even myself, where I wept and didn't understand why, into a room where I was supposed to know many things for certain, where I could never break down. I was supposed to know titles and themes and how to use words like *heuristic* and *hegemony.* I was supposed to teach fiction and explain "hidden meanings" and point out the significance of the epiphany.

With my students, I used stories about Dave and the boys like giant cardboard cutouts that I dragged in and set up and pointed to. *Sons! Husband! My life!* My life with them was proof that I was normal, certification that I was allowed to talk about the muscles and heartbeats in Hemingway's sentences at swanky little Hope College. When I made this little show, I couldn't imagine my life without Dave and the boys. My family! They were my way into living in the normal world. My only way in. I loved them. I loved talking to my students as this woman, this normal woman, who could amuse and delight and surprise.

Helder said the goal of therapy was to make a container to hold all the disparate selves.

I was going to need a big container. One that could hold hordes.

"A very strange, upset, concerned person called you," the department secretary informed me. "I didn't get her name. I really couldn't understand a word she was saying. This might be her number." She handed me a slip of paper with the scrawled digits.

It was Bernie, calling about my mother. A month had passed, and they were still in Wisconsin, still well within range of a visit. My mother had planned to spend a week or so with me and then ride out hurricane season, the rest of the fall, in Wisconsin, with Bernie. But all week my mother, it seemed, was complaining of debilitating leg pain. She couldn't walk. Couldn't eat any of Bernie's food.

"I'm concerned but I feel completely helpless, with no solution," Bernie told me. "She's really angry at me that I am calling you, she's very perturbed. She told me she is a very private person and if I told you anything, she'd never confide in me again. So we need to be discreet, Heather. I think I have to take her to the emergency room. This will be against her will."

"Is it really her leg?" I asked Bernie. It was for "leg pain" she'd gone to the hospital for extended stays after I was born, after my brother was born.

"I was going to the Sunrise Service at six-thirty this morning. She left me a note in the bathroom that said she would not be able to go to church with me, that the pain had gone to her knee. I went back for the eight a.m. service, and then when I returned from that she was up and about and she did seem better. She wants to go home. I'm worried about her traveling. I think her doctor should give the okay. She said she has several doctors. I think the new one is named Pistachio. Does that sound familiar?"

"She doesn't go to doctors," I said. I wondered if Dr. Pistachio was as invented as it sounded. I asked Bernie: could it be an emotional problem? Did my mom seem more anxious, more nervous than usual? Had she said why she wasn't eating?

"She's always nervous, I guess, isn't she?" Bernie feared an embolism like the one that had killed my mother's father. My mother seemed forgetful. Had I noticed that? "I don't know why she is such a private person," Bernie said. "It's so difficult to deal with! I'm so open—you can read me like a book. I share all my frustrations and joys and feelings with friends. All I can tell you, Heather, is to pray. I'm going to try to get her to a doctor. I'll keep you posted."

That evening I called Bernie again. I asked if I could talk to my mom.

"I am enjoying myself so much! The pace is so relaxed and pleasant," my mother said in grand and formal tones. "We have daily walks and Bernie has an outstanding minister. Love going to the little Lutheran church where she is a member."

"Are you doing okay? Do you feel okay?" I asked.

"Oh, I'm fine," she said grandly. "Just spoiled!" She tittered. "That Bernie has prepared some great meals and has really spoiled me! It's almost too much! I can't eat this much food! Oh my goodness. Haven't even washed a dish! We think of you often!" Then she said she knew how busy I was at work, a lot of pressure, a lot of deadlines, how sorry she was that I had to work so much. Would I, she wondered, ever get a break? I knew she was waiting for me to say it was okay to come visit.

I didn't say anything. This cheery, formal version of my mother was just one version cycling through. *Don't get sucked in,* Dave was always saying to me. Kind of like Helder's container idea: Notice everything, but don't buy into it. Hold it. "Heather, you understand everything. You really do. I don't have to spell it out. I'm not sure Bernie picks up on my cues sometimes and I can't be rude, I couldn't hurt her feelings for the world! But it's so nice of you—you really do read between the lines. I'm a very laid-back person! You understand!"

I waited.

"I have to get back home," she whispered. "Right away."

My students complained, as did the boys, that I read into everything. But for so long, I hadn't read into things nearly enough. My mother and I had operated on a normal surface, conspiring to keep the disturbance beneath a secret. Now I read clearly: My mother had leg pain and wanted to go home. But I was also pretty sure I could read something else: My mother was having a psychotic break and needed the safety of home. She knew I knew the code.

For the first time in my life, I felt I could see all the versions of my mother at once. For the first time, I recognized my mother and saw chaos for what it was: chaos. It was something I knew, but not something I was in. I felt clear and strong and calm. I didn't need her to see me or know me; she wasn't going to be able to do that. And I could see what needed to happen next. I could hear Helder whispering in my ear: *Sure, help her, do the good-daughter thing—but do it for yourself and with no attachment to any outcome. Nothing you do will hold. Nothing will change. You can live with a lack of clarity.*

My mother returned to Orlando. She didn't visit and she didn't refer to it in any way, ever. When I spoke with her, she hardly seemed to remember the summer, my marriage problems, her trip to Bernie's, her vow to stop speaking to me—any of it.

"Love the class," a student said to me after class. "You're, like, so positive. Even with the people who suck so bad, you find something nice to say, and it's true! I wish there were more professors like you." She slung her backpack onto my table. "Are you always like this? Are you like this with your stepsons? Are you exhausted when you get done?"

And then she burst into tears. She blew her nose in napkins from her backpack, apologizing. "I'm not usually like this! I am so sorry!" I wished I knew who she was. Had she been coming regularly? She said she didn't think she could stay in the class, even though it was her favorite. She knew what she was supposed to be writing about, but she couldn't bear to do it. She didn't know what to do. She leaned over her knees, hugging herself.

"You don't have to write about anything upsetting. There's not a topic you *should* write about. I say go with the easiest thing, always." This was the opposite of what I'd said in class.

She leaned back down onto her knees and it all came out in one giant paragraph. Her roommate was date-raped at a frat party and wouldn't go to counseling; the guy asked out their suitemate, who agreed to go. "I'm totally overwhelmed," the girl said. "I'm freaking out." This was why she couldn't write. She couldn't think of anything else. Then she laughed and wiped her face on her bare arms. "I can't believe I'm like this," she said. "I'm, like, psychotic."

No, I told her, with great confidence. She wasn't psychotic. I wrote down the name of the counselor I liked best at the college and I told her if her roommate wouldn't go, it would be good if she did.

"You think I need a shrink," she said. "I can see why." She laughed some more and put her hands over her face. "Oh man!"

"Your homework tonight is to not do the writing homework. I want you to not do the reading, either. Your homework is to make an appointment with Jeanne. In class, write about tiny things. Nothing upsetting. Go slowly. The feelings are overwhelming, but they're not you. They're the feelings. You are separate, and you are strong and amazing and good." This was direct quoting from Dr. Peter Helder, Jr., Vulture 101. I had added *strong, amazing, good.*

We hugged and she walked across the atrium, and then she joined a group of other students, laughing.

We could be wrecked inside, and pissed off and exhausted, and still be happy to see our friends.

We could be so many different things at once.

I arrived for my next therapy session confident and bored, which seemed to me a sign the therapy was working. I was handling my mother better, which is why I had come in the first place. I knew I might never have a professional diagnosis for her, but I was confident that the lens of schizophrenia was clear and focused: through it, she was much easier to see. For the first time in my life, I sat in the waiting room without an agenda.

Helder opened by saying sometimes he would talk about other patients, changing key details so as not to reveal personal information. There was this woman, he said, who had a lazy eye. Lots of abuse, very violent childhood, he said. After three years of therapy, she decided she was ready to have a simple operation to repair her eye. She then married a wonderful man and now they were very happy. She still came in around once a month. It had taken her a long time to take that action. But when she was ready, it was that simple.

I stared at him, bored, a little annoyed. I noticed IMAGINE and wished it were not there. What did I care about a woman with a lazy eye? I didn't have a lazy eye. I didn't need a minor operation. I wondered why he was telling me this story. My eyes were fine. But the subject of eyes reminded me what wasn't fine. What I hadn't mentioned in this room. I didn't want it to ruin his impression of me as the nice girl with the crazy family.

I decided to just tell him and get it over with. Perhaps whatever it was that was wrong with me could, like the lazy eye, be fixed. I knew it couldn't. But I wanted to see what he would say.

"There's something else weird about me," I said.

He leaned in. "Go for it," he said. He looked very happy.

"It's hard," I told him. "Because it's going to change the way you look at me."

"Great!" he said. He was grinning wildly, as if to say, *Come on in!*

I told him about not being able to recognize people. How at the party the night before I called him, I'd left in a panic because I kept introducing myself to someone I evidently had worked with for years. How I couldn't tell Janis and Beth apart until they started talking. How Dave was terrible with names and I never forgot names, but I often didn't know if I knew someone or not. I avoided department meetings, functions at the boys' school. People expected me to know them, and I didn't. I told him how I'd carried around the face book at Hope when it was still a printed thing with everyone's photograph, name, and department, but even with the directory, it was hard to tell people apart. I blamed it on Michigan: midwesterners were bland, homogeneous, indistinguishable. Women were easier, because they had jewelry and purses and shoes I could remember. I was good at people from the back and far away.

I told him how when I was little, I'd found a deck of cards—some kind of FBI or civil service preparation, perhaps—with photographs of faces of 1950s men and women on one side and data on the reverse: name, age, place of birth, occupation, a few habits (*smoker, golfer, race car driver, travels to China*). I'd carried those cards with me everywhere, memorizing the facts on the back and matching them to the hairstyle on the front.

I tried to tell him what I had read so far about face blindness. "It's in fusiform gyrus twelve," I said, which I'd thought would sound really smart, but made me realize I didn't really understand face blindness at all. Fusiform gyrus, conceptual configuration, covert recognition—when I had the article in front of me, it all made sense. But when I tried to explain it to Helder, it was as if I didn't know anything. I felt like my students when I returned their failed quizzes: "But I studied!"

Helder was very excited, though. He suggested the experience of living with a schizophrenic was very similar to the face-blindness experiences I was describing. Never really knowing what to look for, never knowing exactly the reality of things. The two experiences seemed to amplify each other in very complicated ways. And he couldn't help wondering: Had my mother's inability to mirror me interfered with the face-reading mechanism at a crucial developmental stage?

No, I said. Nothing in the literature pointed to anything like that. This was a whole separate thing, I said. Early on, I'd read a few articles that had made me consider this. But I had discarded the theory. It was true that babies with cataracts turned out face-blind: you had to see things at certain stages in order to get the face recognition processor laid in correctly. But my mother hadn't *blinded* me. She wasn't *that* bad.

"You have to consider how the mother in a situation like this might influence the developing brain," he said kindly. "And all that trauma," he said. He believed chaos alone might cause the infant brain to wire itself in dysfunctional ways.

No, I said. Face blindness wasn't caused by psychological trauma. If it was related to schizophrenia, it was, I believed, genetic, neurological, congenital. As the session went on, I was getting very angry at him. He hadn't read all the articles I had read. He didn't know. Why had I even brought this up?

He said, "I think this is trauma. I think this is going to clear up as we work together. There is a chance. There is a chance." He was rubbing his hands together.

"No," I said. "It's not trauma."

"I think it is. I think you will be able to see faces again. Could. You could, Heather. Everything you are telling me."

"No," I said. I knew he was wrong. I wanted to protect my mother. I wanted to be related to her in an elegant, fascinating way. Plus, I had only just figured out I must have face blindness. I hadn't yet worked out how to teach it to someone else. I didn't know how to summarize my experience, to show someone who could recognize faces what it was like not to have this ability. I didn't actually know how schizophrenia and face blindness were related, only that they must be, somehow, and that my mother wasn't at fault.

"Let's find out if this can be fixed. Through surgery or retraining." Helder wondered if there was something like Brain Gym for it. He also thought I had to come out, right away. "You have to tell people you have this, people have to know. All you go through to hide, to cover, to keep this a secret—it's making your interactions with people—simple interactions—impossibly complicated. There's all this background noise. It's isolating you. You've got to come out."

I laughed. "No, no, no," I said. Telling was unthinkable. "No one can ever know. They'll think I'm crazy."

I was certain there was some kind of biological connection—as yet undiscovered by scientists—between schizophrenic mothers and face-blind children. I knew face blindness wasn't mental illness—far from it. But some part of me was still in shadow. For nearly forty years, I had thought: *I'm mentally ill.*

"On the first day of class, this is what you say when you hand out the syllabus: 'Hi, I'm—' What do you call yourself? Professor Sellers?"

"Heather."

"'Hi, welcome, I'm Heather and I have'—how do you say it?"

"I say 'pro soap,' like you are for soap. And then 'agnosia,' like 'agnostic.' I'm a face doubter."

"So you say, 'Hi, I'm Heather, I have prosopagnosia.' Did I say it right?"

I shook my head. "No."

"I'm just asking you to keep an open mind on two counts. Practice telling one person. And know that this condition *could* change for you. It's a possibility."

It wasn't a possibility, though. I would always be face-blind. I knew that for sure. And I couldn't imagine telling anyone about face blindness—ever. Even if I didn't have my particular mom to love and hide, face blindness was too weird. It was too hard to explain. I barely understood it myself, and I had spent hundreds of hours reading about it. It sounded crazy.

Our next sessions were contentious, and more than once I said this would be our last. Helder had to accept that face blindness was fixed, incurable, or I was quitting. And he, just as dug in, insisted that I come out.

"It's not a mental illness. You experience it as overwhelming confusion. That's exactly why you have to tell people!" Helder urged me to tell and he urged me to research a cure, to get clarity on what was face blindness and what were the feelings and emotions around it. What was me and what was Mom.

But I couldn't do it. I couldn't bear to think of my mother loving me but unable to face me, to stare into my eyes, to care for me emotionally, to offer me her face. Like any daughter, as much as I wanted to separate from her, I wanted to be deeply connected to her, I wanted to redeem her, I wanted to protect her. I wanted to love and to understand, in that order.

Four

My mother was not my first choice to drive me to Tallahassee, but she was the one who had agreed. Then she changed her mind. She would not condone this behavior after all. I told my father he had to take me. He didn't say yes but he didn't say no. The day before we were to leave, I gathered all my belongings in the foyer. My black Schwinn road bike, three spider plants, all of my books and records, a garbage bag of bedding and another of clothes, a pink comforter and matching curtains from Kmart that my mother had purchased for me. Then I wedged five egg crates of stuff—blow-dryer, radio, an old popcorn popper that Ruby had given me, shoes, clothes, art supplies—into the trunk and backseat of Fred's car. I watered the plants and set them on plastic bags behind the seats. I locked the car and went and sat in my room and thought about how good college life was going to be.

But I was nervous too. I didn't know anyone in Tallahassee, not a single soul. I didn't know anyone here, either. But I didn't have enough money saved up to make it in Tallahassee for even one full year. So what was the point of going? I'd just love it, and then I'd have to come back to Orlando and go to community college. And I'd be ruined for community college, having had courses in philosophy and a wonderful university boyfriend who was probably a poet. I'd be spoiled and stuck-up and unfit for Orlando, and I'd end up killing myself. Florida State University. How on earth did I think I was going to make it there?

Chicken was browning for dinner. I noticed Fred was having trouble walking. Moving from the stove to the fridge, he had to hang on to the countertop, push himself along. It was five in the afternoon. He was insistent and loud and garbled, yelling at me to set the table. I'd already set the table. "Mow the lawn!" he yelled. I pretended to go mow. I sat outside in the corner of the backyard. By the time dinner was ready, Fred was weeping on the sofa. He wanted me to sit with him. I sat next to him; I held his wet hands and I wanted to get away. He was upset now because no one had come to dinner. Ruby hadn't materialized for the last couple nights, maybe longer. "Where is everyone?" he cried. He shook his hands, with my hand trapped in there. He begged me to call people up and invite them over. He named old friends of his, his first lawyer, a judge he considered a friend. His stockbroker. "Call him up, call him up," he said.

"It should be just us," I said. "It's my last night."

"We got this nice dinner here. Going to waste now."

I got him another drink. Straight gin, two ice cubes.

"No, no, no," he said. "Nothing decided. You're not leaving."

He hit the table. It was like a sunset how his mood changed, from weeping to rage, purple to dark.

I cleaned up the kitchen, mopped the floor, wiped down the counters while he watched television out in the den. I told myself I was like a character in a fairy tale, and I told myself I was a whiny, melodramatic, spoiled baby: lots of people all over the world had it way worse than this. I was dusting off the swinging doors when he wandered in. He held on to the fridge to remain upright.

"Time for inspection," he said. He rubbed his hands on my shoulders. I stepped back, behind the bar stool. My main concern was his being sober enough the next day to drive back from Tallahassee after he dropped me off.

He pulled one of the heavy pans off the stove, where I'd set it to dry itself. "They have two sides!" he hollered. "They have two sides!" His words were slurry and I felt so sorry for him, wavering there in the kitchen, waving the pan around, his face full of judgment and condescension and confoundedness.

I smiled. I just needed to get through the next seven hours. I said, "You can be the person who does the backs from now on. I'll do the fronts."

He shook his head. "What?" he yelled. "No."

"Seems like a good plan to me."

Even as he swung, I could see that he would miss me. I ducked and the pan hit the counter hard, but I didn't hear a sound. I saw only the divot in the Formica where the black line was broken. He dropped the pan and lurched toward me. I came out from behind the bar stool; I didn't want to be trapped in the corner. I wasn't scared. I wasn't anything. This was just a night, this was just a night. He grabbed me. He pulled my hair, put his hand hard on my rear end and clamped it there; I was wearing my little red shorts. Then he socked me in the temple with everything he had—not much. He was crying. He stumbled; his foot was hooked around the rung of the bar stool. I tried to stabilize him, to lean him more on the counter and get out of his grasp at the same time.

I slipped out the front door, past my stuff. Half walking, half running, I went down to the little bridge that spanned the channel between Conway Chain of Lakes. People honked as they went by. I waved. I waved to everyone, all the time. They were all probably crazy Belle Isle guys with a buzz going who didn't know me, but I didn't think it hurt anything to wave back, just in case it was someone I might have known, if I was a different girl.

I got up at five, showered, and made us eggs and grits and toast. Fred was in his bathroom. I loaded up the car with the last of my things: makeup bag, a pillowcase of clothes, my little white suitcase from when I was a kid. In it, I had packed *The Nothing Book*, all my love letters from Keith Landreu, menus from restaurants Wayne had taken me to, and the leather belts and purse Wayne had made me, plus letters from my mother, all the poems I'd written when Fred and I had lived in the terrible roachy place on McLeod Road. I knew I had way too much stuff. I knew I wasn't coming back here ever again. I had to take everything I wanted, plus anything I might ever want again, when I was older, when I wanted to look back.

I put my ear to Fred's bathroom door.

"Occupied!" he said.

Finally he came out. We stood in the foyer. I was jangling the car keys. "Well," I said softly. "I loaded up like you said."

"The deal's off," he said. "You're not going."

"Daddy," I said. I laughed. "Everything's in the car. Everything's all set." I was thinking how else I could get up there. I could hire someone to drive me. Maybe I could take the bus.

It took hours on the telephone to persuade her, but my mother drove me downtown to the bus station. As we scuttled oh-so-slowly along the back streets of Orlando in Suzy Q, her new used white truck, she said my father loved me so much, so very, very much, and neither of them wanted to see me go. He'd come around, she said. She said that if I left now, and she certainly hoped I would not, I shouldn't expect to be able to come back. "You can't waltz in and out," she said. "Once you take this step, you've made a permanent decision, Heather. With implications for forever. When we get to that bus station, you have to really, really be sure."

"Well, I'm not sure." With my mom, I had to pretend the opposite of what I thought—and I couldn't quite figure out what that was in this case. So I kept mostly quiet. I was so scared she would change her mind. Again. It seemed wisest to act uncertain, temporary.

I said something like *Let me try, and fail.* I said it was, in actuality, the last thing I wanted to do. I made the whole thing sound like an experiment that would last only a few days.

"It's an expensive mistake, Heather Laurie, a costly mistake."

But I could see she wasn't going to stop me. I took my suitcase and boarded the bus. I couldn't believe she let me. I sat in the front row, catty-corner behind the driver. I could see his face in the giant rearview mirror. I couldn't wait for him to close the door.

My mother waved and waved, not crying, not happy, just serious and forlorn behind the wheel of Suzy Q. She was watching me like a hawk. Would she make a scene? I could see her charging across the street and up the little steps, grabbing me, screaming at the bus driver, *She is a minor! I'll charge you with kidnapping!*

Finally, we launched. I watched my mom until I couldn't see her anymore for certain. I held my purse tight in my lap and wished the driver would go faster. Almost an hour later, we were still not out of Orlando. I couldn't think about my parents: I had to sit straight and still, and it seemed that if I could stay like that—not worry, not look ahead or back, just center myself exactly in the moment—I wouldn't risk them changing their minds.

From the short time my family had lived in Tallahassee, I remembered it as pretty, hilly country, with a capitol building and a cemetery with a French prince, the graves all aboveground. But nothing looked familiar to me. Instead of libraries and cool-looking professor-y people, I saw a crazy, wild street lined with bars running through the middle of campus like a freight train. It was the opposite of what I thought I'd find, but it was still good to be on my own and to be so far from home. I got off that bus and breathed the hot, still air and thought: *This is my life beginning now, and it was all my doing.*

The night was hot and the sky was spooky; the clouds were thin and creepy, not like Orlando at all. There were hills. The sidewalks were bumpy. Walking down a steep hill toward a motel I'd seen on the way in, the Ponce de Leon, I kept banging my little white suitcase against my leg.

A cab prowled up to me. "Where you need a ride to?"

"No," I said. "I'm fine." I kept thinking any second my mother was going to pull up. Any second it was all going to be over.

The driver yelled something at me but I waved him off. I was city-smart, street-smart. I was from Orlando, not some Podunk country town. I wasn't born yesterday.

In the morning, I filled out paperwork and the registrar's office gave me a room assignment: 006 Jennie Murphree Hall. It was in the basement. I got my keys, but we couldn't move in until after orientation. I wrote a check for food services. I bought the full plan. I was hungry.

Orientation was in a dorm on the other side of campus. I walked up the street where a line of kids wrapped around the building. I looked for the end of it, my garnet and gold orientation folder sweaty in my arms. I was sweating all over. My feet were sliding around in my sandals. All these kids were dressed so nicely. The girls had smooth, shiny hair and gold jewelry, and the boys wore khakis and loafers, and they were talking away, hundreds of them. People called out to their friends way up and down the line. It was like a party where everyone knew everyone else, or like high school between classes, only richer and more. *Sheep!* my mother would have said. *Let's get out of here while we can still think!* She would never have stayed in a line like this, mingled with people like this.

I wanted to go to my motel, but a good rule of thumb was *Do the opposite of what my mother would do.* I wanted to run, go back to Orlando, go anywhere else. I stayed.

Guys came out of nowhere.

I said hi, I gave out my phone number whenever asked, but I often couldn't figure out who I was talking to. Guys came up to me and knew my name and it was heady and distracting, but I also felt popular for the first time. I affected a ditzy, spacey persona, giggling and flipping my hair around. Sara Simko, whom I couldn't shake even in college, told me I should be more careful, not give out my number, not be so friendly to everyone. I was getting a reputation before classes had even started. Well, I wanted a reputation.

The best of the tribe were the geology graduate students, who were gorgeous and shirtless and stoned and attentive; they didn't say "babe," "rad," or "hated." We walked around the campus. They showed me all the places Jim Morrison had lived. I pretended I knew who he was. I didn't know he was dead until years later; he was alive to them.

In a rusty green Ford pickup, we drove out to the sinkhole called Big Dismal. They passed the joint, through me, to each other. I pretended this was my new self, but I knew it was only an afternoon self. I didn't want to be stoned. I wanted to be the opposite of stoned: that's why I had come to college. I drank beer. It was cold and sharp and from a green glass bottle, Rolling Rock. It was so much better than my father's beer, Schlitz, my childhood beer. I had two beers now.

At Big Dismal, they explained karst topography, limestone, aquifers and their insistent fragile habits, and I lay down on the pine needles and the world spun around. Florida floated on lace, on fragile ancient bones, and this was why it caved in on itself. I was falling in love. I traipsed along, holding my skirt up higher than I needed to. At the edge of the sinkhole, I took off all my clothes and folded them at the edge. The ponytailed geology graduate student took my careful pile and set it in the notch of an oak. I swung off the rope swing, my body slung out over the terrifying inky green water ten stories below. There were cars down there, and trees and bodies too: the grad students had known the last two divers who died. They had drunk beer with them the night before at Crazyhorse. Naked in the air, I felt like a piece of silk. I went so far down so fast that my eyes opened. In the cold, black water, I felt less unusual, safe. I knew who I was.

There was a party in Hooverville, an old boardinghouse on College by the cemetery. I took a nap. I got dressed up in a white sundress and high heels. At nine, I left Jennie Murphree. But at the party, I couldn't find the guys I knew, my Big Dismal friends. I walked down the hall, up the stairs, back down, into the apartments. I looked everywhere. Everyone appeared stoned, slowed down, happily bored. Women were flinging their limbs around like they didn't really want arms, feet, heads. Men were laughing silently, in slow motion, on a sagging gold sofa. Most people were barefoot. There were beads in the doorways and Indian cloths on the couches. The men all looked more or less alike. But no one acted as though I was familiar. It was too loud and too quiet. I felt like I was seventeen years old, which I was. I was way, way out of my league.

I looked at people as I passed through the rooms in the apartments, doors open to the hallway. Did the geology guys see me and just pretend not to? Were they blowing me off? Did I secretly not want to find them? Did they secretly have girlfriends? Did they have to pretend we had never met? I wondered if they were just kidding when they invited me, if they were hiding from me because they really didn't want me here at all. I wondered if I kept walking by them. I had my hair up in a bun. Maybe they didn't know it was me.

I never saw the geology boys again, but I looked for them every day, everywhere. I said hello to guys I thought were them, but the look-alikes walked right past me. Every day I saw people I thought were Wayne, or Keith. I saw Ruby all the time, too, at the grocery store, the hair salon, driving down Tennessee. Sometimes I thought my mother was following me.

In 006 Zero Alley, Jennie Murphree, my roommate, Tiffany, prayed for me and everyone we knew. She had been praying since day one. She was also praying that at the end of the semester her parents would let her go to Indiana University, where she'd wanted to go, where all her friends from back home went. Florida State, Tiffany told me, was a very inferior school. And no one played euchre. She hadn't made the cast of *Oklahoma!*, which made no sense to me: if there was anyone who should have been in *Oklahoma!* it was Tiffany Crowther. She would not have needed to do any acting at all.

Tiffany prayed and prayed that God would somehow get her back to Indiana. When she prayed, she didn't get on her knees. She prayed in her chair, at her desk. It looked just like studying. Her parents, she said, had not been saved. They felt she was in a cult. I was shocked. She assured me they were Christians, but they were not committed to Christ. "I just pray," she said, looking like a forlorn mother.

At ten o'clock we turned the lights out. While the other girls in our dorm stayed up all night with their illegal boyfriends and our RAs smoked pot, Tiffany and I told each other our life stories. It was fun to remember Easter baskets, my mother's cocktail dresses, the art my father had bought, how shy I was in kindergarten. My mom was strict, with all her rules, but she loved golf and tennis and the theater. My father was wild but so much fun. It wasn't such a stretch to make us sound like any other family. We didn't have close relatives or go on family trips, and my parents were divorced, but other than that, my childhood wasn't all that different from Tiffany's: four square, the Coke song, crushes on boys, the perils of algebra, cruel classmates. I came across as a hardworking, boy-liking go-getter, sporty and serious. I liked my story.

....

About four weeks into the semester, on a Saturday afternoon, I was sitting on my bed, brushing my hair, staring out the window. I saw a man I thought was my father, his silver Afro waving in the light. He stomped up the hill. But I was always seeing people who looked like other people. Not until I saw his car, a pale yellow banged-up Ford Fairmont, did I know that this was no mistake. Attached to the Ford was a flat trailer with sides, covered with tarp. Houseplants were poking out the windows of the backseat. *My* plants.

I would have thrown a tarp over the whole scene if I could.

I ran outside. Fred stood by the dumpster, smoking a cigarette and drinking from a white plastic flask just like the ones sold in the university bookstore. A short, rotund, redheaded woman climbed out of the car, bristling. She was holding a little white box. She handed it to me. She socked Fred in the stomach. "Shit! This is illegal parking! Shit, you bastard, you're gonna git us another ticket! Goddammit, Fred Sellers!" she shouted. "Can't you read? Don't ya read?"

"Heather!" he was yelling. "Girl child!" He turned in a circle amid the U of buildings that enclosed the alley. I opened the box, hoping no one was seeing any of this. In it was a nightgown, a grotesquely wadded thing I feared might have been plucked from my father's personal collection. My father's companion introduced herself as Louise, my stepmother. I didn't have to like her, she said, but she would love me as her own chirren. She had six grandchirren, she said.

"Luigi," Fred said. "New stepmother." He laughed and laughed.

"You're not *married*," I said. I didn't care if she could hear me. I set the box on the hot hood of the car. I wondered what had happened to Ruby.

"Hell, yeah," he said. "Be nice to her. Start unloading." He rolled his hand around in the air, finger pointed as though directing a great roundup. His nails sparkled with clear polish.

"You can't park here," I said. There was no space in the dorm room for all this stuff. I would need an apartment.

"Shit, that's what I'm saying. Did you hear her? Hear her? Fred? Did you?" Luigi barked. She strutted around in her white pants. "This is a pile," she said, looking at my building. "No AC? It's like slavery days. You live in slave quarters. They're treating you like a slave at the fancy-dancy college. Shit. You pay money for this?"

"What is that?" I said, pointing toward the ramshackle trailer.

Fred said, "I built it! That's a great cart! We look like the Joads!" He hooked his thumbs into his pants. I looked at his ankles. He had on panty hose under his pants. I knew it was silly, but I hoped Louise hadn't seen these things. "The Joads!" he yelled again, at Louise. She ignored him. They were perfect for each other.

Even though Tiffany wasn't home, I wouldn't let them come inside our room. I said there were no men allowed on the floor. I carried in everything myself: my bicycle, my winter clothes, a green metal bookcase, the boxes of books, the two milk crates of records, Midnight the stuffed cat, the potted palm plant I'd rescued from the neighbor's trash. I made stacks along a kind of border down the middle of the room. "I'll purge, I'll purge," I promised Tiffany when she came back, standing in the doorway with hands on hips and mouth open, looking like a midwestern milkmaid.

The next morning I met Fred and Louise for breakfast at the Waffle House on Tennessee Street. Fred wrote me a check for a thousand dollars. Louise said there was plenty more where that came from. Fred hollered at her, "You don't know what the hell you're talking about!" People in the Waffle House stared. "You know what Grandpa said! Tell her the truth!" she hollered at him. They squabbled, slapped at each other's shoulders, and glowered, and she pretended to spit at him.

"You are supposed to get five thousand a year from your grandfather," Louise said.

"I'm spending your inheritance," Fred said to me, and he laughed and laughed. I didn't ask. I didn't want to know. It would be better for me, I knew, to pretend I hadn't heard any of it. I didn't want to get my hopes up or down. I didn't take Fred's check. It sat there on the table like a citation.

Fred said he wanted to come to classes with me. I was trying to think what to say when Louise pounded on his shoulder with her little ruddy fist.

"Shit, Fred, you asshole. It's Sunday!" She punched him over and over, scrunching up her features into a little pig face.

"How's Ruby?" I said. Louise took a sip of her coffee and scowled. She was resting up for the next explosion. Under the table I kicked Fred. "I sure do miss her." To Louise I explained that, of all Fred's girlfriends, Ruby had been my absolute favorite. Louise set her jaw, held out her coffee cup, and yelled. "Honey! Hey! Honey! Goddamn college students don't know how to work. We worked!"

"Hey, yeah," Fred said.

The couple at the table opposite turned and stared at us like we were a television show.

"Listen," Fred said, leaning in. "Listen to your old man, now. You want to major in accounting," he said, pointing to the check, "then that's a gift. If you don't, it's an interest loan. Got that? With interest!" He took my wrist and twisted it, hard, in his sweaty hands. "Got it?" He said I could spend the year at FSU and then finish my AA at Valencia. He grinned and showed his huge teeth, and Louise wiped syrup off his face using her spit.

"Don't be like some them women and wait too long to get pregnant," Louise said. "You'll find yourself barren. With college, that's what happens now. These girls are all barren by the time they get theirselves straightened out." She made a clicking sound with her cheeks, *Giddy up!*

I kissed Fred on the cheek and fled.

I didn't see him again for almost a year.

Tiffany said she and her friends had established a special prayer circle for me and my family. She wondered how long all my stuff would stay wedged and piled in the room, if she could help me get rid of it. There were two mission projects that needed donations, she said. There was a lot of need.

I'd been anxious to get our room back to the way it was, but suddenly, when she said this, I wanted to keep all of it, every single piece. This was my stuff. All my stuff in the world. I wasn't going home for Thanksgiving. I wasn't ever going home. Now, it was clear to me, I had to keep this stuff. I climbed over the bookcases and boxes, got in my bed, and rolled to face the wall.

All that fall, I kept seeing my mother. Which was impossible. Then I really did see her. I was walking across campus. I saw a white purse. A head with waves of short, thick hair. She popped into a hedgerow. I went right up to the bushes.

"Mother," I said. "Mother." I was mad, embarrassed. I stepped into the hedgerow so people walking past on their way to class wouldn't see me or her.

"What are you doing here?" I hissed.

She was terribly, terribly worried. My father had told her I was running wild. Going barefoot. And clearly I was not wearing a foundation garment of any kind. Where was my bra? Where was the support hose she had mailed me? What did I think this was? *Who* did I think I was? If I thought for a second she would fund this kind of display, well, I had another think coming.

"I have to go to class," I told her.

We walked back to the dorm. She and Tiffany adored each other. She understood completely Tiffany wanting to be in Indiana—the Midwest was really the only place where you could trust people, not be ripped off, make true friends, friends for life. Farmers, people who worked. And real food! Not all this stuff from Mexico. My mother professed a love for church. "The values our country was founded on!" she said urgently, and Tiffany nodded and they had a quick little hug. During this exchange I lay on my bed with my legs open, staring at my Willie Nelson poster. I kept my mouth shut. I watched my mother carrying on in this manic friendliness. It was as though she were impersonating someone she could only ever pretend to be.

My mother agreed to take some of the stuff that wouldn't fit in my dorm room. She gave me a nonstick pan, gardening gloves, and two more packets of support hose. She gave me a flashlight that didn't work and a watch that needed a battery. Then she drove back to Orlando.

"Your mother is such a super sweetie," Tiffany said.

I rolled my eyes. I liked how normal this made me.

On Saturday mornings, I woke up at six and rode my bike across campus to my job at the science center. I felt like the only person awake, the one good true person. At seven a.m. I was all ready to go, with my stopwatch, my bin of #2 pencils, my test books and score sheets. I loved monitoring the well-dressed look-alike students as they took the test that would determine whether they got into law school, medical school, business school, nursing. I roved, glared, hovered, and imagined their flawed, superficial lives. I called the time every fifteen minutes and wrote it on the board. In between, I made up stories about each person. I married them off, I had them betray each other, I had them break down.

Over the holidays, I stayed on campus. I didn't know a soul; I went for days without seeing a single other person. It was only me and the students from foreign countries. A tiny little dining hall was open, but only for dinner, and no one seemed to go there but me. I truly missed my parents. I wanted to miss them. It was the only way I could love them, a crazy cocktail of longing and pretending and absence and hope.

Miss Molly's Day Care was just a mile to the east of campus; I rode my bike there. At first I volunteered as part of a requirement for an elementary education class I was taking, and then I was hired. I never felt like I worked at Miss Molly's. I felt like a child in someone's large, sunny, busy home. Every morning I dropped myself off to play. I sat on the little orange plastic chairs, passed juice in translucent wax cups from a tray, wiped up juice, swept the linoleum. I loved the counselors; they liked to talk about the kids after they left, and how each child was likely to turn out. That semester I was reading a lot of radical psychology and education texts: R. D. Laing, A. S. Neill. I loved the idea of a subversive world where mental illness was defined as just another version of normal, and education was how you made your way in the world, not something that began or ended. I wanted to move to England and work in a day care where we constructed skateboard ramps for geometry and made books and bread and murals. "But you won't know a soul in England: you'll be all by your lonesome!" Miss Jill said after I told her my plan. She said I was brave and adventurous; she wished she were more like me, all independent and bold. But I could tell she really didn't wish that at all. She thought I was weird and pretentious, a misfit, a troubled girl.

At eleven, the morning moms came to pick up the morning kids. The moms came up the stairs and waited on the deck. Some kids saw their moms and made a beeline. Others were playing out back and had to be retrieved by hand.

"Can you get Maisie for me?" a mom said to me from her position on the deck. I had been at Miss Molly's for months and months; I did not know the mom-children pairings. I didn't know if I had seen this mom before. I didn't know exactly which girl Maisie was. I had suggested the kids wear name tags, but I wasn't sure Miss Molly ever opened the suggestion box. It seemed more like decoration.

"Sure, I'll grab her," I told the mom. I looked in the play area for Maisie. I called her, like I was calling a cat. "Has anyone seen Maisie?" I sang. I pretended I couldn't see her; I covered my eyes and walked around, pretending to be silly, singing, "Maisie, Maisie." A little girl was following me. "Are you Maisie Daisy?" I said, picking her up, closing my eyes, pretending it was a game. She didn't respond. I put her on my hip. She was a quiet, light little thing. Pale, like a potato chip. Holding her, I looked around at the other children running around the playground. Some of them stood out. Phil, with his porcupine hair. Red-haired Allen. But the little blonde girls—some days they were indistinguishable. I was sweaty, shaking. I asked again if she was really Maisie or if she was pretending. She burst into tears.

The mom and the supervisor were talking in the doorway out front; they looked serious, possibly unhappy, possibly horrified. I was afraid of the adults. I let Maisie go and she ran to her mother. I pretended to be distracted, but inside I was panicking. I wondered if I was about to be fired. I was ruining people. Something about me repulsed people. I felt dangerous. I felt like an agent of disease. I went inside and pretended to organize the doll area, where I cried, alone.

The next day I didn't go to Miss Molly's. I was going to call in sick, but I didn't; I just didn't go back. Ever.

From age seventeen to twenty-seven, I lived in Tallahassee, on the fringe of the university, taking classes and working—tutoring, teaching swimming, babysitting, conducting phone surveys, proofreading, then teaching freshman comp, babysitting, sewing, modeling for the art department. I changed my major from accounting to international relations to art history and finally to English, where, though I would have been unable to articulate it at the time, the students and professors were shabby and individualistic, a little more celebratory of eccentricity and, therefore, easier to tell apart.

I pretended I understood everything; I pretended my life both was and was about to be romantic, novelistic. I felt like I was in the swim of things, in an underwater kind of way.

I simply stayed in school until I'd gotten enough credits

and written double enough pages for a Ph.D. and taken all the 9000-level classes: that was as high as the catalog went. Or I would have stayed on and on. I performed poorly on my doctoral exams, mangling dates, authors, and concepts. I wept after the second half-day of orals, I'd done so shamefully. That afternoon I stood alone in my apartment with a cup of Swiss Miss and all my half-read compendiums of literary history, wondering what on earth would happen next, and how. I didn't feel anything like a Ph.D. It was not the beginning of something and wouldn't be for a long, long time. I got the degree. I didn't celebrate. It was only the end of childhood.

Five

I pored over the face-blindness research with a new focus: to convince Helder that his trauma theory was cracked. As children, we are profoundly loyal to our parents, and to their pain: I wanted to be related to my mom, not ruined by her. I found a book by Andrew W. Young, *Face and Mind.* The day it arrived, I took it straight to bed with a highlighter and a big pot of tea. I read hard. I drew stars in the margins. Like an eager-to-please freshman, I underlined continents of text. The vocabulary—*intermodal matching, blindsight, reduplicative paramnesia*—was difficult and thrilling. I felt smart, as though nearly knowing this difficult material was the perfection of something.

Andrew Young defined *prosopagnosia* as "the inability to recognize familiar faces after a cerebral injury." Prosopagnosics were mostly stroke victims, he said, except for a few extremely rare mental patients who experienced recognition disorders that might illuminate prosopagnosia. More on the mentally ill, he promised, in Chapter 8. Mostly, he said, face blindness affected middle-aged men. I began writing him a letter in my head.

Many of Young's sentences were impossible to comprehend. But this is what I loved about the way my mind worked, my way of learning: I didn't mind confusion. I read these sentences over and over and over and let their strangeness wash over me until finally they opened up. For me, reading a hard sentence was very much like recognizing a person. I just kept looking and looking, not letting the not-knowing scare me away, until I got something that made sense.

In spite of the awkward scientific vernacular, I loved Andrew Young: he became my imaginary best friend and colleague in this period of my life. I wanted him to test me. I wanted him to fix, if not my brain, then my spirit. Since the book was already five years old, I assumed his research had progressed. Had he maybe figured out how to insert an updated version of the face processor? Super Face 2.0? Maybe Helder was right after all: maybe there was some kind of patch. I wanted to mail my brain to Andrew Young at his research lab in England, with a little note pinned to the cerebellum: *I don't think I've had a stroke. But I can't remember faces. Call me!*

Andrew Young explained how many steps were involved in recognizing a face—and he had flow charts that made the process, at last, clear. He explained that recognizing beauty, gender, age, race, and emotion were all performed separately, by different processors, different systems, all of them using a lot of brainpower but none as juice-hungry as the face recognizer. I loved Andrew Young, and I was beginning to love face blindness. Because of face blindness, I was getting to learn about things I'd never known existed. I was getting a clear look not just at how I saw but at seeing itself. I'd already come to understand that faces present, in their elaborate design, the most significant visual pattern in our environment. I already knew that in the world of objects—chairs, cars, pencils, trees, etc.—faces are special, and they aren't read the same way as other objects. But now I understood that faces are so important to human beings—social survival being tantamount to survival, period—that we tend to resolve as faces even the chaotic, random patterns made by a scribble, a cloud, a wisp of smoke. I began to appreciate face recognition in a whole new way. It might be weird that I couldn't recognize faces, but it was astonishing that anyone could! The ability to distinguish hundreds of faces, despite the many similarities between individuals, represents the ultimate achievement in human perceptual classification.

I trotted into therapy bursting with paragraphs of theory for deluded Peter Helder. Trauma wasn't the cause of my impairment. The chaos in my childhood homes wasn't to blame. There were so many things that could go wrong with this exquisite, subtle, fragile recognizing system. There could be thousands of reasons mine didn't function. Sadly, there could be no repair.

Slowly, I was learning to articulate the way I saw faces. It was just like learning how I saw my mother. I'd never had a way to stand outside any of this weirdness I'd taken for granted my whole life and *see.* Now I'd found, with Helder's help, a little platform to stand on, so I could look at things that had been, for me, unknowable. I made notes and lists and wrote out little scripts so I could teach Helder about how I saw and didn't see, so that I could truly know it for myself.

One thing the face processor does is let us see the parts of the face *and* the face as a whole, simultaneously. Very few people—normal or brain-damaged—would be able to find their lover's nose in a pile of noses, but on the right face, the brain could magically sort out all the separate features and read them as one unit: *my darling, her special little beak.* The face processor understands the separate eyes, cheeks, nose, and mouth, but it also "reads" the topography of the whole face all at once.

For me, faces didn't tell anything special. A nose was a nose, just as a pen was a pen. I didn't have the ability to commit features to a special kind of memory and store them in a special face place. Instead, I had to study a person to figure out who they were. It took time and patience, and I relied heavily, as did dyslexics, on context clues. That white word on red signs at intersections—you could know it was STOP without truly reading it. That man in my kitchen, doing the dishes, wearing a burgundy polo shirt that was more than a touch too big for him—I knew it was Dave without seeing his face.

The ability to recognize people from context—albeit inconsistently and with difficulty—undercut its credibility. One day I drove down to Kalamazoo to give a reading and meet my friend, an artist, for lunch. I knew who she was right away. But after the reading, I couldn't find her in the lobby. She found me on a bench, bereft. She had simply put on her coat and hat.

I recognized people all the time—in my own way. I

pretended to know people who knew me, and I either figured out who they were or I faked it. Either way, I kept my confusion secret. If I told people I had recognition problems, every time I did recognize them I'd look like I had been lying. Face blindness was too weird. It was unreliable. It wasn't one thing. And just behind that weirdness stood the secret superweirdness, my mother, her disorder, and I couldn't entirely separate the two.

But with Andrew Young in my back pocket, I started paying more attention to what I saw when I encountered someone. I walked into school, and an elfin man cocked his head and did a little tentative nod-grin—Stephen Hemenway, no question. It wasn't his face that gave him away. It was his look. It was as if lazy, untrained workers deep inside my brain ambled out of the chairs where'd they been playing cards and smoking cigarettes while I stood there, nodding vibrantly and stalling for time, waiting for the reprobates to rummage through my brain and deliver the crucial information I needed—*Who is this person talking to me? Janis from History?* they flung down. *No? Try Barb from your department. Or that friendly woman from church?*

The process was exhausting and distracting, and many times a day I just walked right past people because it was so much work, such an effort to stay calm while this frenzy was going on in my head. In public, I was automatically on high alert: Out for a simple stroll, I scrutinized every person I passed, hunting for cues while trying not to draw any attention to myself. I pretended I was in a rush. I made myself seem grumpy, preoccupied.

Helder wouldn't let up. "By this time next week, I want you to tell someone. One person." I decided to get it over with, if only to prove to him what a bad idea it was.

At yoga class, an opportunity presented itself. Our instructor, Gingah, said good-bye to Carol, but it wasn't Carol, it was Carrie. Carrie corrected her and Gingah explained how she was terrible at names but wonderful with faces. "I never forget a face!" she said as students trickled out of the room.

I lingered, holding my satchel. "Could I tell you something?" I said to her as the last student left.

She shined her eyes at me. "Of course," she said. "Heather, of course!"

"For humans, names are stored in a very different way than faces. Names are abstractions, and they're difficult to recall. They aren't sensory, like faces. So names are really hard to remember—for everyone, actually. It's a completely different process from faces."

Gingah leaned down and retrieved her little bottle of Fiji water. She slowly crossed her arms. Then she took a sip.

"Name retrieval is very, very difficult for a brain whose main wiring matrix is devoted to interpreting the sensory world," I heard myself say. I heard how strange I sounded. But I couldn't stop. I went on in my teacher voice, the slow, perky cadences I used in the classroom. Gingah started packing up her stuff. I kept going. Once the face clicked into place, I explained, the name retrieval process began. It was the last thing to occur during the recognition sequence. Name retrieval wasn't a visual process; it had a completely different cognitive footprint. Face recognition was like calculus: there was a formula, and you just ran the program. Name retrieval was like history. Advanced history. You had to *think.*

What made it so hard to get the name was this: Information about a person—age, gender, race, face topography, your feelings toward this person, what they did for a living, *who* they were to you—got stored *separately* from the name. The person information was right there, in the front office. The name data was stored down in the basement. It was a long flight of stairs to get there. For most people, those files opened automatically because they contained *sensory* information. You could taste baked goods and smell dry cleaning, and see all those images in your mind's eye. The person identification information existed in pictures, in stories. You couldn't forget it if you tried (the topic of all songs about failed love).

Names, however, were arbitrary; a person named Debra wasn't a Debra—she just got labeled that because her parents had to pick something. My stepson Jacob could have been called anything; he'd still be himself. Names were labels, stand-ins, substitutes for the thing itself, and that required a different kind of remembering.

Gingah was all packed. She stood up again. "Well," she said. "That is certainly a lot of information. A lot of interesting information."

I felt as I had on the edge of the high dive as a second grader. I knew I wasn't going to jump in. I wasn't going to tell her that I couldn't recognize faces. I just couldn't do it. I helped her carry the mats to the car.

Helder thought the yoga thing was no big deal. Try again, he said. "You have to come out. You do not have to do this alone."

I had to understand how much people would want to help, and how much easier life could be without all the faking and mistakes. "If you worked with a deaf person or someone visually impaired, you would make the accommodations, willingly, joyfully. You wouldn't judge them. You wouldn't think less of them. Tell people you need them to say who they are. Your life will be so much simpler; you'll be freed up in so many ways. Can't you see that?"

"No," I said. "I really can't see it."

I wanted to move to a new place again, where people would introduce themselves. It was so much easier to be new. I applied for a permanent position at St. Lawrence, where I had just done a stint as a visiting professor. I applied for fellowships in California, Boston, Texas, and Orlando. I got one interview, at a school on the Mexico–Texas border. It sounded wonderful to me, sunny and new and anonymous.

Helder was shocked. This was a terrible time to move. I was making real progress. There had been so much growth. He asked me whether this move was going to be with Dave or without Dave.

I didn't know.

I saw Dave for dinner a few times a week. The idea of divorce was out in the open. His position was unwavering. "You know I love you. I'm not going anywhere. And you know how I operate. I'm a Libertarian. I'm not going to try to make you conform to my whack-job—"

"I never said whack-job."

"You kind of did. But you are going to do what you are going to do. I'm not going to interfere with your business. If there's some reason you don't think I'm the person you want to be married to, far be it from me to try to convince you otherwise."

We didn't talk about money anymore, or houses, or drinking, or car insurance. We didn't talk about my job applications to faraway places. We didn't talk about my therapy or the boys' homework or missed doctor appointments. After our dinners out, we hugged and kissed, told each other "I love you." I went home to my bed. He went to his.

Helder asked, "Have you thought more about filing for divorce?"

I thought about it all the time. I couldn't stay with Dave. But I couldn't figure out how to leave him.

Helder pressed me to take a step, any step. He said things that made me cringe, like "Author your own life" and "Lean into our relationship, what we have here." All this uncertainty, he said, was ruling my life.

"I don't know about that," I said.

I called my mother on the spur of the moment one morning, surprising us both. "Mom," I said. "Quick question."

"What can I do for you, my dear person? You name it!" She was expansive, loud, fresh. I wondered if she knew exactly who I was. Lately it seemed as though she was covering for her forgetfulness, not remembering the last time we spoke or what we had talked about.

"Do you ever have trouble recognizing people, or do you know if Daddy did?"

There was a long silence. It was ten in the morning, a day I wasn't teaching. I walked, with the phone, to the kitchen, and reached under the sink. I was tempted to pour myself a shot of whiskey. I was shaking all over. Still, she didn't speak.

"Can I call you back? I am right in the middle of something. I am so, so sorry. Can I call you back, maybe at six, or eight, or eight-thirty? Which of those would be good? I'll use the signal. Would that be good?"

"I can't say if I'll be here, but okay, sure," I said. I knew the answer before I called. My mother wouldn't be able to know if she saw faces or not. She didn't have the ability to witness her own experience. But I wasn't asking in order to get information. I wasn't pretending we were normal people having a normal conversation. There was a sliver of a chance my mother would say something useful or important regarding face blindness in our family. I had to know, before I went any further, what she knew and did not know. Even if it was nothing.

I called Fred.

"Do you have trouble recognizing people?" I asked him, shouting into the phone. "Did Mom?"

"Wah?" he hollered back. "Wah?"

I broke the question down. Did he have trouble with faces?

Another round of yelling.

"I'm terrible with names," he said. "I can't remember names!" About my mother, he said, stop asking. He wasn't telling me. If it affected my medical history, my health, I said, he had to tell me. He said no. Not at all the case. He was going to his grave. He was living to be a hundred. He planned to outlive me. He hung up hard.

For the first time in my life, I was relieved that my parents had no idea what the hell I was talking about. I was not an extension of them, and this significant, defining feature was mine alone. Face blindness was kind of my moat. Maybe it always had been. Inside, I was safe.

Six

After a few weeks, *Face and Mind* was almost entirely highlighted in bright yellow. One night, I sat down with the boys on the sofa and told them I had an important announcement. Jacob said, "This can't be good." It was good, in a way, I explained. I had a rare neurological disorder. I wanted them to know about it so they wouldn't be hurt or confused when I had trouble recognizing them. Dave was sitting on a stool in the corner of the living room. He had a beer in one hand. His laptop was on his thigh. I thought he should be listening. I felt I was going about this all wrong.

"You don't have anything, Heather." Junior stood up. "But I gotta go, sorry."

"Wait," I said. Dave told him to sit back down until I was done.

I explained, in simple terms, what I had learned. I asked the boys to let me know who they were if they were aware that I wasn't recognizing them. Like if they ran into me downtown or came by my office unexpectedly.

Junior covered his face. "Who am I?" he said in a singsong voice. "You don't know who I am?" He was half mean, half kidding.

It was just a tiny glitch, I said. I used hair, and context, and voice, but I made lots of mistakes. It wasn't a mental illness, but it had been very frustrating for me. When I saw them out in public, I said, I might not know who they were. Or I might.

Jacob said he wore a tie-dyed T-shirt all year round, so that would make it easier. "You know me," he said.

"Except at our school that is basically the uniform, tie-dye," Junior squawked, his voice cracking. "I gotta go," he said again, and this time he flew out of the room, slamming the front door.

"Everyone has hair. I don't see the problem," Jacob said. He patted my leg. He went to his room.

"They're fine," Dave said. "They're just boys. They're interested in their Nintendo and when is the pizza going to appear, and that's about the extent of it." He was fiddling with his computer.

I sat on the couch and stared at the carpeting for a long, long time. This wasn't an easy thing in general, but for the boys I suspected it hit too close to home, because of their mother. I said this to Dave. He didn't think they thought about their mother at all. "They think of her every single day," I said. "Every single day. She is with them every single day."

I called my doctor and told him I wanted to be tested for face recognition.

He said, "What?"

"I believe I have face blindness," I said. I didn't say prosopagnosia. I didn't want him to think I thought I was smarter than him, a prima donna, a showy, knowy bitch.

"You're having vision problems? Confused?" he said. "Headaches?"

"I'm not confused," I said. "I'm fine. I'm sure I have face blindness. I want to be tested for it."

"No," he said. "That's extremely rare. You don't have that, Heather. Insomnia, shortness of breath, diarrhea? Heart palpitations? Numbness?" He was one of those doctors who speak in lists.

"I can't recognize people," I said assertively.

"I'm terrible with names too. It's not really a serious problem, Heather."

I resisted the temptation to launch into a discussion of person identity nodes and name retrieval processes. I said, "There could be a tumor, or something—a stroke, maybe something from the car accident. I don't know. That's why I want to see a specialist. I have to pursue this. If I can get it fixed, I want to do so."

"You're having headaches?"

I wasn't, but I said I was. Yes, headaches.

He said he'd write the referral, I could see a neurologist, get an MRI. "But you are fine, Heather."

Dave thought I was subjecting myself to needless trouble and anxiety and expense, but he said he'd be there whenever I needed him to be. He visited me every couple of days; I visited the boys in the afternoons, bringing them socks, pizza,

Gatorade, pencils. On weekends, we ate out, impersonating a family. I bugged the boys about their grades. In my driveway, after the boys got out and jogged up the street to the apartment, Dave bugged me about bugging them. "They're not used to being talked to like that," he said. "I don't want them to have complexes."

I couldn't give up on how I wanted the boys to be raised. As long as we were married, I felt entitled to vote. "It's not going to work unless we unmarry," I said. I told Dave I was thinking about a do-it-yourself divorce. I had books from the library. There was a book for Michigan. We could be like we were before. "If I'm the girlfriend, I can keep quiet," I said.

"You know I don't like to give advice," Dave said. "But objectively, I think this is a really bad idea, it would be really bad for you. You shouldn't have married me. And you shouldn't divorce me." He'd said this before.

The brain, I had recently learned, has one task: to make sense. It is a visual organism, and for things to make sense, the eyes have to be level. The perceiving system does not function properly if the eyes aren't level. If a person is walking unevenly, because of back pain or a sore foot, the legs automatically compensate, one limping, dragging, slowing, or kicking out so it takes longer to arrive and complete the step—whatever it takes to keep the eyes at perfect level. The whole body works, in fact, for the eyes. Your knee might be torqued, your femur out of alignment, but the incoming visual information will route correctly. The brain cannot handle tilted.

Dave and I were tilted.

"It would be a trial separation. If we aren't yoked financially, car insurance, all that stuff, we'll get along better."

"So why did we get married?" he said.

Because I wanted to leave home; he knew where I was from. Because he had the map from one place to another. Because I loved him and, despite my parents, he loved me, even us.

I was beginning to think of prosopagnosia as a key part of who I was, and to consider how it might have protected me or steered me through my childhood. The condition demanded a relationship with ambivalence, an acute ability to not-know, a comfort with postponing certainty, a familiarity with chaos and doubt. What was negative capability if not a kind of prosopagnosia? I considered everything from a place of profound uncertainty, and considering my mother in this manner must have helped me cope. Not knowing her was possibly the only way to have loved her the way I did. I was used to being blindsided: *Oh, you aren't who I thought you were at all.*

Generally, Dave encouraged me not to talk to my mother when I was tired, alone, hungry, or upset about something else. He vetted her letters for me, promising to let me know if there was anything important in them. He strongly believed schizophrenia wound down in the elderly—they just didn't have the energy to make everything topsy-turvy anymore.

"I'll try every hour on the hour," my mother would say on the answering machine, and she did, leaving the same message each time. Then weeks would pass when she wouldn't call or answer her phone. Sometimes her neighbor, Pilar, left a message: "We are a little worried about your mom. She doesn't appear to have gone to the grocery store. She won't eat anything we take over. She says she has trouble with her legs."

When we did speak, I never mentioned anything about my research, my theories. Sometimes she went on about how she and my father had raised me to be an intelligent, special person. "I just can't believe you work for so little money. You should be making decent money. With all that education? All those years of school? It's ridiculous. It's a crime." I kept my mouth shut. I pretended to go along. I was accustomed to pretending; it was only weird now to recognize it as that, pretending.

In the same conversation she could plummet. "I was a terrible, terrible mother," she would say in drastic tones, weeping. "I don't know how you can forgive me." I stayed away from the past; any question about my childhood and she would clam up, hang up, not call back for days. She changed the subject if I mentioned Dave, the boys, house-hunting, my marriage.

I was proud of how I handled her now. I pretended my mother was a near-extinct, exotic bird. You had to be very subtle and cagey in your approach. You had to hold out your hand and pretend you wanted anything other than for her to land there. I loved the feel of her feathers, the glance of them on my palm, the whisper, and I worked for it.

Whatever secrets my mother harbored, I'd always thought I had to *find them out*, or that someday she really was going to tell me. I always felt I had to *know*—the answer, the story. I'd organized myself around the feeling that I was wrong for not knowing. Now, for the first time, it occurred to me that I had known all along, that I was the one responsible for articulating this knowing, and for telling what I knew.

I re-saw everything; I remembered things I'd never before considered. The mother who made perfect Chex Mix. The mother who was passionate about *The Sound of Music*. The mother who adored my father. The mother who, when she drove across the Intracoastal Waterway, said she felt that this time the truck was going over, we would die, and it would be for the best. I held all of these contradictory memories together and realized I knew now how to remember her: I understood how it all fit together. I started to write down the story as best I could.

My mother used to say that the best years of her life were when she was little, following her father around the golf course, where he was greenskeeper. Shagging balls in a plaid jacket that was a micro version of his Pendleton gear, with her own miniature set of wood-handled clubs—this was when the world was open and beautiful for her, when time swept out from the golf course, never-ending. She'd said her father was the only person who ever understood her, and when he died on Christmas Eve when she fourteen years old, it was the end of her real life; she was never the same again. The packages for him sat under the tree for weeks.

Something else had marked her that year; she'd hinted at it, shrouded it in mystery. I thought rape was a legitimate explanation, the source of all her checking, the fire drills, the drills where we had to pretend we were being kidnapped and escape. But the details kept changing. Two things had happened to her, maybe three. Someone she knew had disappeared. Nothing had happened to her when she was fourteen; she'd never said her whole world changed. "Stop pressuring me. I will never tell you if you keep on like this, Heather."

Maybe grief had tipped the balance, but illness had been running the show ever since. Illness was life itself. Illness was truth and safety and manners and being aware of everything but the illness as a thing itself.

In 1955, my parents cut short their honeymoon to Niagara Falls. ("She kept hitting me and, yeah, I hit her back," my father told me, and he sounded, fifty years later, still reluctant, surprised, and not sorry. Was this the deep, dark secret that he'd have to kill me if he told me? No, he said. He would never tell me that secret. Never ask him again.) Then a trip to Europe was scuttled, over passport photos and fingerprinting. My mother tried teaching. She hid, she told me, in the classroom closet "to see how the children would behave when they didn't know I was watching." She tried substitute teaching. It took them nine years to get pregnant. Sometimes she said they were desperate for a child. Other times she said they were happy just being the two of them. Still other versions had them on the brink of divorce.

In a perfect and elegant counterpoint, as I began to recall the past, my mother started to lose her memory. She didn't seem to be remembering our conversations, and this new forgetting had a different flavor from her usual lack of apprehension. She'd call me twice, three times in a day, each time saying: "Hi, honey! Is this a good time to get caught up?" Each memory I picked up seemed to correspond to a memory she had dropped, for good.

I called her more now, unsure how much time she had left as *her.* Tell me anything, I said. Tell me any story about your life. Any illnesses? Tell me any little thing.

"I'll think. I'll get back to you. Someday I am going to write it all down. I've always wanted to write."

My mother didn't even like writing checks: her signature could be copied, the routing numbers stolen. The conversation was over. I told her I loved her and we said good-bye.

A couple weeks after I brought up the idea of do-it-yourself divorce, Dave came down to my house, late. He got under my covers. He said I was making a terrible mistake. "You're divorcing the wrong person," he said. "You're letting this marriage get caught up in what you really do have to leave behind. I'm tired of being collateral damage in your life. Please don't leave me and the boys, Heather. It's wrong. You'll regret it. It doesn't make any sense."

But I had already filled out the forms. I told him I didn't think I could figure out how to make it work. We cried in each other's arms. He left.

Yes, I had used him. I felt like a creature, a parasite, a crab. I had lived in Dave, used him as my shell, and now I was going out of him and leaving him empty.

I told him I loved him.

I didn't tell him that I loved him and I couldn't be with him. There aren't words for that.

Seven

The neurologist's receptionist said she was sure I was fine. "Everyone gets confused. I do all the time." She dragged out the word "all," making it into a blanket.

In the waiting room, fluorescent lights hummed. A woman had her lumpen legs propped up on the coffee table, making a bridge to a pile of *Better Homes* and *Michigan Living* magazines. Two very old women in wheelchairs who seemed to be twins stared at the walls, looking mad, bored. I sat as far from them as I could. I pretended to read about midwestern destination vacations. Leaves were the big draw.

"Heather Sellers?"

Startled, I leaped up, dove through the doorway, and followed the nurse down a thin corridor.

"You think you're confused?" the nurse said as we walked, reading the form on her clipboard. Her name tag said *Bettina*.

"No," I said. "I'm not confused. I can't reliably recognize people."

Bettina sped up. I scooted along behind her down the

narrow corridors, clutching my paperwork. The office was much bigger than it looked from outside. I'd never find my way out alone.

In the examining room, she weighed me. "We all get that sometimes," she said. "I bet you are Just Fine." She patted my shoulder and I got off the scale and said, "No. This is a real problem." But I forced myself not to tell her what I had learned. That we must have recognition to survive. The infant has to be able to lock on to the mother's face, her gaze, her identity, in order for cuteness and likability and pity to occur. So the organism will be likely to be fed, carried along with, and touched. To survive, we have to be seen.

Bettina strapped the cuff on my arm, took my blood pressure. Why did they do this in every office, for everything? We watched the needle pause at its favorite numbers. "One-oh-nine over eighty. You're perfect," she said. "See?" She left.

I waited and waited and waited in the windowless room. I sat and waited. I walked around and waited. I went through the cupboards. Paper cups, boxes of gloves that looked like condoms with fingers, tongue depressors. There was nothing in this room for a brain. On the back of the door was a poster with a giant ear; I was studying the peachy coils when the doctor walked in, knocking. I jumped back, busted.

He had *Yntema* stitched in blue across his white coat. The way he rocked back on his heels, reading a page in my folder, I sensed he liked wearing the white coat too much.

I grabbed my articles from my satchel and didn't sit down. I'd brought three: "Right Lateral Fusiform Gyrus Dysfunction

During Facial Information Processing in Schizophrenia," "A Network of Occipito-Temporal Face-Sensitive Areas Besides the Right Middle Fusiform Gyrus Is Necessary for Normal Face Processing," and my favorite, carefully highlighted: "Where Am I? The Neurological Correlates of Self and Other."

Dr. Yntema had thinning white hair, a wiry little body, small feet. He motioned me to sit down. "Dr. Mathur indicates confusion at work, forgetting names?"

He had a way of sending his words over to me that said, *I have yelled at people who love me.* I couldn't sit. I made a little barking sound. My palms instantly glazed with sweat. I wiped my hands on my dress. I moved closer to him and leaned on the counter.

"No," I said. "You're confused." I smiled to show I was clever but kind. "I'm a professor and a writer," I said. "I'm not forgetting names. I'm great with names."

He frowned. "What do you teach?"

"English," I said. "I'm not confused." I smiled at his chin. "I can't recognize people. I first noticed it in college, but I have probably had it my whole life. I am sure I have prosopagnosia." I handed my articles over. He would not take them.

He asked me the date. The president. My address. What day of the week it was. I told him: October twenty-third, Bush, Twenty-fourth Street, Thursday. "Those are all things crazy and confused people *do* know," I said. "This isn't about confusion."

He said, "I know you know this, but can you tell me where we are today?"

"Down the wrong path," I said.

"Married?" he said.

I sat down in the chair. "Yes."

"Why the hesitation? You aren't sure if you are married? Not *that* married?"

"No hesitation," I said.

He said, "Marital stress? Job stress? Abuse? Alcohol?"

I smiled and said no, no, no, I was doing really well. I was happy.

"You do not have prosopagnosia," Yntema said. "I have never even seen a case. Remember four words: *house, car, tree, window.* You will be asked the words later."

"Someone has to have it," I said. My articles sat there between us. I stood and gave him my hands, as he requested. I gave over my arms, and he pressed and I resisted. I gave him my knees and he banged on them. They responded appropriately, with kicking.

"Head trauma?" he said. "Daddy knock you around a little bit?"

"What?" I said. He was coming at my head with his hands and flashlight. I put up my palms. I said loud and clear: "In the grocery store, I have gone up to the wrong man, thinking it was my husband." I paused. Yntema looked at his pen, his flashlight. I leaned back. He closed the gap between us.

"It's not like you went up to a fat black man thinking that was your husband."

I wanted to call for help. I wanted to get out of that room.

He said, "There's sexual abuse. Right? Am I right? I'm right. Daddy getting a little drunk? Can't keep his hands to himself?" He was hard as a wire.

He said, "Close your eyes." He said: "What were the four words?"

To rule out a brain tumor, I had to lie perfectly still in a tiny tube in the basement of the hospital at nine at night. Dave said he would be glad to come with me. When we got there, I couldn't go in the tube. I shivered in the cold, low-ceilinged room in my yoga pants and sock feet, a thin white T-shirt. The giant machine loomed.

"I can't do it," I told the girl behind the glass.

She stared at me like I was a fish in a tank.

I looked at the long tray on which I was supposed to lie, and the tiny tube into which I'd be inserted. For an hour. Not moving. I didn't see how I'd come out alive. I asked her if my husband could come in. I got out of the machine completely and Dave hugged me in the hallway. He was already taking off his necklace. His crucifix. His wedding ring. The ring he wore on his other ring finger, the ring that he said married him to the boys. The tray holding our jewelry was a tiny, tiny version of the tray I had to lie on.

My toes stuck out of the end of the tube and poured sweat. Dave held one foot in his bare hands. The machine roared. And pulsed. I felt like it was *giving* me a brain tumor. Then it got louder. Jet engines pulsed; the tube vibrated. An MRI makes you feel like you are being ground, like glass, into pulverized bits. I had to take a break. I had to take another break. I wept. Dave held my foot and said, "It's okay, it's okay, you are doing great."

After the scan, out in the car in the hospital parking lot, Dave held me and I jabbered on and on. He didn't say anything. He was warm and good and quiet and whole. The next day, I returned *The Michigan Divorce Book* to the library and I threw away the forms I'd photocopied.

The brain scan results came out fine, completely normal.

I was, to say the least, an incredibly difficult person to not-live with. I hounded the boys, I obsessed about my family, I spent hundreds of hours on research. I was alone in my own little world. Sometimes I didn't even ask Dave how his day was going. The details of the discussions we had in those dark, cold, horrible late-winter months don't belong here. He had more reasons to divorce me than I him, but he did not want us to break up. When I suggested couples counseling, Dave said if that was what I wanted, of course. He'd give it four sessions with a neutral party. He wouldn't see "Svengali," as he called Helder. He presented me with a dozen candidates in three towns. But in the end it was I who wouldn't go. Dave was the only person on the planet who knew me, who knew my whole story, but the person I was wasn't the person I wanted to be anymore.

In March, I filed for divorce and got a case number.

Getting a divorce was like buying a handgun: it was a potentially dangerous thing to do. There was a waiting period. During the waiting period, I received a letter from the National Institute of Neurological Disorders and Stroke in Bethesda, Maryland. It was from Carol Rowan, chief of public inquiries in the Office of Communications and Public Liaison. The letter opened, "I am sorry to learn that you may have prosopagnosia and can certainly understand your desire to obtain an accurate diagnosis and any available treatment." Rowan suggested writing to Antonio Damasio and included his address at the University of Iowa. I'd never heard back from him; he was no doubt besieged with mail from weird brains. Rowan went on to say that her search of the Internet identified the Harvard Vision Sciences Laboratory and the Harvard University Prosopagnosia Research Center as a good place for prosopagnosics wishing to be part of research studies. In closing, she wrote, "You mentioned your mother has schizophrenia; you may wish to contact the National Institute of Mental Health for their materials on this topic." She provided their address, website, and phone number.

In retrospect, it seems odd that I hadn't found the Harvard site on my own. In all the months since I'd first discovered prosopagnosia, I'd Googled movie reviews, recipes, festivals, myself, David Junior and Jacob, skin conditions, dog care information, maps, travel, and words I wanted to know. I'd Googled *Reivers* and *parapraxis* and the names of authors as I prepared lecture notes. But for face blindness, once I'd discovered the hard-core research databases, PubMed and PsycLIT, I stuck with them. Obscure scientific articles were safe. Google seemed like wolves, the whole naked world. I still kept prosopagnosia far off to the side of my regular life, a secret.

Immediately after reading Carol's letter, I drove down to my office and logged on to the Internet. I went to www.faceblind.org, the Harvard site. There was a "Contact Us" form. I explained that I was coming to Boston in a few months, in late April, to meet with my textbook publisher. Was there a study I could be part of? Could I meet with the directors of the research lab? Had anybody looked for a link between prosopagnosia and schizophrenia?

Brad Duchaine, head of the Harvard lab, wrote back right away. Yes, he said. We'd love to meet with you. There were two studies I could be part of.

On the website, a face-blind professor in Sweden, Cecilia Burman, had posted a tutorial on the condition. First she showed a stone, close up. Easy to recognize: it's a stone. Then she showed six stones, each quite different. She gave the stones human names. Then she showed a rock-strewn beach. A stone wall. A cobblestone street. Now could we find Joey or Margaret? She showed six rocks out in a field, stranded. This was *exactly* what it was like to be face-blind. It was one of the happiest moments in my entire life, seeing those images of rocks on grass, rocks by other rocks. I e-mailed Cecilia and told her how useful her visual explanations were. She wrote back and told me about the face-blind support groups and a book by a gay man who compared coming out as face-blind to coming out as gay.

The prosopagnosics on the list serve were strange and funny and fascinating. Most of them said they had been born with the condition, and a surprising number saw it in their children. There was a militant contingency who adored their face blindness: they called people without prosopagnosia "neurotypicals," or "NTs," as though *we* were the ones you'd want to be, and other people were not only boringly predictable but also a little flat, walking around recognizing everyone, taking the brain for granted.

In my world, and in my mother's world, things could always be more than one thing. My whole life, I'd been primed to look beneath the surface, to trust my feel of a thing. Maybe the face-blind militants were right. Who was to say what was an ability and what was a disability? Who defined "normal"?

But like schizophrenia, which could similarly cause a person to see slant, face blindness had devastating side effects. I was *only* comfortable in ambivalence. I didn't trust my decisions. I wasn't married, I wasn't divorced. I did and didn't have children. I was always looking at new houses, new jobs, new cities, new places to be new. Prosopagnosia was not a mental illness. But just like schizophrenia, it kept its host constantly guessing, always on the run.

I asked the online face-blind support group: How many of you have told the people you work with about your condition?

Dozens of people wrote back, with advice ranging from "Don't do it!" to "Do it yesterday, your life will be so much easier." Tell only a few people. Tell your boss. Tell anyone but your boss. One man said he'd just that morning written a letter to George Bush to ask for accommodation for all of us, under the Americans with Disabilities Act. "People must wear name tags in the workplace," he argued. A man in London said he had been fired after he told his office. "Maybe there were other performance issues," a woman posted. A face-blind woman in California said that after a year of struggling with the decision, she had come out, but afterward no one introduced themselves, and she feared people now considered her unstable.

One wise woman wrote me privately. She said telling people was a process. It took about five different explanations—five times, she'd found, for people to understand what it was, what it meant, and why you knew them sometimes and not at others.

I e-mailed her back right away. Do you have a script? I asked her. And what do you say to the people who do not believe you?

As little as possible, she said.

I asked her if she'd heard of a connection between prosopagnosia and paranoid schizophrenia.

No, she said. She had not.

Eight

Boston was a city turned inside out, taken apart at the seams. In the backseat of a cab, Brad Duchaine and I stitched under the Big Dig, which was much bigger and diggier than seemed possible. The dank tunnel walls didn't seem like the kind that would hold. The air smelled of clay and fish and fuel and salt.

Brad Duchaine, renowned neuroscientist, wore Chuck Taylors, frayed jeans, and a tan T-shirt with a monkey on it. All of Brad was perfectly frayed and faded—his backpack, his hair, his watchband—except his super-sharp eyes. I thought he'd be older. I thought he'd be in a suit. I felt like I was on a date.

Brad was explaining his research. "We think we are looking at a syndrome," he said. Many prosopagnosics who appeared to have the disorder from birth also reported problems hearing, driving, and recognizing cars, just as I did. He thought prosopagnosia was the key to finding out some very interesting stuff about how the brain processes objects. "We think we've got a pathway into understanding something about consciousness itself. Until very recently, we thought of the brain as one seamless intelligence, because that's exactly how it feels to be in a brain. But now we see that there are separate processes, different groups of computational machines working simultaneously." What was so groundbreaking was the understanding that these systems didn't interact with each other or have awareness of each other. "Did they give you the Benton and tell you you were fine with faces?"

"Yes," I said. I told him how easy it had been to tell the photographs apart on the face test I'd taken in Grand Rapids, at a second neurologist's office: I'd just used the hairstyles to differentiate the men.

Most of Brad's other subjects had had the same experience. Multiple neurologists, flawed testing protocols, misdiagnosis. Most of his subjects had easily passed the Benton Visual Retention Test, which had been in place since the 1970s, and Brad had just published a paper on what was wrong with it: it wasn't really measuring face recognition, since the hair and ears and other details gave additional information.

Brad asked me if anyone in my family had prosopagnosia.

"They wouldn't know," I said. I took a deep breath. Here was my opening. He was going to be looking inside my brain; I felt like he was going to know everything anyway, like he could already read my thoughts. "To figure this out takes a lot of self-awareness, and an interest in one's own interior experience. My mother is a paranoid schizophrenic. She wouldn't be able to discern face blindness in herself or in another person." My words took up all the room in the wide backseat. This was the first time I'd said anything like this out loud, to anyone other than Dave and Helder. I had the feeling I would be struck down or dissolve. I held on to the door handle with one hand. But the cab kept crawling forward, and Brad's face didn't move.

I took another step. "I'm sure face blindness is related. That's what I really want to find out about. Did her brain give me this, because of the schizophrenia somehow? Or did my experience with her, as a child, somehow provoke the face blindness? Do you know of any potential connections?"

There was a long, pregnant pause.

"No," Brad said. "Turn, stop—here," he said to the driver. "No," he said to me. "That wouldn't be related at all. We think face blindness is genetic."

He sprang out of the cab and paid the driver.

I followed him. What did *genetic* mean? Genes. Wasn't schizophrenia genetic too? I felt like a kindergartner, struggling with something as basic as colors. But I didn't ask any more questions. I followed Brad across the plaza, past the light post, through the revolving door into William James Hall, where the Harvard psychology department is located, past the armed guard, and to the elevators.

In the elevator, Brad pushed the button for seven and said to remind him to get us lunch; he would forget.

Then he said: "Up we go."

The walls of the vision science lab were painted black, and so was the ceiling. Black drapes swept across the room, creating numerous cubicles. It was like being on stage in a surrealist black-box theater: no audience, all curtains. I loved it.

The thick curtains smelled dusty, and Brad pulled them

around us like skirts, making a little room. He turned on a bright lamp. I sat in the folding chair while Brad booted up his laptop, complained about its slowness. I wanted to go slowly. I wanted to remember everything. I wanted to ask him, again, about my mother.

"Do you think I have it?" I asked.

"We'll soon see, but what you've said so far fits with what prosopagnosics are saying about their experience."

"What's the cure?" I asked. "Is it surgery or more like rehabilitation?"

"No cure," he said. "Here's the first test. These are famous faces, with the hair removed. This is the sample, so you can practice how the test works." He nodded to the screen. "Is this face familiar?"

I said, "Yes." I sat there, staring at the screen. "No cure? There's no cure?" I had come all the way to Boston and there's no cure? I was right, and Helder was wrong; but I was surprised at how bereft I felt, hearing these words. I had been hoping for a cure all along.

Brad said, "There's one guy in California who claims he may be having a little luck with retraining, but most research shows that attempts to learn face recognition have resulted in *worse* identification skills, actually."

"No cure?" I said. "At all?"

"When you're ready," he said. He nodded again at the laptop. "This test isn't timed," he said. "Take as much time as you need. Type out who it is. Don't worry about spelling."

A face flashed on the screen—just the face; the ears and hair had been cropped out.

"Jim Carrey?" I said as I typed. I was off to a good start.

"That's me," he said. "I just put that in there for fun. That was the sample."

"Do you look like Jim Carrey?" I said.

He said he did.

Many, many faces flashed by. They were new, unfamiliar faces; my reaction, time and again, was that I had never seen them before. I correctly identified three faces: Nicolas Cage (those eyebrows), Julia Roberts (those teeth), and Martin Luther King, Jr.—he was the only black man they ever used in these tests. When I was finished, Brad read the names of the others and asked me if I knew who each of them was, so he could determine if the test was testing known faces. Brad Pitt, George Bush, Mel Gibson, Jennifer Aniston, Tony Blair, Winston Churchill. Robert Downey, Jr. Condoleezza Rice. The whole sexy crew. Yes, I said. I have seen these images in my life. I should know them. But I can't recognize these people. He smiled. I smiled. I was really, really happy to be failing.

The next test was a breeze: identifying emotions on faces. I knew who was happy, I knew who was sad, afraid, disgusted, and surprised. Brad explained what I already knew from Andrew Young's *Face and Mind.* The system that processed reading emotions on a person's face was completely separate from the system that read the features and correlated face to identity. Face-blind people can tell if a person is sad or happy, but they can't tell, by face, who that person is, if they're familiar or unfamiliar.There existed a visual processing system just for face recognition, separate from identifying facial beauty, emotion on faces. Brad and his research partner, Galit Yovel, were studying one very specific aspect of face processing: Does face detection (knowing that a particular object is a face) come before or after face identification (knowing whose face it is), or are these two processes concurrent?

Brad showed me upside-down faces and asked me to match them to their owners. I couldn't. Interestingly, "normal" humans are also very bad at identifying upside-down faces. They perform, with upside-down faces, as face-blind people do with all faces. The human face processor only works with upright images of faces. Monkeys, on the other hand, are adept at recognizing individual monkeys, regardless of orientation.

The next test Brad gave me was designed to establish that my object recognition was normal, so we could declare that I had a face problem, not a problem recognizing objects in general. "You'll see pictures of guns. If you've seen the gun before, hit the red button." I matched the guns. I did the same for images of houses, landscapes, cars. No one does extremely well on the guns, Brad said, except gun collectors. (I didn't even want to think about face-blind gun collectors.)

The next test was titled Bald Women. It featured faces of ordinary humans, but as with the celebrities, with the hair and ears cut away. I couldn't match them. They all looked the same. Once in a while, as with Nicholas Cage, a pair of eyebrows jumped out, and I hit the white button: *Different.*

Brad ran my results and came back with a printout. "Yup," he said, smiling. "You're pretty bad at faces. One of the worst, actually. I've tested only one person who is worse than you."

I beamed. I was face-blind. Harvard-certified.

"We know so little," Brad said. "But we're getting inside the black box. I'm optimistic we're going to learn lots in the next ten years."

"Ten years," I said. "I'll be almost fifty."

On some level, I'd expected the testing itself would be a kind of cure: that I would return to Michigan with a better brain, improved perception. Now, as I leaned on the glass and watched people walking across the campus, I realized I was not ever going to recognize people by face. Things weren't ever going to be any different. Prosopagnosia research wasn't for prosopagnosics. We were simply providing, with our unusual wiring, a pathway into the black box, insight into consciousness and how it works. Other people would benefit. For example, we might help the government improve its software for identifying terrorists at airports. Right now, computers were terrible at face recognition—although, like me, they were excellent at gait.

There was a lot that I would simply never know. I was never going to know when I became face-blind. Whether I'd ever known faces normally, ever been headed down that path. I was never going to know how I might have turned out if childhood had been even one notch easier. I was never going to know—really know—what my mother's life had been, what her illness had been, if she'd been diagnosed and kept it a secret—any of it. She would remain a mystery, and I had to let her go.

What I did know was a hell of a lot about the nature of not-knowing. Which is, by definition, the opposite of mental illness. It's philosophy.

"Monkey MRI!" I said, reading the sign over the door. In the window a bumper sticker warned: *Please do not feed the scientists.*

In a glass control booth, Brad and Galit fired up their laptops. In the adjacent room, I lay on my back, perfectly still, in my socks, black yoga pants, and paper-thin white T-shirt. My lucky MRI outfit.

Galit was worried I would fall asleep. She kept talking to me over the microphone. I'd taken a Valium, but I assured her I was wide-awake, never more awake in my life. I was checking for monkey hairs as I lay on the hard little bed. I worried, with all these electrodes on my head and chest, that Galit and Brad could read my thoughts. My arms were pinned at my sides, hands folded over my stomach. Humming under my right hand was the *Same/Different* box, with its two buttons. My face was packed with sponges and cloth in a white plastic cage with metal wires. I could be shipped to the Alps. Mark me FRAGILE.

Galit said the first test would take two hours. It would reveal the exact landscape of my face-processing area. Was it missing, defective, or just not plugged in? I would look at face after face, and they would study activity in my brain.

Galit was dressed all in black, like a cat burglar. She peered up at me. "If you are scared, you can squeeze the ball. I'll come right in—right away—and zip you out." She pressed the ball into my hand, then scooted out of the room and closed the door.

I wanted out. What was the point of this, if there was no

cure? I was helping science. But I didn't want to help science. Science was fine. I wanted to go home. I closed my eyes.

The last time I'd done this, Dave had held my foot, like it was a baby bird he'd raised himself. Now my foot just lay there, sweaty, frozen, at the far end of my body. I wondered if we'd ever connect again, me and Dave. It felt like he and my mother were part of my old life, and this tube was sending me into my new life, reconstituting my molecules, resetting my counter to zero.

When I opened my eyes, deep in the tight tube, I saw a little mirror, the kind that comes in a lipstick case. I looked into it and my stomach whooshed, like I was tipping backward. I was falling out of myself. Where the heck was the Valium floor, the cottony dulling, the pleasant fog?

The Simpsons came on the screen, behind my head, reflected in the little makeup mirror, and I jumped. Galit's voice blared into the speaker by my ear: "WE ARE NOW TUNING. WE ARE NOW SETTING UP. BE PATIENT, PLEASE. THANK YOU."

The machine roared and banged.

"IF YOU ARE READY TO BEGIN, WOULD YOU PLEASE SQUEEZE THE BALL?"

I squeezed. An oval photograph of a woman's face—just a face, no hair, no ears—raced across the computer screen, flashing at different points like a laser show. Then another face skittered across the screen like a skipping stone and was gone. One after another, faces skated across the monitor, black and white and bald. They all looked exactly the same. Was this the real test? Was it a trick?

"WHENEVER YOU ARE READY, PLEASE BEGIN." I

pressed *Same. Same. Same.* The faces kept coming, dozens of them. They all looked exactly the same. An occasional face had dark eyebrows. When I saw those eyebrows, I clicked *Different.*

I wanted out. I had my panic ball, but I was scared to squeeze it. If we stopped, we'd have to start over.

The machine quieted to a dull roar. Galit stared up into the tube at me. "You are saying *Same* a lot. You understand the test?"

I said yes. I said I wished there was a button for *Not sure. YES.*

She asked, "Can you go a little longer? We are getting really good stuff."

I said okay.

After three hours, we finally stopped. I said thank you. I put on my regular clothes. In the elevator, Galit said that she was very grateful that someone so claustrophobic was willing to help them. She would call me tonight with the results.

I felt like a million bucks. I felt molecularly altered. I was part of their life's work, part of their magnum opus. I was fresh. I was done. Not cured, but *seen.*

That evening I walked around Boston feeling smart and complete and helpful. I felt like I'd run a marathon, finished an advanced degree. On the Common I heard French, Dutch, Chinese. Everyone in Boston looked focused, like they had a thesis statement.

Back in my hotel room, I took a long, hot bath and waited

for Galit's call. I wished Dave were with me. I wanted to tell him about the funny monkey sign. I wanted to tell him about the MRI and everything I'd learned and how messy the lab was—at Harvard! I wanted to ask him about his day, and see it in my mind's eye as he talked.

This, of anything that had happened so far, was always the thing that felt the most like healing: telling Dave what I saw, what I knew, and having him see it. And then getting to do the same for him.

When the phone rang, at 10:34, I jumped off the bed like electricity.

"I have terrible news, I'm so sorry," Galit said. "We lost all the data." She explained that technicians had been working on the machine over the weekend. She and Brad had tested the equipment and thought everything was okay, but evidently not. "We have nothing," she said. "Can you come in again? I hate to ask. We have nothing."

"No," I said. "I took the Valium. I don't have another. I'm leaving in the morning. And I'm claustrophobic. There isn't anything you can do?" It was Harvard!

Actually, there *was* something she could do. Her husband was a cognitive behavioral therapist who specialized in claustrophobia. Possibly he could help. He could be at my hotel—like that.

I called Dave.

"How was the big book meeting?" Dave said. His voice was pushy cheerful, like a thing catching up to itself.

"We talked about that *last* night." I took a breath and tried not to be rude. I looked at the ceiling, where there was a faint stain in the shape of Marie Antoinette's head. "This is the face thing. Today was the functional MRI."

"The face thing!" he said. The cell phone crackled.

Dave said no, he didn't think a strange man should come to my room and experiment with cognitive behavioral therapy. He thought I should just come home. I knew I was face-blind. He believed me. I didn't need proof. I'd helped these people as much as I could. He missed me. He was slurring his words, like he had stones in his mouth.

Dave said, "Do they like the book?"

"This isn't those people. This isn't that. That was the meeting two days ago. The textbook publisher meeting. We already talked about it! This is the face people."

I hated how I sounded.

"We're breaking up," I said. And I disconnected.

"Are you ready to kill the monster?" Iftah, Galit's husband, leaned forward, smiling, rubbing his hands.

"I am not," I whispered.

There was no reason to be afraid. This fear was just an old remnant signal from the brain stem. The brain is very dumb! Iftah said. We can learn to override it. There is no fear, only fear *of* fear. There is no such thing as claustrophobia.

We were sitting on a sofa by the elevators in my hotel. He talked. I took notes. He asked me what I was afraid of in the tube and I told him: suffocating, not being able to get out.

He said I could get out.

No, I said. I have to squeeze the ball and wait for your wife.

But what would happen to you while you wait? What is the danger you fear?

I wanted to go to bed. I didn't want to get in the tube again. I didn't need to cure my claustrophobia; it was the least of my problems. "Well. I'm afraid I'll die. I feel like—"

"It is a feeling state. You see? You won't really die. You can't. There's no deadly spiders or deadly toxins . . . nothing in the tube is really dangerous. You just want to get out. You don't need to, though. Nothing bad can happen in the tube. You just lie there. Right? In a tube. It's a tube," he said.

The more he talked, waving his hands, pleading, the better it sounded. When we were babies, ten thousand years ago, we were afraid if we were in a small space, in a crevice, and with reason: if a baby was wedged in a tight space, it was dependent on someone else to get it out. Our heart rate went up. Our fear response increased our chance of survival. Not anymore. Not for a long time. But the limbic brain, the oldest part of the brain, still *thinks* all tight spaces are equally dangerous. This brain—good for a baby, good for a cavewoman—was a very dumb brain, an old brain. It was not a helpful part of the brain for people who lived in cities, in our century, with elevators and cars and MRIs. The old remnant brain sent a strong powerful signal in situations where there was no longer any danger. A long time ago, a plastic tube would not have been something you went into willingly. Now it was safe. The old brain hadn't caught up with civilization. It was always erring on the safe side, and its version of a safe side was thousands of years out of date.

I smiled and nodded. How did I not know all this already?

He talked about his other patients. There were many situations now—bridges, skyscrapers, glass walls, airplanes—that would have been dangerous ten thousand years ago but were in fact not dangerous to the modern human. The old brain just didn't know any of this, and there was no way to get a message to it. We had to draw on the new brain and remind it, willfully, to ignore the old alerts, no matter how convincing they seemed to be. We could override those impulses.

"It's a monster in your brain. We kill him!" Iftah announced, grinning like a kid. He stood up. He motioned to me to stand. He put his fists in a fighting position.

"Right now?" I said. I thought we were just having a talk.

He was nodding, waiting, smiling, rocking on his toes. He looked at the door to my room. "We give it a try. Galit is so upset. She feels so badly."

I was moved by the lengths to which he was going to help his wife.

This was not the person I was used to being: I walked down the hallway, grinning, with a stranger following me. I unlocked the door to my room. At the threshold, Iftah hit the front of his forehead with his palm. "We must use this," he said, and smacked the back of his head with the same hand, "to overcome this."

In the room he said, "Well, what is scary to you in here, this room?"

"You."

He laughed. "What would be really scary?"

I walked across the room, nudged my suitcase out of the way, and stood by the small closet. "I would go in here."

He said to go in. I did and he closed the door.

"What will freak you out now?" he said through the closed door.

I could hear and feel his body leaning against the door. And the monster leaped. I couldn't believe I was sitting in the dark in a closet in a hotel room with a man, a stranger, leaning on the door. I had never been further from who I was, and at the same time I suspected somehow I was becoming myself in there. This, I realized, was *the gap*. It was funny and fascinating.

He jangled the doorknob. "Do you see the monster?" he said. "Is he near?"

"Yes," I said. "He is here." I was smiling. It was like the monster was on the screen in the MRI tube, and I was clicking at him. I was scared, but not in the way I thought I would be. It was so goofy. I was outside the scare, having it—it wasn't having me. Maybe for the first time in my life.

"Are you laughing at him? That is good! That is good! See!"

Iftah banged on the door, hard. I shook, startled, and then I was still. It was quiet. The monster grew. I kept watching him. He didn't take over. There was a gap. I was able to see the monster. I could see just what Iftah was talking about.

I heard Iftah leave the room. He came back, running, threw himself against the door, rattling the knob, pounding.

Again and again and again. He screamed. Kicked the door. I sat there and stared at the monster, and Iftah was right. Each time he pounced, the monster grew bigger, but never as big as before. Whenever I jumped or startled, I turned up the volume on *watching*, and each time I did this, the fear got smaller, always much smaller than the time before. Until it was just really hot in that closet, and extremely boring.

I came out of the closet. "I am cured," I said. "You must go home to Galit." I was automatically picking up his accent, his cadence.

"I see this. No Valium needed." He threw his hands over his head. He shook my hand. He was so handsome and happy. It was the weirdest evening. I wanted Dave to see it. I should have called him back.

In the morning, in a new building, in a different room, I sailed through the test; I wasn't scared at all. Galit would e-mail me the results by the end of the week, but clearly, she told me, I was profoundly face-blind. In the fusiform face area, there was not even a flicker.

She said, "You were very calm. Very different from yesterday."

I was not the same as yesterday. I was different.

Flying home, I tried to conjure fear. I wanted to practice my monster technique. But I was not afraid of flying, and my ten-thousand-year-old baby brain had no trouble floating above the clouds. We had three seats all to ourselves, me and my brain.

Dave said he'd tried marriage four times now and he was done trying to change. This was the problem with me and Dave: all I wanted to do was change.

4

One

"Take a stand," Helder said in every session. "Take a position, stake a claim." I didn't need to feel good and calm about it. I needed to override the old system: I could count on it feeling wrong. Getting past the feeling state—that was our work. "State a belief and end the sentence with a period, not a question mark." Face blindness, he felt, had so secured me to uncertainty that to believe my own point of view was a challenge.

"How?" I kept saying. "How?"

Helder wanted me to see the divorce through. It was hurtful to Dave to lead him on. I didn't want to get divorced, because getting a divorce is painful and sad and ugly and consuming and flat-bottomed and heavy, as failure mixed with confusion always is. Although I had filed for divorce in March—almost two years to the day since Dave and I had married—the court date was so far off, it wasn't real. I had kept my distance from Dave since the end of April, though, after I came back from Boston. I knew if I didn't we would hug and feel terrible about everything all over again and want to not hurt each other. We'd go out to dinner and talk and talk and forget why it had been so hard, that it had been hard at all. I knew I wasn't ever going to fully understand my relationship with Dave. He was my family. It was like divorcing my arm.

I pretended I *had* to. I pretended Helder was making me. I'd been someone else when I married Dave; none of this seemed fair to him. But on July 11, I would, on my own, make it official.

We could always get back together again later, I told myself.

* * *

Wednesday mornings were divorce days in the Ottawa county courthouse. Wednesday, July 11, was the hottest, steamiest, stickiest day of the year so far. I put on a pink Zoë bra, my best bra, and a white linen skirt and suit jacket that I'd originally bought for a job interview. Dave had helped me pick them out. I hadn't slept at all. I kept going over my list of why we had to get a divorce. Every minute, I resisted the urge to call Dave and say, *Don't let me do this* and *I am so sorry.* What if I didn't show up for the hearing? Could I still get divorced later? Would it count against me?

Dave was not contesting. With respect to the divorce, he was in default, which sounded drastic but simply meant he wasn't fooling with the paperwork. He was Bartleby-ing this one: he preferred not to be divorced. Dave did not want to separate, he did not want to buy a house, he did not want to fight, he did not want to discuss how much or exactly why he was drinking;

he did not want to have home-cooked dinners together. But he wasn't fighting it. There was nothing to argue over, no children between us, no houses, no boat, no car, not even a stereo or a weed eater. There were the dishes Junior bought me for Mother's Day, but no one knew where those were anymore. We'd never lived together. *Pseudo-relational,* Helder had called it. A sham marriage, Junior had called it. I wanted to think of it as a good first draft. I had made a mistake in knowing who I was. I had a long way to go, still, in recognizing myself, and I felt selfish that I hadn't known more when I'd married Dave.

We'd had our last fight a couple weeks after I'd come back from Harvard with my diagnosis. With the boys' support and a flurry of e-mails to their girlfriends, I had planned a night at my house with David Junior and Jacob—pizza, Dr Pepper, and Trivial Pursuit on my porch. Dave would come too. Dave agreed to all of it. Peter Helder said it was a great idea to stay connected to the boys. But not the Dave part. "You're separated. You aren't married. You have to stop pretending." Helder used the word "fantasy" a lot, and I countered him: I'm divorcing Dave, but I'm not ending the relationship. This is my *family.* I can't have *no people at all.*

I cleaned the house that morning and thought about how much fun it was to know teenagers, to have them *want* to come to my house. Last time we'd gotten together, Jacob's girlfriend, Courtney, had given me a pair of nearly new leopard-patterned stilettos that didn't fit her quite right. "You are the only adult woman I know who can give these a good home," she'd said.

Dave called at noon. Jacob couldn't come, he told me. He was at a friend's house and they'd gotten involved in some project—cutting down trees or something—and he wasn't going to be done in time.

"But he has a previous commitment," I said. "We've had this planned for so long."

Dave took a long pause.

I told myself: *Stop, breathe. Call him back. Wait.* "Fuck this," I said. "No. Why doesn't he have to come?"

"Sweetheart," Dave said in a wide-open way. He never, ever cussed. "We can postpone. We postponed before when you had to. I've never once told the boys they had to be somewhere and I am not going to start doing so now. I can assure you. This isn't that big of a deal." His voice was very even and very hard, and he spoke so slowly it made me want to do drugs.

Late that night, I carted the untouched liters of Coke down to the apartment. I'd had a couple of glasses of wine, half a bottle—too much for me. David Junior and Jacob weren't home. I found Dave sitting on the floor in his closet, sorting coins, a tumbler of wine balanced on the safe before him. He collected gold. He knew the price of silver daily. He kept guns. I pointed to these things.

"Don't," he said.

I was not good at the Libertarian thing, I said. I sat down on his bed and explained in great detail exactly why his program worked great for a group of individuals but not for anyone trying to be a family, a collective. He called me a communist and I said I was proud to be a communist, red was my favorite color not by accident but by design. We were being ridiculous, but since we were angry, it wasn't funny, it seemed almost realistic. He called NPR a radical organization and a security threat.

He brought up *Good Night and Good Luck* again—a movie he'd walked out of. I said hurtful things about the Drudge Report, the boys' eating habits. He pointed out that I was the one who was sick all the time; they were fine. Maybe I should consider Doritos instead of organic arugula. He mispronounced "arugula" and I corrected him, in a bitchy, marmy way.

He said he was just minding his own business, minding his own business. Why did I make him out to be a monster? His face turned a color I hadn't ever seen before: storm. He stood up from his safe, a maw filled with stuff I didn't understand and didn't want him to keep in a safe. He had lumps of gold in his palm. He took off his wedding ring. He shook it around in his other palm. He had a habit of doing this whenever he ate nuts. I watched the ring rattling back and forth in his palm.

"You took a vow, Heather," he said. "A vow. For faster or slower. For better or worse. You're really going to cut and run?" He had tears in his eyes. He wavered in the doorway. "Throw this away? I'm tired of trying to convince you I'm a good person. I don't need all this constant aggravation." He said *constant aggravation* the way Fred said it—the way he said it to me, to my mother.

"You know what?" I said. It wasn't me talking, but I was going with it. "Fuck it," I said. And I sauntered out, swiping a pile of neatly ironed and folded T-shirts off the edge of the bed as I left.

That night, I took off my ring and put it in a tiny heart-shaped box on my bedside table. I imagined Dave's wedding ring, engraved with my secret name for him, in a bowl with those gold lumps, deep in the heart of his safe: what he loved and needed most, locked up by fear.

I'd altered my daily route. Of course, I couldn't help but see him everywhere. Face blindness was a problem. But so was life.

I stated my name, my address.

"This is being recorded," the judge said. "Please speak up."

I said it again. This time I pretended I was on *Law & Order*. I sold it. I leaned into the mic and answered the questions, trying not to wiggle. I didn't enjoy getting divorced. But I had trouble resisting performance. What with the podium, the microphone, the good lighting, an audience corralled behind the tiny wooden gate, I felt like I was at a reading. I felt like an officer of the court. I felt like a lawyer. I felt strong and beautiful and unkind.

The judge's robe was wrinkled and sticky looking. He stared at my folder. He looked very judgmental.

"Property divided?" he says.

"No property to divide, Your Honor," I said. I licked the inside of my cheek. "We never lived together after we were married." I wanted to add how we'd tried. I wanted to produce my notebook of house information sheets: Exhibit A! I wanted credit for organization. For trying.

There was a long pause while he sifted through the paperwork.

I said, "Does the court have further questions?" I felt like I was on television.

The judge didn't answer. He grinned. He stamped my forms. "I wish my whole day could be this easy," he said. He smacked my folder. It was done. Getting divorced had taken less than two minutes.

As I walked up the aisle to get the papers I'd have to take upstairs for stamping and filing, I said, "May I approach?" I couldn't resist. I said it mostly to myself.

Outside, on the courthouse steps, in the hot morning sun, I wondered: *Now what?* I was divorced. I didn't have a plan for the rest of the day. Seagulls were screaming. A police officer was writing a parking ticket near my car. I was divorced.

"You rocked," a woman said. She was sitting on the wide white courthouse steps, smoking a cigarette. "You should be a lawyer," she said. Her friend in a red sweater said, "You were so great, you were so awesome, it was all, like, *Go, girl.*" She was smoking too.

"Man, I *wish* you were my lawyer," the first one said.

I wanted to hug them. I said thank you. I said, "I wish I was too." I breathed in their smoke. It helped.

In my bright orange truck, I blasted Tom Petty. I took off my jacket. I flew down Lakeshore Drive in the fabulous pink Zoë bra and my beautiful white linen skirt. My folder of divorcedness and my jacket wilted on the seat beside me. Like things that had expired. Things someone just got out of.

I drove around for hours, singing hard. Not happy, just getting it all out.

Thursday I was divorced and Friday I was divorced. All summer I was divorced. Dave and I didn't speak. I didn't see the boys. It wasn't like being single. It was like having been somewhere. The only thing I liked about it: I had been married. I had officially known someone. I had been legally known by someone and normal and real for a while.

Nothing else about it was relaxing at all.

Two

When I called my mother to tell her about the divorce, she said, "Oh, that's okay, honey." She said it as though I'd told her I had gotten my hair straightened: *That's okay, honey, curly just didn't work with your features!* "You really took on *a lot* with those boys! And they were getting into the mail. That made me very, very nervous. You might or might not have noticed I stopped writing to you. I felt I had to discontinue when I realized those boys were reading your mail. I know that hurt you."

My father said two words: "Goddamn him." He sounded very sad; I thought I heard him crying.

"No, no," I told him. "It's not Dave's fault. Dave's a good guy."

"Then what's the problem?"

"It's complex."

"Complex," he said. A coughing attack ensued. "Bullshit." He announced that he was marrying his housekeeper, Lola, a woman who spoke no English.

"No," I told him. "This is not a good idea."

I called back later that day. I spoke to Lola in my terrible basic Spanish. She sounded young and afraid. "It is for convenience," she said in Spanish. She said she meant to take good care of my father. "I believe you," I said, and I wanted to help, but this was illegal and a bad idea. "You two can't marry," I said. "Fred must move up here, by me. He has to move to Michigan."

I had filled out application forms for Appledorn, a retirement center a mile from my house. I had toured the facility. There were two vacant rooms, adjoining. It seemed perfect to me. A woman in my running group had her mother here; she visited three days a week, brought toothpaste, orchestrated hair appointments. It seemed possible, even fun.

Helder was horrified by my plan. Bringing Orlando to Michigan was, in his opinion, an awful backward slide. But to me, it seemed as if it would be less distracting to have my parents corralled, close by, cared for; to me, it seemed a way to get things under control.

Appledorn's paperwork was explicit: they did not accept anyone with mental illness. For several nights I tossed and turned, trying to imagine what would happen to my parents if they couldn't get into a decent, normal nursing home. Finally, I signed in the little box affirming that my parents didn't suffer from mental illness. Surely there would be doctors involved at some point; surely I could pretend not to know their conditions. Age and dementia were masking the craziest parts of these two people. True, it was difficult to imagine my father, with his ponytail and panty hose, among the stolid, ancient Dutch farmers. Nor could I see my mother dealing with strangers coming in and out of her room, dispensing medications, and preparing food for her in a large, hidden kitchen. It would be a torture worse than death for her. But these were things I did not need to think about. Somehow, it would all work out.

When I called my mother to talk about the details one Saturday afternoon, she didn't know who I was. "I don't think I can help you," she said. "I feel terrible. I feel like I wish I could. So very badly. But I can't. Thank you for calling!"

Helder said, *Fantasy, fantasy.* Be careful, he said. Having them here could easily derail normal life. He was concerned about my focus, my avoidance of dealing with my face blindness. "You have some momentum. A giant forward step. This is a real engagement with life, and you have to tell people now, 'I'm face-blind.'" He vultured all over the room, flapping his wings. "There's no drama here. There's no crisis in face blindness. It's just a plain, simple, clear thing. Would you please tell people?"

"I don't see it happening," I said. I wanted credit for the divorce. I wanted pity. Had I not done enough?

The way I'd lived with Dave—not "*with* with" him—was too close to the way I'd lived as a child, Helder preached. "You're a very relational person, and we are meant to be relational. In divorcing Dave, you've come out of hiding. You've come into a fuller sense of who you are. Now you have to come out as face-blind," he said. "It's way past time. Tell people. Lean into relationship." He leaned in his chair. "It's not a big deal." He grinned and opened his palms. "Easy! Just tell! Tell your bike group!"

"Aren't you supposed to not give advice?" I crossed my arms. "You're really very pushy and bossy and directive. It's not effective." I was frowning.

He laughed. He said yes, he was pushing. Absolutely.

My whole life, my mother and father had pushed the theory that *something mental* was wrong with me: *Heather is emotionally troubled, she needs help.* No one in my family was uncertain. I was the only one. I hadn't fit into my family. But like them, I had a thing that made me separate from the world. I blended into my family enough to survive; I had dual citizenship. Face blindness was both passport and extradition.

Helder said: Let the story go. Let the story go. Don't try to make a story out of it.

I knew what he meant. We explain ourselves to ourselves, and it's never accurate, it's often unhelpful, and the self-story becomes obsolete, but we cling to it. Okay, I said, so I let the story go. Done. But I didn't know how to explain it. Without a story, who was I?

He laughed and pulled back, wide-eyed. "You don't need a story. And yes, you do know how to explain it. You've been explaining it to me in no uncertain terms for almost a year! It's the faking—all the work you have to do to try to figure this out, every second of every day—that is what distances people. That is where the problem is. Let people in."

"No," I said.

"You said to push you. You said that."

Andrea was always late. I was always early: I relied on being found, so as not to have to struggle with and fail at finding. The intimate restaurant was crowded and I sat at a table with my back to the wall so I could see the whole of the restaurant, monitor each person who came in. I studied the menu of spaghettis and sandwiches. I had once considered Andrea Reesman my best friend and closest colleague. When I'd first come to the college, we had kickboxed and shopped together. Both single, we'd gone to art openings every Friday night, and on the weekends, often we'd take the train to Chicago, treat ourselves to art and restaurants and triathlons, where she often placed in her age group. But in Holland, I would find myself in long conversations with a tall, handsome woman—downtown, at the grocery store, at the mall—completely unsure of who it was I was talking to until she said the name of one of her faculty or cats, or cocked her head a certain way: Andrea. Over the past couple of years, we had drifted apart. We hadn't had lunch in almost a year.

Now in her late fifties, Andrea had recently become the college's head of business management, and she'd ditched her northern California flax jumpers and loose linen shifts and Birkenstocks, cut her long black hair super-short. Today, I was on the lookout for an elegant woman in a boxy suit, a matching purse and pumps, and perfect hair in a pouf—a kind of dressy raven. I checked each person who entered to see if she looked at me, if she was headed toward my table. And then a woman flung herself into the chair opposite me.

"So sorry I'm late! The hideous meeting refused to end." She strung her big pink purse on the empty chair across from me and took up her menu. She whispered huskily, leaning across the table. "The man in charge of this committee I'm on is a stupid, stupid man. The president and the provost are right there in the meetings and he just gets away with it!" She picked up the menu and said, "Can we drink at eleven-thirty in the morning, do you think? If I order wine, will we get fired?" She grinned, sweet and wicked—Andrea all over—and I could see she was fighting back tears. She worked very hard for the school. She and the committee head, the man who was driving her nuts, were both up for promotion to vice president. Only one of them would be chosen. She recounted in great detail all her frustrations with him, with the school politics. It was fascinating. She could see all the players and the issues with a clarity I could never muster. At meetings, on committees, I never even knew exactly who was who—or, it seemed, what was what.

As Andrea talked on, I waited for an opening to say, "I'm divorced—and there is more." *There've been times we have talked and I haven't known who you were until you mentioned your cats or our plans. There've been times I think you waved to me, but I'm not sure—there are so many people who look like you. I don't want you to think I'm rude. Our friendship is so important to me. I wonder if I have walked past you and not greeted you. I have a condition, face blindness. It's the reason you called me aloof, why we aren't as close as we once were. Sometimes I know who you are. Sometimes I do not. I probably come off as defensive, distracted, strange. This is what I'm dealing with: prosopagnosia.*

Behind her, a waitress seated a group of men, then came over to us. She said, "Hi, Heather." She wasn't wearing a name tag.

Andrea ordered coffee.

I ordered tea.

Andrea talked for most of the lunch. "He is so stupid!" she concluded when we were done eating. "He's a short-sighted, entitled, ridiculously petty, incredibly wealthy man." She laughed. "Okay. I'm done. High road. How are *you*?" She checked her watch and squawked. "Heather. I have talked the entire time. We didn't get to you!" She thanked me for listening and held her arms up, staring around the room and making the little hand motions for signing a bill. "Do you see our person?" she said.

I looked around. A waitress scooted past, loaded down with a tray of lunches. I didn't know if she was our server or a different one. They all wore white shirts and black skirts and little green aprons. I turned back and looked at Andrea. I visualized Helder on the couch. Don't apologize, he'd said. You aren't sorry you have it. There's nothing to be sorry for. Just explain. Tell the facts. No drama. *I have a rare neurological disorder.*

On the sound system, Frank Sinatra was singing "My Way." Andrea turned all the way around, searching for our server; she had a one-o'clock meeting. Then she turned back around, in slow motion. Her mouth was agape. Her face was expressing surprise and dismay. She was using more than her face. She held her enormous purse tight to her chest. She leaned low over the table, shrinking down into her chair at the same time. Then she put her face on the white tablecloth, where her plate had been. She let out a small squeak of pain. "Why didn't you tell me? Why didn't you tell me? He's sitting right behind me, with the president and the provost and your dean! He's right there," she whispered, hoarse. "Heather!"

I looked at the men at the table behind Andrea. I'd seen them come in, the quad of men, and I'd noticed them eating. Men in suits, clean, prosperous, powerful men, each with short gray hair, crisp white shirt, tie and jacket. Men in uniform. Men I'd never seen before in my life.

I was speechless. I looked at the top of Andrea's head. I wished she'd lift it off the table. "Do we work with them?" I said gingerly. Maybe Andrea was wrong. Surely these weren't those men. Normal people occasionally mistook people; this happened all the time. Perhaps it was happening now.

"Why didn't you say anything?"

Frank Sinatra finished his song, holding out that last syllable for what seemed like a week: *wayyyyyyyy.*

The moment for telling had passed.

I waited a few days before trying again. I decided to take the safe route of the telephone. No actual faces, no not-recognizing debacles, no horrific face-blind implosion while I was trying to broach the topic. I called an old friend from college, Bland Lawson. He'd helped me write my papers for Brit Lit, had a party for me when I got fired from the law office, taught me to dance the two-step and the waltz. He played a concertina.

He was unmarried, wore straw hats, dressed in seersucker, and lived in Myrtle Beach with his mother. Bland was the perfect person on whom to practice weird shit.

"Hello?" he said. His southern accent undid me. I heard ice tinkling. Bland drank mint juleps for real. He ironed his seersucker suits with starch.

"Hey, Pinky," he said, wide as the sky.

"I'm face-blind," I said. "Prosopagnosic. Greek. *Prosop-* is for 'face,' *-agnosic* is like 'agnostic.' I'm a face doubter. I can't see human faces. I doubt them." I heard his ice cubes shift, fall. "It's like golden retrievers. Would you be able to pick out your own dog from a lineup of twenty other golden retrievers? No," I said quickly. "You would not."

"What?" Bland Lawson said. It was a word he wrung three syllables out of. "You are calling to tell me you can't find your dog? Or you can't find my dog." Bland enjoyed being deliberately obtuse.

"Prosopagnosia?" I said. I hadn't talked to Bland in over a year. "It's Greek?"

Long pause. I could see a couple of ways my delivery might be adjusted.

"I can't pick up my step-kids at school. Honestly. I can't find the boys when they're with a group of kids dressed similarly. You can read about it online. I also got divorced from Dave, but I am really just calling to practice telling you I can't recognize people by face."

There was another even longer pause, filled with another sip.

"Thoughts?" I said. "Reactions, questions?"

"No," Bland said. "You don't have that. I'm a hypochondriac. And I have never heard of it."

I'd liked telling Bland. It hadn't gone well but it hadn't been disastrous, like the Andrea lunch, which made me redden with shame whenever I thought about it. I wanted to tell, and have the person *know*, really know. I wanted to be believed.

I called a practical, sturdy acquaintance, a professor of photography who taught at a nearby college and had a hearing-impaired husband. She was perfect, I thought: she would have a response, she would share it, and she would enjoy talking about vision and perception; she'd be sensitive to disorder because of her husband.

We met for coffee. She found me at a table in the back.

"Hi, Teresa," I said. "Ready? I'm jumping in with this thing."

She leaned forward and laughed. "This seems big."

"I got divorced. But that's not why I asked you to come out. I have a rare neurological condition that makes it hard for me to recognize people, including you. It would be helpful to me if you could tell me who you are when we run into each other."

She burst out laughing. She sipped her coffee. She laughed some more. "You think you have everything, Heather!" she shouted. Because of her husband, she always talked full volume. "You are making this up!" She laughed and laughed. Then she got serious and said in a challenging tone, "How did you recognize me now?"

I took a sip of my coffee. I debated. What would Helder do? Think. Should I tell Teresa that her super-loud voice, her distinctive choppy hair, her distinctive body outline, and her North Carolina–Cuban accent distinguished her in West Michigan, made her easy as a billboard for me? That this ease of recognition was probably partly why I was always so happy to "see" her?

"I knew we were meeting, Teresa," I said, speaking slowly in my new Teaching Prosopagnosia voice. "You came and sat with me. I'm not stupid. It's a very specific impairment, it's just the face." I drew a circle around my face with my fingertips. "Actually just the interior features, nose, cheeks, eyes, lips, et cetera."

An aghast frown came over her face and took over her whole body. "Heather Laurie Sellers!" she shouted. "You recognize people, Heather. I mean, you just do. I've seen you do that a million times. I don't think you have this. This is so silly. Have you been on the Internet? I want to hear about the divorce. I told you that you shouldn't have married that man. Did I not? Do you remember? My husband and I both told you to your face: *You are making a huge mistake.* When did all this happen? You never tell anyone anything."

I told her I was working on that.

"You just wanted those kids. You just wanted to be a mother."

I knew, for certain, so few things and one of them was this: my love for those boys was *not* a bad thing. So I said so.

There was an awkward pause.

"Usually, Teresa," I said, "I'm working so hard to figure out who the fuck I'm talking to and what's happening next, I don't take a stand. I don't say anything at all."

There was another long silence. She finished her latte. I'd never seen her so quiet. She stood to go. She said, her voice suddenly soft, "I don't feel like we're really connecting, Heather. You've changed." She said it as an accusation; she sounded disappointed.

I took it as high, high praise. *Yes,* I wanted to say. *I have changed. I have moved closer to the person I meant to be. Sometimes, like now, I can almost even see her face!*

We hugged, but our hearts weren't in it. Tea spilled on my purse, and my purse got my pants all wet.

Telling turned out to be exactly like going off the high dive. The first time was hell. And then, soon, I was running for the ladder, scrambling up, eager to fling myself off, wondering what kind of special spin I could include, how I could make the telling, the falling, more beautiful, more fun, more creative, more interesting and effective.

It wasn't anything like how I thought it would be. I thought people would ask me questions about the disorder, my childhood, my mother, my family, how long I had it. I thought they would say, *Did your parents try to help you?* And that I would dissolve into tears or, worse, weirdness in the midst of the questioning. But no one asked anything at all. The disorder itself was such a tricky thing to understand, it stopped people short.

I called my colleague Lorna, a professor in the psychology

department. We ran together a few times a week. I was eager to tell Lorna about my condition because she was a new friend and I didn't want things to go awry. Already there'd been incidents. On campus, more than once, I'd mistaken her for someone I didn't know. Recently she'd invited me to come swim and dine with her family at their house. When I got out of the pool, I went inside to change. Walking to the bathroom, I ran into a strange little man with his head wrapped in a towel. I screamed. It was Lorna, coming in from the pool.

I wanted to be closer to her. I didn't want to lose her as I had lost Andrea.

We met for a run on a wide empty road that circled a windmill, passing sheep, ponies, tulip fields. It was early; the sun was still coming up. Lorna was talking about her marriage and how strong she felt with Bruce, her husband, whom she had met and married when they were teenagers. I thought this was as good an opening as I was going to get.

I asked Lorna if we could do a few more laps. I had a couple of important things to tell her. She said of course. I told her about divorcing Dave. She said she was very, very sorry. How was I doing? Actually, pretty well, I said. But there was more. I needed one more lap to get up my courage. "Can we run one without talking? I have to tell you something that is so hard for me to talk about."

"Of course," she said. "Absolutely." And we ran, and I listened to our breath and the sound of our running shoes on the road, and the cadence calmed me down.

We eased into a walk. I said, "I have a condition that's hard for me to talk about, but I have to tell people. It's very strange and unheard-of. I am getting ready to tell the whole campus community about it. Before the semester is officially underway, I am sending a mass e-mail. Lorna, this is a very weird thing, but I actually can't recognize people reliably," I said. "Sometimes when we run into each other, it takes me a few moments to figure out who you are. I am afraid sometimes I may not know at all."

"Prosopagnosia?" she said.

I stopped short. I grabbed her shoulders. "You know about it?"

"I was just teaching this to my class last week!" she said. "The students were fascinated. You will have to come to class."

"You *teach* this?"

"It's on the test! It's in the book! Of course!"

The sky changed from gray-blue to peach melba, streaks of vivid raspberry, and the air was warm and smooth, as though it had been well cared for all night. We ran and ran and ran and ran, and then we walked, still talking. Lorna knew all about face blindness. She said another colleague in Psychology was doing research on it and would want to know all about my experiences at Harvard. I told her how hard it had been, telling people. Lorna said I would find myself repeating the explanation many times. Telling people once would never be enough. Remember how long it had taken *me* to understand it?

"Yes," I said. "My whole life."

"Telling is a process," she said. "You'll always be teaching people, Heather. Thankfully, that is something you are really good at."

Lorna said there were two kinds of prosopagnosics: those

who compensated by being friendly to everyone, and those who retreated, hunkered down, avoided interactions. I was, seemingly, both types in one, a super-friendly super-avoider. But people saw me as bubbly and confident and friendly, and it was going to be hard for them to accept this truth about me. I had covered it up so well for so long. I should be prepared for them to be surprised and confused and dubious. "It's difficult for people to believe you won't know *them.* They'll think you know *them* because they want to know they are important to you. It will be very hard for some to believe, because it runs so counter to their perceptual experience, but also their experience of *you.*"

We hugged, at the edge of the river, by the old windmill. I knew now I'd tell everyone. I'd tell them over and over for the rest of my life. And the telling would get better and better. Above our heads, while we hugged and hugged, a great blue heron flew like a slow arrow in the sky. I pretended it was the vulture: a blessing, welcome, welcome. Welcome to the visible world.

Three

"Lay it on me, Heather," the vice president of my college said. He was one of the important men I hadn't recognized at the Andrea lunch. He was steely in a friendly way, with perfect silver hair, gleaming skin, a suit so black it was blue. I liked him a lot. He was a cyclist and handsome and fair and effective, well-spoken at meetings, piercing the bullshit like a needle. I needed his okay in order to send, the next day, the day before classes, the e-mail I'd written, announcing my face blindness to the whole school.

I pressed my hands on the notebook where I'd outlined my speech. I looked at my notes. Then I looked him in the eye. "I can't recognize people by face. I need to tell everyone so they can help me by introducing—"

"Oh, I have that too," he said. "I'm terrible with names. You aren't alone. Boy, do I have that."

"Well," I said.

He looked at me kindly, nodding.

"This is different." I explained *prosopagnosia.* I taught him how to pronounce it. I told him about the difference between vision and recognition, the stages of apprehending a face. I told him how majestic it was that most people *could* do this. I emphasized that it wasn't about names at all. I explained how name retrieval came *after* recognition and identification in the complex sequence associated with simply saying "Hey" to someone. Remembering someone's name was really hard for everyone to do because names are abstract concepts, not visual images, not physical, like a face.

"Dr. Smith," I said. "I recognize people all the time. But the disorder makes it difficult for me to *reliably* recognize people. It's been hard on my social life. It's a factor in the classroom. You may have noticed I've avoided sporting events, graduation, commencement, the pre-college conference—and anything where people are in uniform. I avoid small groups of familiar people. The entire committee structure of the college is, for me, a nightmare. I need people to know about this," I said. I sounded so calm and clear. "I need their help."

The vice president slowly wrote the word *prosopagnosia* on his fresh yellow legal pad. He was quiet for a moment. Then he told me a long story about his son and his son's learning disabilities. At first I didn't understand. Then I realized, as he recounted the years of testing, the behavior problems, the family's struggles, that the vice president wanted to show he was with me, next to me. He was providing a matching story.

The sun poured into the spacious wood-paneled office and I felt strong and empty and grown up. I almost *fit.* I couldn't even imagine anymore how I'd ever been convinced I was mentally ill. The girl who'd thought that, the girl who tried so hard to please her parents, to fit with them, was faded, a specter.

And then he asked me, as if he'd read my mind, "What did your parents do about this when you were a kid? What did they try?" I could feel him speaking as a kind and good parent.

I smiled. I said, "Here is what I'd like to share." I handed him the e-mail I'd drafted. He read it. He didn't ask me any more about my parents. I wasn't hiding them. I wasn't ashamed of them. They simply weren't relevant to this action I was taking.

He asked me some more questions about my condition and what I'd learned from my research. I'd never felt more clear about prosopagnosia or who I was—and wasn't—in relation to it. I felt like I was describing my arm, why it looked the way it looked. I smiled and I heard my teacher voice, pleasant, calm, a little loud, but in a good way, festive. Until you can explain a thing clearly to someone else, you don't really know it, I was always telling my students. I said, "I just want people to know about it. When I pass them without saying hello, not to take it personally. To feel free to say who they are. My working relationships are so important to me." Smooth, I thought. Team-player-ish.

"By all means," he said, rising from his chair. He swept the e-mail across the table toward me. "Send!"

I walked across campus. I could see myself, friendly and tall, long dark hair, sandals: a new student would see me and think,

She looks like a nice professor. In the August heat, students were unpacking tubs and duffel bags from vans while grumpy fathers frowned at flustered mothers and younger siblings sat on the grass, bored.

Up in my office, I turned on my computer. I assembled recipients from my address book and then copied my e-mail. I took a breath and hit *Send.*

It felt like dropping myself off in a new place, all alone. Who would I be now? Who would I become? I wanted to take the message back. What had I done? *People will think I am nuts. They'll think I'm making this up.* My hands and feet were pouring sweat. We know you're alive, I heard Helder whispering. I wiped my palms on my blouse.

I turned off my computer as though that would quiet things down, stop the sending. I took the elevator downstairs and went out the back doors of Lubbers Hall. "That's not it. That's not it. That's not it," a girl said. There on the sidewalk, backs to each other, each with her arms firmly crossed, stood a mom and her daughter. I walked up to them and said, "Can I help you find something?"

The mother said yes and the girl said no, but she held out her orientation folder. "We're, like, totally confused." She was nearly in tears. She could tell me, a stranger, anything. She could not, in these hours of leaving home for good, look to her mother.

"My daughter is Sarah VanderVeen, and we just learned there's another Sarah VanderVeen here. Do you think there's going to be confusion? We're looking for the dining hall. Phelps? Felts? How do you even say that word?"

"We don't have the dinner coupons," Sarah VanderVeen said. "Mom."

I looked at the mom. She was trying so hard. I looked at the daughter, one of the Sarah VanderVeens. Yes. There would be confusion. There would always be so much confusion. Many, many things would go wrong.

"I know where you're going," I said. "It's Phelps. And it's on my way."

I felt the mom breathing out, wanting to talk to me. She looked so kind and normal. I bet she was from Illinois or Indiana, lived on a farm, quilted, helped with 4-H, belonged to a book club. But she held back, and her daughter, Sarah VanderVeen, walked next to me. I looked at her little printed schedule of classes and her dorm assignment. "Girls love Dykstra," I said, though I heard mostly the opposite. "And you have great classes, you've gotten so lucky. Gibbs is an outstanding history teacher. You'll love her."

"Sarah loves history!" the mom said. Then she covered her mouth; I could feel her doing it, like I had eyes in the back of my head.

Sarah shuddered.

I told her how perfect it would all turn out.

"I wish she could have you as her teacher," the mom said.

It wasn't until later that evening that I realized I would not recognize that Sarah VanderVeen if she came to my office or if I saw her again on campus. I was still getting used to not-faking. I was still getting used to me as I really was, as I had been all along.

A couple months later, Brad Duchaine called me from Harvard. He wanted to know if I would be willing to explain my condition on television, if I would be willing to appear on the *Today* show. The very next day.

I said, "Let me call you right back." I called Helder, and he laughed and laughed and laughed. "Now you are telling the world. I love it. And it's very efficient!" He asked me: Did I want to do this? Did I see a downside? I would miss a day of work. That was a downside. But I knew that if I'd seen a show on face blindness when I was younger, my life could have been much easier, much sooner. "I think I can explain this really well, and I don't think many people can. I think there are a lot more people who have this disorder than we know. I have to do this."

A couple of hours later, a producer was sitting in my living room, out of range of the camera. Standing by my bookcase was a very cute sound guy—Chuck Taylors, messy buzz cut, thick lips—with a box of dials strapped to the front of his body. "We're good to go," he said.

The producer, Nancy, said to talk like we were girlfriends just having a chat. Giant lights and a silver umbrella made me squint. My eyes watered. My hands were sweating.

Nancy leaned forward, smiled. "This had to be hard on your husband. You couldn't recognize him. You got divorced."

All my furniture was moved against the walls and a giant

silver-white screen was behind me. I was dizzy; this all felt *pretend,* when the very point was to *stop pretending.* I was angry at her for turning questions into statements, for making Dave look bad.

Helder had said to enjoy myself and to talk slowly. I took a deep breath. I talked slowly. Dave-slow. "That would make a good story, but no. Dave was really great about the face blindness. He helped a lot."

Nancy got back on her cell phone.

The windowless production van was parked outside. Through my windows, I spied neighbors on the sidewalk, talking and pointing at the van.

Nancy set the phone on the floor between us again so her producer in New York could hear everything. "But surely it was part of it. You went up to the wrong man? That had to be really hard on . . . your husband." She looked at her notes. "Dave. David. Dave? David?"

I explained that this was exactly what was so hard about the disorder. I never knew when I'd recognize someone and when I wouldn't. It was much more complicated and much more confusing than that.

"On the phone you said you thought you were mentally ill."

"Yes."

"Talk about that. Just chatting, like we are just girlfriends, chatting. Terrifying. It must have been terrifying."

"Well," I said, "I knew something was wrong. I walked past my closest friends and they'd come up to me and I wouldn't know right away who was who. I had long conversations with people who clearly knew me very well, and I had no idea who

I was talking to. Then I made a vow: no more faking. That's when I 'came out.'"

"Recently, I take it."

"Now," I said. "I'm in the process."

When she asked me about my parents, how they had handled my confusion as a child, I said the line I'd gotten from Helder that morning. "That would be a whole other episode." I smiled. I said no more.

She waited for me to say more. I could hear the equipment humming. I looked into the camera. I could see my face in the glass on the lens. I smiled at myself. I smiled at America.

After a long, awkward silence and another brief conference on the cell phone, the producer said, "She won't talk about it. She won't say."

The producer put the phone back down on the floor. She didn't sound so "girlfriends" anymore. She sounded like she was trying to sound like Diane Sawyer. "There's no cure for what you have. You were probably born this way. If researchers came up with a cure—surgery, training, a pill—would you do it?"

"No," I said quickly. "I wouldn't ever change my brain."

"Really," she said. She let her jaw go slack, her mouth hang. "You don't want to be cured." She said it like you'd say, *You don't want a brain.*

I speechified. I pretended I wasn't talking to television, to a camera, but to a convention of philosopher-therapists. Face blindness, in my mind, had saved my life. It was the means by which I learned to recognize myself. It was true that face blindness had isolated me from the world, been hard on friendships, made work difficult. But I loved face blindness now. I thought of it as great training for being a writer: I had to go over each person, again and again, paying attention to the tiny details that made them distinct. Face blindness might have been better training for writing than graduate school had been. Writing and face blindness required the same patience, the same commitment to slowness. They forced a similar kind of willingness to hang out in frustration and ambivalence. Failure rates were high in both camps. In both, writing and recognizing, one had to hang back, leave spaces for the truth to emerge in its own time. I had come to the point where I couldn't imagine my life without face blindness. It was how I knew how to know the world!

Nancy said, "Really. You wouldn't take a cure. You wouldn't want to know your husband's face, your own face?"

"I *do* know them," I said. I was calm and clear and not-sweaty. "I know them when I'm looking at them. I always have them with me. A face is just a label, a handle. I'm committing much more important parts of a person to memory. I'm not on the surface. I'm focused on *the essence of the person, the soul.*" This sounded lofty and I laughed and the cameraman said, "No, it's good." The soundman said, "Sincere. And fascinating." He adjusted his cool dials.

"You have no photographs displayed in this house," the camera guy said. He was burly and warm, dark hair, big and brilliant-looking.

The sound guy said, "She's face-blind, man. That's part of it. Right?"

I said I wasn't sure.

"Albums, snapshots, video—we need visual components." Nancy had the cell phone to her ear. "Are they upstairs? Where's your family? Where are your photographs?" she said to me. "Yes," she said into the phone in the same breath. "We're getting photos of the mother, the family, right now. Yup. Yup."

Nope, nope, I thought. You are not.

The cameraman said we were losing light. "We need high school yearbooks, family photos, definitely photos of your mother and father. Think visual! Do you have siblings?"

"There aren't any," I lied. "I don't have photographs." The past was rushing in. I had to lean hard against the door to my childhood to keep it from flooding in.

After another series of calls to New York, they filmed me typing my book—this book—at my dining room table. The camera guy took a vase of black-eyed Susans from my kitchen counter and set them by a pile of books they'd chosen from my bookcase. He loved the light streaming in through my dining room windows. It looked pathetic, the way they set it up, like a bad straight-to-DVD movie about a Struggling Writer. A jar of *pencils*!

They asked me to look thoughtful, stare out into space.

I can't do that, I said. I can't do this. I can't impersonate a writer. But I did it.

The producer rushed over to an antique mirror I had hanging by the door. The glass was old and wavy. "This is perfect! Come and check your lipstick, like you're on your way out."

I couldn't do that. I explained again: It's a perception problem, a processing problem, it's not *visual.* It was so important to get that right. Nothing ever looked wavy, I said. It was hard for us to remember noses, lips, eyes, but faces weren't altogether missing, or distorted. I reminded her about the new research: face recognition skill lay on a continuum. As many as one in fifty people—two percent of the world's population—were significantly impaired, unable to easily distinguish faces. People needed to understand the disorder for what it was or they'd never be able to know they had it.

"We will get it right," the producer said. She told me not to worry. "But let's just get you adjusting your hair, you know, like you're going out, looking in that mirror. One last little final check."

We got in my truck and drove around town. The producer instructed us to look for people I might know but would not be able to recognize. I kept telling her: I'm not going to know. And I recognize people all the time. If they are in a place I am expecting to see them, I'll know. But if they are out of context, or I haven't seen them in a few weeks, I may or may not. It's not a disorder you can rely on. And I'm not going to know when any of this is or isn't happening. It's unfilmable.

We parked behind the shoe store downtown. A man waved at me as we walked across the parking lot behind the shoe store. "Do you know him?" the producer said. "Jim, Jim, are you rolling?"

"I don't know," I said. I was quick trying to think, *Who could that be?*

"I think we just missed it!" she yelled at him. "We just missed it. It happened. We missed it. Okay, we need another one of those. Be ready, guys. Tell us when that's about to happen again, Heather, okay? We need you to communicate with us. We need your help here. You are the only one who knows."

I trotted along Main Street. I was the only one who *didn't* know, of course. But it didn't seem like they were going to get that.

Down Main Street, the cameraman walked backward out in front of me. There was a microphone hanging over my head on a boom: I felt like a little fish on the end of a line. I walked "naturally" in my purple dress. I pretended I was window-shopping. I checked out my butt in the plate glass of the Lokker Rutgers store. My butt was looking good.

No one came and said hi. No one asked, *Is this television?* Suddenly the sidewalks, which had been crowded with shoppers, were empty. The producer said, "Weren't there just a whole bunch of people walking down this street?"

The camera guy said, "We lost all our background. I've got no background."

The soundman said, "In New York we'd be fighting people off. This is really, really weird. Not one person has tried to get in the shot. It's like they're *avoiding it.*"

"It's the Midwest," I said. "They're going to give you privacy. They're being polite."

"Where would there be people—people who know you?" the producer said again. She was standing across from me with her arms crossed. Her entire career was founded on recognizing people and showing them to other people. She wasn't going to get prosopagnosia. Not today. It would be like me understanding calculus.

As we walked back to the truck, the cameraman said, "How do you know who I am?"

I couldn't tell if he was kidding or serious.

After they left, I called my mom. I told her, "Write this down: Tomorrow morning, seven twenty-five a.m., the *Today* show. I think it's on NBC. It might be ABC."

She was excited. She read it back. "National television! My beautiful daughter! I will be watching. You can count on that! I will be watching with all my ears and eyes! Oh, my beautiful daughter."

She didn't ask me why I would be on television.

Maybe she thought: *Of course my daughter will be on television.* Maybe it didn't matter why: it was her *daughter.* Or maybe this was triggering a fairly complicated paranoid response; television was one of her least favorite things in the world. Perhaps she had to keep a superbly narrow focus in order to muster and sustain the only appropriate reaction: excitement. If she asked for details, if it became too real, it would be too threatening. What if the topic of the program somehow led people to her? *I will protect you, Mom. I will always keep you safe.*

I called my father. I told him I was going to be on the *Today* show. He should watch, tomorrow morning. Did he want me to call him and remind him? No, he said. No, no, no, no, no.

Daddy, I said. I'm going to ask you a question.

"Wah?" he said. He sounded flat, and close to death, but he had sounded that way for twenty or thirty years. I got all choked up. I knew he wouldn't answer and I knew I would ask anyway. "What was the secret, the thing about Mom you won't tell me?"

He said this: "If you tell anyone, I will kill you. If you tell her I told you this, I will kill you." His voice was suddenly hard-edged and clear. I sat forward in my seat; I curled my big toes under my little ones. I froze.

"I wrote her papers." He was working hard to speak, forcing the words out, but they were all coming out. "In college. She wasn't passing any of her classes. For one, I paid the TA to change her grade to Pass. For another, I wrote all her papers. And she got her degree . . ." There was a long pause. Then he said: "She kept hitting me! And once I beat the shit out of her! But she got her *degree*." He hollered the word "degree." "She not know!" He sounded on the verge of tears.

This was the secret? I envisioned my mother, bound up with psychosis, flailing against my father, not able to read, concentrate, write, get through the day evenly. "I'll never tell," I said. "That was sure real nice of you. To help her."

"Bye," he said.

"I love you," I said. I didn't know if he heard. I liked it to be the last thing I always said.

I called Dave. I had to tell him the big secret. He was at work and he went out and stood on the balcony to talk to me. I heard the wind in his phone. "He's not a bad guy," he said. He joked about how funny it was for an educator to have academic fraud as a family secret. I told Dave about the *Today* show. He warned me not to be surprised or hurt if my parents forgot to watch it. I knew they'd watch it. This was the climax, this was the perfection of everything, this was my official entrance into the normal world. I knew they'd watch it.

I asked Dave if he'd mind waking the boys. I wanted them to see it, to understand face blindness, to know I wasn't crazy, like their mother.

He said he'd try. He planned to watch. He would be late for work in order to watch and he was there for me if I needed him, or anything at all.

Four

I dragged the dog up onto the couch with me, and clicked on the television. I wouldn't have recognized Matt Lauer without the helpful little label that popped up on the bottom of the screen occasionally. It would be so great if in real life the name of everyone could pop up, just when needed. "Face blindness—fascinating," he said. Then he said it again, exactly the same way. "Face blindness—fascinating." I went and got my tea.

There were commercials, and then, after a piece on Britney Spears, who had not yet lost custody of her children, Matt Lauer said it again, "Face blindness—fascinating!" and then, in the way of television narration, a series of nesting boxes, the story opened and unfolded and then there was Holland, Michigan, my little town, footage of Eighth Street, where I was walking down the street in my purple dress with my straw purse. *My arms are really long!* I thought. My gait was syncopated, horsey. Then there was a pretty-faced woman talking to someone; purple dress, huge hair, straw purse. Oh. It was me. There were some facts on face blindness. Sufferers couldn't recognize their own friends and family. While it could be caused by stroke, now researchers felt it also ran in families, and genes were involved. There was a graph, a chart, a person getting an MRI, sliding into the tube. I wondered if that was me. I thought of Iftah and the monster. The tiny ancient brain.

A family was interviewed. A face-blind man cried because he'd never seen his wife's face, and I thought people weren't going to get it, weren't going to understand. I thought of Lorna: it takes five times. This man who had the wife, he could see her face every day. Why was he saying that he couldn't see it? He couldn't remember it, but he could go look at her. I was on the edge of my seat. I was wiggling all over my couch and holding my dog and talking to him. *It's different from this. This isn't it!* I wanted to jump in and explain the parts they were misapprehending, the things they were telling wrong.

Then, at the end of the segment, as music played in the background and the hosts of the show explained where people could get more information, there I was on national television, fake-writing in my living room. This part of the piece came out exactly as I had feared: I didn't look like a real writer but more like a woman who owned way too many cats.

The voice told America, "And so, day by day, she struggles to make sense of her disorder. And her world."

After that a car commercial came on and I jumped around my living room. *Everyone knows!*

My phone rang. My mom was breathless. "You are probably being besieged with calls."

"You saw it!"

"So I won't keep you long. Oh, honey, you were fabulous. You are my beautiful brilliant daughter! So articulate! My goodness! You have lost weight too. You look so strong." Then she said she was more than willing to send me three thousand dollars in order to get braces so I could fix my poor crooked teeth. They were my only drawback, my only detrimental feature.

I paused. I sat down. The bubble burst. I said she didn't have to do that. She said that was the one little thing she noticed that wasn't perfect. She said, "You were so much more articulate than those Harvard people! Those well-trained, brilliant men! You were *better!* I just wish you would have stuck with your expensive dental work. It's all my fault, really."

She never once mentioned the topic of the program, and she never referred to any of it again—ever. For her it must have hit way too close to home.

I called my father's house. No answer, no answer, no answer.

I walked the dog. At Dave's apartment, Junior and his girlfriend were standing on the sidewalk, right outside the back door. They were arguing, both talking at once. Junior said hello and leaned down and scratched the dog's head. Michaela repeated herself loudly. "You were there that day! We studied it in psychology. You were there. Prosopagnosia. It was on *the test.*"

"No," Junior said. "It doesn't exist. It does not exist."

I paused. *Slow down,* I said to myself. *Leave space.* He was a teenage boy. He was focused on his girlfriend, and getting to the beach, and Chee-Zee bread sticks, five for two dollars. My brain, and its funky little glitch, weren't high on the list.

"Junior," I said. "Y'all saw the show? Wasn't that pretty cool?" I tried to sound like a general, friendly person who lives down the street. I tried to imagine how the dog would approach this verbally, were he able to contribute along these lines: gentle, gentle. I tried not to need anything from this.

"Heather," Junior said, and he made a chiding, dubious face, tucking his chin and frowning. A pretty mean face.

Michaela hopped down into her convertible, over the side, her long blond hair spraying across the seatback. "You're crazy," she said cheerfully. "David, you're crazy."

He waved his arms. "It's not a real thing. It's just not. People! Come on!"

"David, you know all the times I haven't recognized you. Been startled in the store. Remember at Walgreens? At D&W, pretty much every time unless you have your name tag? Remember at school yesterday, at the gym? I did not know it was you. You know I didn't."

"You always think I am some random truant psycho thief boy. I know. But that's not a *thing*." He covered his face. "AGH!" he yelled. "There is no such thing as face blindness. You just don't like me!"

I reached up and took him by the shoulders. I looked hard in his eyes. "I like you." I gave him a shake to press the words into him. I said, "Did you see Ken Nakayama, the famous Harvard researcher, being interviewed? He wouldn't really be making this up. It's his life's work."

Junior turned his back to me and jogged down the street. The dog looked up at me, completely confused. At the stop sign Michaela slowed her car, he vaulted in, and they sped off.

Jacob and Dave were upstairs, standing in the living room. Pizza boxes were all over the floor, like little islands of safety in a stormy, chaotic sea. Blankets, socks were strewn about. The apartment had the smell of men living without women.

I tiptoed over and hugged Dave, shook Jacob's hand. Jacob covered his face. He made little shutters with his hands and opened them up and said, "I don't see the problem. I don't see it, Heather. Everyone has hair and ears. Everyone does!"

I leaned on Dave. I'd been so happy in my own house. Why had I come down here?

Jacob lunged forward and yelled in a freaky movie voice, "WHO AM I?!!!"

"Jacob," David said, "that's uncalled-for, buddy."

"Sorry, but I'm saying everyone has hair and ears. Hair. And ears. I just do not see what the problem is." Jacob lumbered down the hall and was gone.

Jacob and Junior were mad about the divorce. I was not who I was when I met them. It felt like a trick to them. I'd divorced their dad and now I was telling the world I didn't know people? I'd be cranky too. David said that wasn't it. They were just teasing.

Dave said I did a really good job, better than Ken Nakayama. Of the face-blind people, Dave said, I was the best one.

"The mom was good too," I said.

"Which one do you mean?" Dave said.

"There was just one mom. Wasn't there? The face-blind mom? The one who wasn't me, the other lady they did."

"There were three face-blind women," Dave said. "They were sisters."

"What?" I said.

We watched the tape. We went over each scene. Dave pointed out which women were different women, and he pointed to a scene I was in where I hadn't seen myself before. He said, "Now, that's the original one, she's just changed clothes. And now that's her again."

David Junior was reading *The Da Vinci Code* and talking about it constantly, and I wanted to look at Leonardo da Vinci's notebooks myself, to see his drawings and pages and notes. I had an idea of what they looked like, but I didn't really know. The college library had two dusty old volumes from the 1930s. When I got home, I dragged them upstairs and got in bed with Leonardo. I picked up volume two and spread it across my lap.

Volume two opened itself to a page titled "Of the Choice of the Light Which Gives Grace to a Face." I couldn't believe it. I loved when books did this: when the book itself seemed to recognize who was reading it, and what would be best to reveal.

Leonardo wrote:

> If you have a courtyard which, when you so please, you can cover over with a linen awning, the light will then be excellent. Or when you wish to paint a portrait, paint it in bad weather, at the fall of the evening, placing the sitter with his back to one of the walls. . . .

I skimmed down, turned the pages. I found a section titled "Of the Way to Fix in Your Mind the Form of a Face." How great would it be if I could learn tricks for remembering faces from Leonardo da Vinci himself?

> If you desire to acquire facility in keeping in your mind the expression of a face, first learn by heart the various different kinds of heads, eyes, noses, mouths, chins, throats, and also necks and shoulders. . . . Take as an instance noses: there are ten types. Straight, bulbous, hollow, prominent either above or below the centre, aquiline, regular, simian, round, and pointed. These divisions hold good as regards profile. Seen from in front, noses are of twelve types: thick in the middle, thin in the middle, with the tip broad, and narrow at the base, and narrow at the tip, and broad at the base, with nostrils broad or narrow, or high or low, and with the openings either visible or hidden by the tip.

I tried to think of how I would have comprehended this passage if I had come across it before knowing this task was one I would never be able to complete. My explanation would have been: *It's Leonardo da Vinci—he's a genius!* He could see all kinds of thing no one else could see.

Now I attempted to imagine Dave's nose, my own, Jacob's, my mother's. I couldn't see any noses. If only this edition had, as perhaps the original notebooks did, Leonardo's drawings, the original museum of captured noses. I needed a cheat sheet, a little flip book of noses and face parts, indices like the cashiers at the grocery store used, big color pictures of *broccoli, cress, kohlrabi.*

To see better, to draw more skillfully, Leonardo counseled a kind of stealing of face parts, the visual equivalent of eavesdropping:

> When you have to draw a face from memory, carry with you a small note-book in which you have noted down such features and when you have cast a glance at the face of the person whom you wish to draw you can look privately and see which nose or mouth has a resemblance to it, and make a tiny mark against it in order to recognize it again at home. Of abnormal faces I here say nothing for they are kept in the mind without difficulty.

I heard my mother's voice, from the distant past. Her taxonomy of noses. How she always said hers was patrician, that patrician was the best kind of nose. At the time, I'm sure I thought she was just making all this up. She had so many odd notions, all kinds of theories for how to sort people into bad, and worse, and bottom-of-the-heap. I didn't really comprehend what she was talking about when she described faces, but I often didn't know what she was talking about. She had lots of rules and policies no one else subscribed to; she saw lots of things that weren't there. I hadn't thought of her nose thing in so, so long. *A cute little button nose. It's right for you, honey. There's nothing wrong with your nose. It's a turned-up little nose.*

Reading Leonardo, I knew absolutely for certain my mother was not face-blind. If I was born with the disorder, I could have gotten it from her, her side of the family, but she wasn't face-blind. I hadn't known this was the piece I was looking for. But it was. She wasn't face-blind. I wasn't schizophrenic. We shared our love for Portmeirion china, pleated blouses, songs featuring the moon, sheets dried on the line, and grass and little kids and nonpareils and the idea of kitten heels. Our difficulties had come into contact, but these difficulties weren't what tied us together.

"So it really could come from Fred." Dave was sitting across from me; we were at a restaurant on the lake, overlooking the beach where we had taken a walk on our first date.

Every week we went out for dinner, and Dave listened and always had some insight into my mother, the boys, me, or us. His acceptance—his embracing—of the range of human experience was a kind of genius. I couldn't live with him, but I didn't see how I could live too far from him. It was selfish and strange, my friendship with him. It was keeping him from moving on. Almost every Saturday we went to the Blue Star Antique Pavilion—Dave talked silver and gold with the codgers working their booths and I sniffed out vintage Pringle sweaters, and linens. The vendors always called out when we walked in the door, "Well, it's the Happiest Divorced Couple in West Michigan!" as though we'd won a prize. I knew I needed to give that prize back soon. But not yet.

"My father never talked about noses," I said. He never referenced a chin, or a jaw, or talked about the eyes. I'd never seen him go up to someone on the street and say hello.

"I wonder if there were times Fred didn't recognize you," Dave said. "If this explains why he hated to leave the house. Why he didn't really have friends. Why he gave all those homeless guys as much money as they asked for, thought of them as familiar, as close friends. Could he tell them apart? I bet he couldn't."

Did the new theory explain, in part, Fred's heavy drinking, his failure at employment, his inability or his refusal to fit in with the world? In the dark bars, the regulars sat, like students in classes, in their same exact positions, on their same stools, came at the same times, wore the same clothes. The bartender called them by name. Maybe at work there were too many people to keep track of.

Maybe even his cross-dressing was a way for him to say *I know this is me,* Dave theorized, like when you put a red tag on luggage.

Face blindness could make you lose yourself to yourself, but not exactly in that way, I said. I didn't think face blindness explained everything about Fred. A disorder wasn't really an explanation—ever; it was always more like an extra limb. I didn't feel like I needed to know which of my parents had passed it on. Maybe they both had. Maybe I got it a whole other way. I would not ever know, and the great triumph of the year was that now I could sit and not-know the hell out of something and it was a perfectly pleasant, non-chaotic way to spend time.

"He's really good with strangers," I said. "He was always super-friendly to people he didn't know. And frustrated around everyone else."

Dave said for a paranoid person to be really successfully paranoid, you would have to recognize people. It wasn't strangers that freaked you out, it was known people. This, I thought, was a fascinating point. We talked about it for a long time. We finished our dinners, ordered another round of drinks. The sun was down, but the sky was still full of aqua and pink, the lake a perfect mirror.

"You know I will always love you," Dave said.

"Yup, I'll always love you too," I said.

Five

The week after I sent it, I got thirty-eight responses to my e-mail. And they kept trickling in, months later:

> Thank you for the email but how long have you known and why are you telling us now?

From a prof in religion:

> When did you know you had this?

I decided to save the e-mails as one would save get-well cards. Replies weren't required. I decided that no matter what they actually said, people were trying to say, *Thanks for telling us, let us know if we can help.*

I noticed as I went from class to the library, from the library to the dining hall, from my car to the coffee shop, a lot more people on campus were saying, "Hello, Heather."

No one was saying who *they* were, but they were greeting

me by name. Suddenly, I had all these new people to not know.

> It must be really hard for you because you are such a vibrant and outgoing person. You are such a people person.

I wanted to write back and explain that prosopagnosics were prone to acting this way, all showy, because we were desperate to be seen. Because we didn't recognize people, a deep part of us feared it was *us* that was invisible.

> This is Amy Van Dort. Do you know who I am? When I write to you do you know it is me?

My friend Lisa e-mailed me and asked if I could pick up her toddler at day care; then she called me. She was nervous. She had talked to her husband. "How will you recognize my kid?" she said. I told her the truth: "I won't. But he will recognize me." I told her to tell the day care people. They would have to give me the right kid. "You can tell me what he's wearing."

"We're just not comfortable with it," she said. "I'm sorry."

The e-mails kept coming in, a couple a week:

> We live in such a caring community isnt that lucky?

> This is Brad Pitt. Hey! Gotta keep ya laughing! (Really it is Jack. Hahaha).

> This explains a lot. I always wondered why you give me such a funny look, like you do not know me or like me.

(I do not like this person.)

> I have seizures. Do you think i could come and talk to you about the brain and these things sometimes? I could treat us to coffee. I know you are busy.

> You are so brave!

> You are so courageous.

> Hug hug hug. You are so courageous, Heather.

> I got your email. How courageous. This is Bob Luidens. I have a beard and grey hair. I will always introduce myself to you. But I have a question. How is it you never noticed this before? What about your parents? If you had such a serious disability, wouldn't they have taken you to a doctor?

> I think I have this. Not as bad as you. Can we meet for coffee my treat?

Four people on campus wrote me with similar stories: after reading my e-mail, and taking the tests at the Harvard site, they each thought they were face-blind. I wrote back to each person right away. We met individually that week, and I met two of them again the next week. I was convinced: these were face-blind people. I encouraged them to join the online support group, to contact the researchers at Harvard and MIT, and to read Andrew Young's wonderful, difficult book. The most important thing, I stressed, was to tell everyone. People needed to know. Otherwise, one misunderstanding after another steadily eroded one's confidence and well-being. Things were so much easier, once everyone knew. Tell!

They insisted on remaining anonymous.

I remembered the feelings of shame and fear, so wrapped up in my experiences with my mother and her illness, that had kept me from wanting anyone to know. But with all the fervor of the newly converted, I wanted everyone to know everything. I wanted everything *told.* "You have to tell," I said over and over, as politely as I could. I was aware I sounded exactly like Helder, calm but definitive, serious and all therapist-y. I sounded exactly like Peter Helder when I had loathed him most intensely. But I assured my face-blind colleagues I would never reveal their identities. I would keep their secrets, absolutely. And, we joked, we were safe with each other. We wouldn't recognize each other at our faculty meetings.

I made plans to meet Dave and Jacob and Junior for lunch. I had just sat down in a booth toward the back when I got a tap on my shoulder. "We're already here, sweetheart." It was Dave. "We're right here. You walked past us, sweetheart, but it's okay."

I joined them at their table.

"You looked *right at us,*" Jacob said. He threw his hands

out wide and held them there, exaggerating his stunned condition.

"She's faking," Junior said.

"Didn't see you," I said. I smiled.

"Right at us!" Jacob said, waving his arms around.

"Jakey," David cautioned. "Be nice."

"But she looked right at us. And then sat over there!" Junior cried out.

I looked at Dave. I took his hand in my hands. "I'm not mad, but I think I'm going to go. I know no one at this table means any harm." I looked at the boys, who were looking hard at the tabletop. "But if you had a hearing impairment, or dyslexia, I wouldn't doubt you. I would be kind and supportive—at least, I hope I would be. I guess I would keep trying to understand. No hard feelings. It's a very weird disorder. It's hard to understand. It took me my whole life to figure it out." I stood up. They looked really sad and hangdog and I felt like I'd been clear, but also too harsh. "I'll see you at the pool later, Jakey?"

"I'll be there," he muttered.

"How will you recognize him?" Junior piped up, his voice high and cheery. He made little window shutters over his face with his hands and flapped them open and shut. His father told him to knock it off. I laughed and said I knew they'd find me. "I'm easy to find," I said.

Months later, I would hear Jacob explaining to his friends that I had a rare neurological disorder, one that had affected Kurt Vonnegut and affects Jane Goodall too. He was always soft-spoken, and he sounded kind and gentle and a little proud as he explained how I didn't know him sometimes. When

Jacob and his friends sat in a circle on the living room floor, playing Dungeons & Dragons, I couldn't tell the boys apart, not even Jacob, except for Teddy. "So, keep dyeing your hair blue, man," Jacob said to Teddy. And the conversation turned back to superpowers, and charisma points, and whose turn it was, and why Flinchie's family appeared to love him so much. Junior and I never spoke about face blindness again. He enrolled in a college, Michaela dumped him for the second time, he dropped out mid-semester, and Dave said I shouldn't worry; he said the kid was finding himself.

In the year to come, Fred ended up in a nursing home on Orange Blossom Trail, a nursing home that had been a Holiday Inn when I was in high school; he still knew who I was when I called, but he never wanted to talk for long. The last time I'd spoken with him, he'd had a cardiac event an hour later, been rushed to the hospital. It was days and nights on pins and needles, with midnight calls from the hospital. Was I his daughter? Was I the person who could say do not resuscitate, who could tell them his wishes? Yes, I was this person. I faxed the paperwork. I hired people to help. I called him every couple of hours. He yelled at me. "I'm fine," he said. "Fine."

He always asked about my mother. "Is she better?" he always said. "Is she doing any better at all?"

"She has memory problems," I told him each time. "Her memory is failing her. She always asks about you." This wasn't true, but I couldn't help but say it. I wanted him to know she loved him back. I wanted them to continue to recognize each other. They were each, in so many ways, all the other had. I told him, "She has good days and bad days."

"She always did!" he said every time. "She always did misremember! 'Bout raining outside!"

Whenever I spoke with my mother, I told her I loved her. She always responded, "Your father loves you so, so much."

"I love you," I would repeat.

"Your father loves you so, so much, honey." It was an admission, a deflection, a makeup exam—all at once.

Lately, she'd been talking about when I was born, how happy he was, what a great moment that had been.

And then she said, "When you coming down?" She always asked this. "When you coming down?"

I could not say. I couldn't go back down just yet. I was careful about the last words. *I love you. I love you. I love you. She loves you. He loves you.*

I wanted them both to know, to be sure of me. I wanted a tight little circle like that, here with me in the giant look-alike world.

Dave and I stopped going out every week; instead of the happiest divorced couple in West Michigan, we became a divorced couple in West Michigan. He wrote me an e-mail one day. Friends of mine were introducing themselves to him. That morning at the coffee shop, Pat Roehling had said, "Hi, Dave, it's Pat!" He called it collateral face blindness. David James and

Suzy always called out, "Hi, Dave, it's Dave and Suzy!" They hadn't done this last year. *I'm not the one who can't recognize people,* he wrote. But it was funny and helpful, since he could never remember people's names. I could tell he was smiling when he wrote it. He closed with a question. Did I want, by the way, to go out for a drink?

Yes. Yes, I did.

It was always going to be hard to know about Dave.

Someone else wrote me. I don't even remember who it was. But it's the question that matters the most.

> Do you want me to reintroduce myself to you once or always?

I want you to always.

Afterword

Off and on for many years, I tried to write a book about my childhood. I'd bring chapters to workshop, to writing group, and I always got the same comments: *How could you live this way? How could you survive this? It's too raw. You don't speak to these people, do you?* I was deeply hurt by these reactions, and also confused. This was my mother. I loved her. This was my family. My life. How could it be *too raw*? I sent a completed version of the memoir to an editor who liked my work. She said no one would believe this childhood was survivable. She said something was missing. She said, "You need a perspective."

I struggled to understand what she meant. Perspective?

Meanwhile, I was a professor, teaching literature to college students. I led my classes through great stories and poems, and we talked about the universal task of growing up: coming into awareness of one's experience, learning to trust one's perceptions enough to claim a perspective. I gave examinations on this material. But I couldn't see my own life clearly at all. I didn't know *what* all I didn't know; I suspected it was quite a lot.

In childhood, it's our parents who give us our standards for experience: "Here's an inch," they say. "And this is a foot." And a child says, "Thanks! I can make my own yardstick now." In my family, there wasn't any kind of calibration demonstration. In the chaos, I struggled to figure out anything at all. In addition, my neurological condition, undiagnosed and unknown to me, made it impossible for me to trust my perceptions. I couldn't see who I was or where I stood. My parents noticed my confusion and anxiety. They thought I was crazy. For most of my life, I thought they had that much right.

And then one day I went home and turned on the lights, and began to look clearly at my childhood. Gradually I could discern what was, and what was not. The disorder that had plagued me my whole life emerged from the shadows, too, and over time, it became knowable and manageable. More than anything else, laying out the story of how I came to see has brought me clarity.

But I discovered something else in writing this book, something even more graceful and vital than the elusive "perspective." In all that darkness, there *had* been love. What I'd felt all along was not a fantasy, not yet another misinterpretation. I loved my parents. I wasn't wrong about that. And somehow, against all odds, my parents (especially my mother) were able to bring their versions of affection into our world, into our family, as well. I'd set out to write a book about how we learn to trust our own experience in the face of confusion, doubt, and anxiety. What I ended up with is the story of how we love each other in spite of immense limitations.

Readers will no doubt have noticed that my brother is not much mentioned in this book. He grew up with a very different set of circumstances from me, often under a different roof. Out of respect for his privacy and his own point of view, I chose to leave him out of this account almost entirely. His story is his own to tell, or not.

My own perspective I do feel moved, even obligated, to share. The discovery that deeply flawed love and deeply flawed vision can coexist has been life-changing for me, and I feel uniquely able to illuminate it. You could say that the gift of prosopagnosia was the ability to live with uncertainty, to be receptive to all that a person might turn out to be, literally and metaphorically. Face blindness helped me stay open to possibility—motivated me, on the cellular level, to try to know and understand what can't be easily seen.

I hope that, at least in some small way, this story will help steer others toward clarity, and toward love, in spite of the greatest odds.

Acknowledgments

To the incomparable Rebecca Saletan, I am most deeply grateful.

I am indebted to Michele Mortimer, for all her help with shaping this book, word by word, punctuation mark by punctuation mark, and to Chuck Verrill, always. Dedicated, detailed, and pragmatic editorial assistance was provided by Karly Fogelsonger and the wonderful Elaine Trevorrow.

Thanks to Abigail Thomas and my fellow students in the solstice memoir workshop at the Omega Institute, where this book's backstory was begun. My writing partners, Ann Turkle, Lorraine López, Debra Wierenga, and Jackie Bartley, have read many drafts and provided much encouragement, insight, and patient fruitless comma instruction.

Sarah Gorham, Jennifer Ackerman, Ron Spatz, and the late Carol Houck Smith supported this work early on. "Tell Me Again, Who Are You?," an earlier essay version of one of the chapters in this book, appears in the *Alaska Quarterly Review*. It was reprinted in Lee Gutkind's *Best Creative Nonfiction 2007*.

Ken Nakayama at Harvard's Vision Sciences Laboratory, along with Brad Duchaine and Galit Yovel, patiently explained basic neuropsychology, provided face blindness humor and encouragement, and the turning point in my life: diagnosis. I am grateful for their kindness, generosity, and wisdom.

Mary Brodbeck, Tammy Hillen, Jesse Lee Kercheval, Rosemary Cantor, Kate Sexton Small, and Ellen Darion feed and steady this writer—thank you for your friendship. Hope College provides a particularly nourishing and supportive community; I'm especially grateful to my colleagues Charles Aschbrenner, Priscilla Atkins, Natalie Dykstra, Lynn Japinga, Lorna Hernandez Jarvis, David Klooster, Marla Lunderberg, David Myers, Barb Mezeske, Kathi O'Connor, Jeanne Petit, Pat Roehling, Carol Simon, and Jane Burroway.

And I wish to extend buoyant gratitude and great affection to Kevin Larimer, Sarah Van Arsdale, Elaine Sexton, Ruth Cunningham, and to everyone at Riverhead, especially Geoff Kloske, Elizabeth Hohenadel, Margot Stamos, Lydia Hut, Alyson Forbes, Lisa Keffer, and the absolutely amazing Stephanie Sorensen.

BOCA RATON PUBLIC LIBRARY, FLORIDA
3 3656 0588385 9